Leading Culture Change

LEADING CULTURE CHANGE

What Every CEO Needs to Know

Christopher S. Dawson

STANFORD BUSINESS BOOKS,
AN IMPRINT OF STANFORD UNIVERSITY PRESS
STANFORD, CALIFORNIA

Stanford University Press
Stanford, California

Special discounts for bulk quantities of Stanford Business Books are available to corporations, professional associations, and other organizations. For details and discount information, contact the special sales department of Stanford University Press. Tel: (650) 736-1782, Fax: (650) 736-1784

Printed in the United States of America on acid-free, archival-quality paper.

Library of Congress Cataloging-in-Publication Data
Dawson, Christopher S. (Christopher Sapp)
Leading culture change : what every CEO needs to know / Christopher S. Dawson.
p. cm.
Includes bibliographical references and index.
ISBN 978-0-8047-6342-4 (cloth : alk. paper)
1. Corporate culture. 2. Organizational change—Management. I. Title.
HD58.7.D383 2010
658.4'063—dc22

2009038158

Typeset by Classic Typography in 10/13 Sabon and Stone Sans display

Contents

Illustrations

Culture Change Cases

Preface

This book is based on my twenty-five years of experience consulting to various organizations striving to shape their culture to become something better and thereby create value. Though mostly U.S. firms, these companies span a wide spectrum of size, industry, and location: more than seventy-five separate engagements in all. As I worked to help these companies realize, define, and then execute their culture change journeys, some very clear patterns emerged:

- *Difficulty.* As you will see in the thoughts that follow, there is no question that culture can, and does, change. Like any change of comfortable patterns, it is exceedingly difficult and requires a good reason—but there is no question that *it is possible.*
- *Evolution not revolution.* Like losing weight or changing a habit, culture change happens gradually over time and can be hard to see day to day. Even when there is a dramatic shift in leadership or company ownership, the "actual" culture changes slowly. Indeed, unless someone sets out to accelerate change in a specified direction, it is not unusual to hear members of an acquired organization talking about "our culture" ten to fifteen years later! "Accelerated" and intentional culture change can happen in as little as three years. In twenty-five years of observing this phenomenon, I have never seen a culture change noticeably in less than a few years.
- *Leadership makes the difference.* Cultures are changing all the time—though there are always forces of equilibrium that maintain the status quo. Pressures in the external and internal environment cause all organizations to adapt—whether they are aware of it or

not. What makes the difference is leadership that first recognizes the need for change, and then acts strategically and effectively to shape the culture.

- *From here to there.* As with any journey—whether business strategy or family car trip—a clear picture of the destination is the single biggest determining factor. Without a destination, there is no journey—though culture will still evolve as a result of the interplay of natural forces.
- *Authenticity.* After a clear destination, there is no more powerful critical success factor for culture change than the behavior of the leadership. And let's be clear, this is not the *words* of the leaders but their *actions* day in and day out over time.

This is a practical book aimed at helping those in CEO and senior executive positions create greater value through the shaping of culture. It is my strongly held view, based on dozens of culture change experiences, that the CEO and top team must be actively involved in determining the scope and priority of the effort. Only the CEO can answer the question, "Will our organizational culture act as an accelerator, or barrier, to successful strategy execution?" Only the CEO can translate that enterprise priority into the appropriate level of attention and resource. With this premise in mind, as I move through the best-practice steps of culture change, I answer this question: "What does the CEO need to know about (human capital levers, Shadow Cultures, change accelerators, and so on) to effectively sponsor and lead the culture change that is required by the strategy?" In the course of answering this question, I will touch on a wide territory of material crossing several disciplines: human capital, psychology, organizational behavior, strategy management, and organizational development.

Beyond those areas of culture change in which the CEO must be directly involved, for example, in managing the top team, my goal for tangential, culture-related disciplines is to give CEOs sufficient working knowledge to make them effective culture change sponsors and leaders. In pursuing this goal, I have summarized some technical areas—for example organization design or behavioral competencies—in ways that might seem like, well, executive summaries—exactly what they are intended to be. Some of the wisdom that I hope to impart to CEOs is a more finely-honed ability to judge how, when, and where they must be involved in the culture change process—at every step. To make those judgments, it is necessary to have some grounding in what best practices are, so they can make the determination between what is their decision space and what is the subject-matter expert decision and execution space. Although human resource and organizational effectiveness experts will find much to learn in the book about culture change, that non-CEO audience is forewarned that many technical subjects are approached through a filter of "What does the CEO need to know?" and *not* "What is a scholarly or comprehensive review of the culture change subdiscipline." Irrespective of the CEOs' experience and technical or functional background, they must understand enough about finance, marketing, and operations to do precisely the same thing as they will need to do in culture change, that is, prioritize strategy and attention with CEO-level domain knowledge.

All of the cases cited in the book recount real events—most of them consulting engagements that I was directly involved with. For obvious reasons I have changed the names of some, though not all, of these companies. The case material remains true to life.

Acknowledgments

This book, ten years in the making, is dedicated to my two life partners—Laurel and Wah Zee. Without them, the book would not have started or finished. Many others made valuable contributions: my son, Ryan Dawson, did a spectacular job of editing—elevating the quality of both thought and writing in the book. My daughter, Shaelyn Dawson, pulled together all the references. My colleagues Greg Love and Muriel Taylor gave generously of their time and made invaluable suggestions from a real-world CEO perspective. Finally, I want to thank my Stanford University Press colleagues, Margo Beth Crouppen, David Horne, and Jessica Walsh, who were extremely helpful and a pleasure to work with in creating the book.

Leading Culture Change

Section I

Culture as the Engine of Value Creation

1 Culture Creates Value

Culture is the engine of value creation. Building a consistent, strong organizational culture is one of the most important contributions a leader can make. Why? Because organizational culture is the prime mover and the accelerator, or barrier, for all other value-producing (or destroying) activities.

A distinctive, well-aligned culture creates a powerful competitive advantage, one that is difficult to duplicate. It is the medium through which any leadership initiative will be executed. Indeed, leadership priorities will *only* be realized to the extent that the culture allows and facilitates those priorities to come about. Culture is a first cause in creating value outcomes, and can be shaped by leaders who channel this powerful force.

The CEO and top team can shape and change culture to accelerate or hinder organizational value. This book is about how to shape culture so that it becomes an accelerator to value creation.

Why Is Culture Underutilized by Leaders?

Impediments arising from the organizational culture pose a serious risk to successful execution of any and all leadership initiatives. In extreme external conditions, overcoming those culture impediments will determine survival. Why is there such fatalism and abdication by leaders when it comes to active shaping of this critical variable? Leaders often speak eloquently about their culture, but then delegate the entire space to the Human Resources function, as though it were an accounting detail they did not need to bother with.

Understanding, defining, and leading the culture of an organization is a primary job of the CEO or top leader and should not be delegated. CEOs should be as knowledgeable and involved in shaping the culture as they are in relating to customers, working with the board, and driving the strategy.

Culture *Can* Be Shaped and Changed

Here is the good news: culture can always be shaped, and often changed for the better! I have seen it happen many times in my consulting practice over twenty-five years—and the literature is full of rich examples that reinforce that conclusion. How is it that culture changes? And can it be deliberately shaped? These are the questions I hope to answer in the pages that follow.

Individual personality and organizational culture have much in common that we can learn from. We all have certain personality traits—some of them established early on and relatively fixed, others acquired through life in the course of experience. When we meet any of life's challenges—whether aspired to as a goal or thrust upon us by circumstance—our ability to deal with that challenge will be accelerated or limited by our personal attributes. If it is our desire to climb a mountain (or if we "find ourselves" at the bottom of one that *must* be climbed), there are numerous physical and personality characteristics of the climber that will make the journey more or less successful. Some of these characteristics could even preclude the journey before it ever begins. We all begin with some baseline portfolio of physical, mental, and emotional attributes: stamina, determination, lung capacity, risk-taking, and so on. These can be developed—to a degree—through focused training and sufficient will to achieve the goal. However, there will almost always be a point at which baseline traits and physical attributes become limiting factors instead of facilitators.

The very wish to climb the mountain (or to recognize that it *must* be climbed due to circumstance) is an attribute of the individual at the bottom of that mountain. There are some, finding themselves at the bottom of the mountain, who conclude, "I am perfectly content here without the bother of climbing this mountain." Others cannot begin their climb soon enough. Some need or drive compels such individuals to climb the mountain, for reasons that are important to them. That "reason" may be reactive or proactive: "I'll die if I don't get out of this valley, over that mountain" or "I'll be better somehow when I get to the top."

There are many parallels with organizational culture in this discussion of individual personality. If the "mountain" is the external environment facing any organization, and organizational culture is a stable set of values and capabilities, we can think of organizational culture as the *accelerator* or *barrier* to those strategic intentions of the organization. In this context, organizational culture may also become a powerful *competitive differentiator* that is difficult for others to copy.

Organizational culture also functions as a *prime mover* or "container of possibilities" in the sense that core values of the organization manifest in a diverse spectrum of possible strategies, structures, and cultures *as well as* corollary limitations. Like the great diversity of achievement that comes from different personalities, different companies have *a priori* cultural attributes that predispose them to success or failure in various endeavors.

Culture as Accelerator and Barrier

There are many challenges in developing a successful business strategy. Is it aggressive enough? Have we chosen the right value proposition? Are we reading our customers accurately? Have we positioned ourselves well in relation to competitors? Even if there are perfectly accurate answers to all of these questions, the successful execution of that strategy still dangles in the wind of the organizational culture. This point is axiomatic: the more aligned the culture is with the intended strategy, the more likely the strategy is to manifest according to plan; in other words, the greater chance it has of actually creating value versus being "just another set of plans." By the same token, the less aligned the strategy is with the organizational culture, the more difficulty it will encounter, up to and including outright failure. Like human beings, many organizations stumble along in spite of themselves—being lifted by favorable economic conditions or industry sectors—and never grapple with their own culture as a source of potential value.

Any strategic initiative will be either accelerated or delayed by the existing culture. Precisely for this reason, leaders must understand their culture, and be skillful in ways to shape or change it. Case 1.1 illustrates an example of an accelerated culture.

Case 1.1. Accelerated Culture

A midwestern phone equipment OEM supplier realized that it needed to reduce its defective returns, which were running at an unacceptable and costly level. It brought in a Six Sigma quality-improvement consultancy to impart methods, tools, and techniques of this continuous-improvement paradigm. The company also had a long-standing inclusive and familial culture in which the founder was still very much involved in running the company—and had been extremely generous during good and bad times to all twenty-five hundred employees. Although there were the usual organizational tensions between different functional departments, an employee stock option plan, frequent company social events, and numerous other demonstrations by the executives in modeling the "midwestern" values of the company all provided fertile ground for the rapid adoption of the new program—seen as a set of tools and methods to help solve a critical quality problem. In preparing the company for the substantial investment of time and effort needed to implant the Six Sigma methodology, the founder went around to every department and explained how important this was to the company, making a personal request to senior managers to put aside petty silo differences and embrace this methodology to improve organizational effectiveness. The consultants commented that they had never seen a Six Sigma program go in so smoothly or so quickly—and they continue to use the company as their premiere testimonial. The company has significantly reduced its defective return rate, and is applying the Six Sigma methodology to other areas of improvement.

If the founder had not created the culture to proactively embrace the Six Sigma change, then the goal would have been slow going or entirely stagnant. It was the cultural attributes of the company that helped it adapt itself so quickly.

How Do You Know When Your Culture Is a Gate or Barrier?

When leadership has been inattentive to organizational culture, or unintentionally created the wrong culture to support the strategy, the result is usually "no result." Following are a few common examples of how culture can function as a barrier to value creation:

- Profitability and other performance measures are slowing or declining relative to peers.
- Initiatives begin with fanfare but then falter or fail.
- There is "tribal warfare" between departments that prevents sharing of information and collaboration.
- Managers play it safe in setting goals because they fear reprisal.
- There is a big gap between what customers really think about the company and what employees believe they are delivering.

The reality of dealing with today's fast-changing environment means that few companies will have continuous alignment between strategy, initiatives, and culture. The most effective companies are modifying their strategies and culture periodically to adapt to the external environment. In some industries such as technology that have predictable change every eighteen to twenty-four months, a culture focused on adaptability and agility may have high survival value. Case 1.2 provides an example of undesirable consequences when the culture is misaligned with the strategies.

Case 1.2. Innovation Misalignment

A global food company had continued to spiral into "commodity hell" after holding a premiere brand position for many years. Over-relying on its legacy brand, and failing to see competitive dynamics that accelerated commoditization throughout the industry, it faced increasing margin pressure. The company became more and more heavily leveraged in debt, seeking to solve the margin compression problem with cost-reduction programs. Consultants were brought in to make the "painful cuts," which they did, eliminating a centralized research and development facility and many other nonessentials. After several years of incremental margin improvement, the leadership came upon the "innovation" paradigm, going headlong into the latest and greatest innovation training programs and consultancies. The innovation program at this company is still only a "corporate initiative," and a thin one at that, after many years. The cause? A completely misaligned culture based on scarcity and fear. Every time the leaders try to push out innovation as a solution to commoditization—and they have done so in numerous ways—they are met with the same powerful "barriers": a culture in which a dominant financial function requires short-term return on any investment and a management culture of fear and intimidation in which new ideas that do not meet with the executives' notion of a "good idea" are publicly criticized and even humiliated at high decibel. The best innovation processes and business initiatives in the world will not succeed in such a culture of scarcity and fear. This company's innovation initiative—which it desperately needs in order to escape commodity hell—has literally been stalled for years due to an "inhospitable culture" that is grossly misaligned with the business solutions leadership is trying to create. Here is a simple example of how one can draw a very direct "line of sight" between value creation and culture or, sadly in this case, value destruction.

Culture as Competitive Advantage

When organizational culture has been developed in deliberate and focused ways over time, it can create a distinctive advantage that is difficult to imitate. There is no better example of this than Toyota. Beginning with the mechanistic paradigm of the early Demming quality control methods, Toyota has gradually iterated a manufacturing culture that is arguably the best in the world—certainly when judged by the value created as a result of this culture. What is most interesting about Toyota is that they have publicly documented exactly what they do—indeed offer daily tours of their assembly plants—and yet competitors have been unable to copy some "secret sauce" in the culture to imitate their success. Toyota is a dramatic standout of how massive value can be created through the establishment of a highly differentiated culture.

At some point it becomes difficult to distinguish between "brand" and "culture"—though an external brand cannot be sustained with a misaligned culture. Insofar as "brand" is a form of strategy—an initiative to create differentiation and customer loyalty—culture will be an accelerator or barrier to the execution of that brand strategy.

Culture as Prime Mover and "Container of Possibilities"

On another level, organizational culture shapes potential value in a more fundamental, causal way. Culture is a *prime mover* in determining a universe of possibilities, as well as creating degrees of freedom on what an organization is capable of accomplishing. Every organization's basic "DNA" allows and defines what is possible for the organization to undertake or even to conceive. The analogy to personality is, again, useful to illustrate the point.

We each have a "package" of defined qualities—our "personality." Though this can change to some degree, there are key elements in most of us that "allow" or "constrain" possible behaviors and outcomes. For example, not everyone has the ability, drive, or interest to become an accomplished pianist. Most everyone can learn to play the piano given sufficient interest and effort. There are real individual differences which place constraints on, and open opportunities to, what any of us can accomplish.

The "DNA" of organizational culture functions in very much the same way. There is that primary DNA in every organization that invisibly shapes everything that is possible for that organization, *before* anything ever bubbles up as an option. The analogy to personality breaks down in that organizations may have successive "lifetimes" in the form of new leadership, acquisitions, and so on, allowing them the real possibility of more dramatic transformation than is typical of individuals (though certainly some instances of personal transformation qualify as dramatic). IBM, GE, and the U.S. Post Office are all excellent models of organizational cultures that have undergone massive transformations of their fundamental core values. IBM transformed itself from the stereotypical "Big Blue" 1950s company that sold "big iron" computer hardware and wore the blue-suit, white shirt, and red tie uniform, into a creative and flexible technology solutions company with a globally diverse "knowledge worker" culture.

A good example of how organizational culture functions as "prime mover" can be seen in the interface of international companies struggling to find common ground around cultural values (Case 1.3).

Case 1.3. Culture Miscommunication

A German-owned and -run maker of specialized CAD software needs a presence in Latin America, where several of its largest architectural and engineering firm customers and suppliers are based. After much debate the German firm elects to pursue acquisition of a Brazilian firm that has been highly creative in developing an innovative new user interface for a similar product suite of its own. After the acquisition is consummated by financial and legal staff, the leadership of the two firms—roughly equal in size and local stature—realizes they must get together to map out a strategy and truly integrate the two firms: a planning retreat is calendared in São Paolo to begin this integration process. From the very beginning of this first watershed leadership event there is friction. The brewing storm begins with the executive assistants making the arrangements; the hosting Brazilians see the event as the perfect opportunity to build relationships—mostly through a series of social events. They propose an agenda with five to six hours of working conference room time, with the lion's share of the time spent in social situations. The visiting Germans see the event as a perfect opportunity to begin the pragmatic, heavy lifting of merger integration and propose marathon working sessions to address issues of strategy, structure, and people duplication inefficiencies. After the two CEOs get involved, a compromise is reached for the São Paolo agenda, but the two teams gradually come to realize that they have completely different values and ways of thinking about the world. The Brazilians want to minimize processes, methods, and structures in order to maximize innovation. They see the first order of business as building trust-based relationships. The Germans want to maximize processes, methods, and structures so that they can create predictable outcomes. They want the innovation and creativity of Brazilians, but find themselves impatient with long aimless meetings and lack of discipline and accountability. After two years of trying to build something—with many well-intended cross-cultural emissaries and missionaries—the leadership of the firm, which has remained largely independent, votes formally to dismantle the company. The lawyers and accountants are paid once again to unwind joint affairs. A great deal of value is destroyed in both companies in countless ways from consulting fees to customer relationships.

Here is a dramatic example of organizational culture acting as "prime mover," resulting in value destruction for both companies and their shareholders. There is cultural "DNA" in both the German and Brazilian firms that defines their beliefs and perceptions, their values of what is important and how to be successful. This DNA in each of the companies, amplified by national identities, defines a fundamental orientation to the world and basic strategy of how to do things that, in this example, create insurmountable obstacles to the establishment of a business synergy that would otherwise be healthy in all other aspects.

The Premise of the Book

Culture can create and destroy value. No reasonable person sets out to destroy value, but many inattentive leaders end up doing so—by failing to either *accelerate culture alignment* or remove *barriers* to strategic objectives. The *a priori prime mover* situation is, of course, present to one degree or another for every company. Like your personality, we all have one. No company has a "no-culture," unless they are a "no-company." The central challenge for leaders in leveraging culture is in recognizing where they may be able to accelerate business objectives via culture shaping, where they must remove cultural barriers to company-critical objectives, and where it is simply unrealistic to think that the culture can be moved beyond a certain degree of freedom to attain a desired objective.

Can organizational culture be changed? Yes and no. Like the proverbial iceberg, there are hidden aspects at the very bottom that are very unlikely to change, and visible aspects at the top that are quite easy to change. The more important question is, Where is the "waterline" on your iceberg, and how much motivation is there to change? We will explore this question in more detail in Chapter 2, since what one believes is an important variable in what is possible. Like individual human talents, highly motivated and disciplined individuals are capable of things that nobody believed possible. Individuals and organizations can and do change at very fundamental levels when there is sufficient reason and the leadership competence to make it happen. Yet it is common sense to remind ourselves that for every company or individual there are real limitations to what kind of change is possible. A furniture manufacturing company is not likely to become a world leader in health care services. However, like Herman Miller, it might become a world leader in innovative industrial design. Large and effective culture change, though inspiring and admirable, is the exception rather than the rule. Most cultures probably do not have sufficient reason and drive to make such changes to their fundamental cultural DNA. That is perfectly okay—shaping a successful culture to execute a more modest set of strategic objectives is still a worthy accomplishment and produces shareholder value.

For members within an organization, culture is an unseen and largely unmanaged force. For the leadership of the organization—especially the very top leader—it is a force, like electricity or gravity, that can be harnessed in the service of specific goals, though never fully "owned" or controlled.

My hope is that this book will serve as a practical field guide for CEOs and other leaders in senior positions of "final" responsibility who see a need to change culture. It is very difficult to change or shape a culture without access to a culture change method, tools, and the "levers" of change. The book will also be useful for those in advisory positions to CEOs, but it is written quite specifically for leaders in a position to shape company direction through setting priorities and allocating resources.

Chapters 1, 2, and 3 constitute Section I, which defines basic terms; provides a working definition of organizational culture; and makes the linkage between strategy, culture, and value creation. This first section is less "how to"—though still not academic or theoretical—tackling the fundamental premise of the book: culture creates and destroys value. The reader interested in the "how to" who already embraces this basic premise that culture creates value may wish to skip ahead to Chapter 3, "Five Critical Success Factors for Culture Change."

Chapter 2 provides a working definition of organizational culture. Without attempting a comprehensive or scholarly review of this interdisciplinary literature, I look at the historical threads in the business literature and where they have brought us with regard to the organizational culture concept. I dispel some myths and establish a working definition of organizational culture for the leader faced with the task of changing it.

Chapter 3 describes the "Five Critical Success Factors for Culture Change" and lays the groundwork for Section II, which is focused on practical guidelines for the CEO faced with the task of culture change.

Chapters 4, 5, 6, and 7 make up Section II, which focuses on the end-to-end process, best practices, and practical guidance for the CEO facing the culture change challenge.

Chapter 4 outlines the Setup phase of the Culture Change Process. Culture change is a major undertaking that not every company needs to embark on. In this chapter I offer a framework and tools to help the CEO determine the level of urgency for the culture change along a red-yellow-green continuum. Also addressed in Chapter 4 are important framing, communication, and persuasion steps that the CEO must take to make culture change a priority.

Chapter 5 focuses on the Launch phase, describing an important new framework for defining the "as is" and "to be" cultures. In this chapter I describe the two "Shadow Cultures" (*Ideal* and *Required*), why they are important, and how they can be integrated using the "Get Real Tool" into a more complete Vision Culture. I also outline what the CEO needs to know about culture assessment, and his or her role in managing the Launch phase of the Culture Change Process. Concluding the chapter, I describe the Culture Change Roadmap, which marks the end milestone of the Launch phase.

In Chapter 6, "Propagating the Wave," I offer practical guidelines and best practices about how to translate the Culture Change Roadmap into actions and initiatives that are in the critical path to the Vision Culture and linked to value creation. I review best practices in the three essential "culture change levers": change acceleration and communication levers, human capital levers, and executive authenticity.

Chapter 7 offers key principles, tools, and specific guidance for celebrating and evaluating progress and completes Section II. In this chapter, I supply a framework to close the loop back to the initial strategic drivers that determined the need for culture change.

Section III is concerned with practical applications and begins with Chapter 8, which describes three common culture change scenarios: moving from a commodity to an innovation culture, moving from the relationship or early stage culture to the discipline or performance culture, and integration of cultures in a postmerger situation.

In Chapter 9 I outline the leadership competencies that are necessary for the top leader of the future who fully understands the importance of harnessing organizational culture as an engine of value creation.

And finally, in Chapter 10, the Epilogue, I circle back to poignant recent events that illustrate the power of culture to separate the survivors during a recession.

2 What Is Organizational Culture?

Before we move on to the many practical aspects of culture change, we need to define what is meant by *organizational culture.* Using the criterion of "What does the CEO need to know about culture to be effective in changing it?" I will offer a quick review of the concept, ending with an operational definition. My sole objective is to bring practical clarity to the culture concept, laying the groundwork for what follows: a how-to guide for changing culture. The colloquial definition of *organizational culture* is far from clear, creating an obstacle for our primary goal: *how* to change it. Organizational culture is a "personality" and a "set of capabilities"—both are necessary components. But before fleshing out that distinction, let's start with the dictionary to get grounded on the concept.

We can quickly rule out several unlikely contenders listed in the *Webster's* dictionary definition. When referring to *organizational culture,* we *do not mean the following:*

- The act of developing intellectual and moral faculties, especially by education
- Expert care and training
- Enlightenment and excellence of taste acquired by intellectual and aesthetic training or acquaintance with and taste in fine arts, humanities, and broad aspects of science as distinguished from vocational and technical skills
- The act or process of cultivating living material (as bacteria or viruses) in prepared nutrient media

When we speak of organizational culture, we mean something more like this definition from the same *Webster's* source:

1. The integrated pattern of human knowledge, belief, and behavior that depends upon the capacity for learning and transmitting knowledge to succeeding generations
2. The customary beliefs, social forms, and material traits of a racial, religious, or social group; *also* the characteristic features of everyday existence (as diversions or a way of life shared by people in a place or time) <popular *culture*> <southern *culture*>
3. The set of shared attitudes, values, goals, and practices that characterizes an institution or organization <a corporate *culture* focused on the bottom line>
4. The set of values, conventions, or social practices associated with a particular field, activity, or societal characteristic <studying the effect of computers on print *culture*> <changing the *culture* of materialism will take time>

As with many terms in colloquial usage there is an assumed understanding that we all mean the same thing when using a term such as *organizational culture.* When someone says, "The culture of General Electric is completely different from that of Dow Chemical" or "Oracle has a very aggressive sales culture," everyone knows what is meant; that is, *here is a set of shared beliefs, attitudes, and behaviors that is subjectively different for those who compare and contrast these cultures.* This is an example of what I call "culture-as-personality." It is probably the more common and colloquial definition of organizational culture—one that revolves around values, style, climate, or "ambiance." In this usage of "organizational culture," we are focused on the overall climate of the company as a social system.

There is another important use of the term *culture*—what I call "culture-as-capability." Unlike "culture-as-personality," which refers more to style and climate, "culture-as-capability" refers more to enduring competencies of an organization. Here is an example:

> Southwest Airlines has developed an incredible customer service culture through empowerment of customer-facing staff with authority to make trade-off decisions that balance the long-term loyalty of the customer with various pricing, scheduling, and other costs. The company's leaders did this by rethinking all of their decision and signature policies, and rewarding reasonable initiative for those who can most directly have an impact on customer satisfaction. They have successfully created a true culture of empowerment aimed ultimately at one

> goal: creating shareholder value by making the flying experience as pleasant as possible, thus taking market share from competitors and generating profit.

Southwest Airlines invested time and energy to create a culture based not only on the engaging personality of CEO Herb Kelleher but also in customer service capabilities that included an organizational capability to carefully select, orient, and train customer-facing employees, for example, flight attendants that revel in singing and telling jokes. It also created internal reward and recognition structures to fully engage employees in the company mission, from profit sharing to funny prizes to unannounced visits from the popular CEO. The Southwest Airlines culture can be fully described only by reference to both the distinctive personality of the founder *and* the many human resource, accounting, and flight operational policies, procedures, and new organizational capabilities that were installed to reinforce that organizational personality.

Here is my working definition of organizational culture:

> Organizational culture has two faces: culture-as-personality and culture-as-capability. Both are critical elements in the practical context of "changing culture." Either of the two definitions is incomplete and inaccurate if taken without the other. Culture-as-personality calls out the qualitative, subjective, and experiential aspects of the "climate" and "values" of the organization. Culture-as-capability calls out the objective, more easily measurable aspects of culture, often described as "levers" that can be pulled to shape distinctive value-creating capabilities.

Let us now take up the culture-as-personality half of this definition in more detail.

Organizational Culture as "Social Personality"

Organizations share many similarities with human personality. Both are born, live, and die in the course of a complex set of exchanges with a changing external environment. Organizations have distinctive social environments—their "culture"—which have a unique collection of traits—their "personality." This is the popular definition of organizational culture most commonly found in the business literature of *Harvard Business Review*, *Fortune*, and *Business Week*. As core concepts in anthropology, psychology, and sociology were applied to the business world by writers such as Peter Drucker in the 1950s, the notion of culture as a distinctive social personality gained acceptance and has grown steadily.

Simply put, this view of organizational culture arises from application of fundamental tenets of personality psychology and cultural anthropology to organizations.

This definition from Edgar Schein comes closest to capturing the business conception of organizational culture that emerged in the 1980s and has developed in popular usage ever since:

> Organizational culture, or corporate culture, comprises the attitudes, experiences, beliefs and values of an organization. It has been defined as "the specific collection of values and norms that are shared by people and groups in an organization that control the way they interact with each other and with stakeholders outside the organization. Organizational values are beliefs and ideas about what kinds of goals members of an organization should pursue and ideas about the appropriate kinds or standards of behavior organizational members should use to achieve these goals. From organizational values develop organizational norms, guidelines or expectations that prescribe appropriate kinds of behavior by employees in particular situations and control the behavior of organizational members towards one another.[1]

In his well-known book *Organizational Culture and Leadership,* Schein articulates the view that these "core values" are largely *unintentional* reflections of the personalities of the leadership, especially founders of the organization. Schein did not design a formal culture typology, suggesting that organizational culture is a complex interplay between the personality of the founder or subsequent influential leaders and the environment. His central thesis was this: largely unconscious values are the root cause for attitudes, beliefs, and observable behaviors that in turn form the framework for various organizational rituals and ways of doing things, ultimately shaping the destiny of every organization.

This personality-oriented tradition spawned numerous organizational culture typologies: for example, Deal and Kennedy's "play hard/work hard," "tough-guy macho," "bet your company," and "process" cultures;[2] Handy's "role," "achievement," "power," and "relationship" cultures;[3] and Schaef and Fassel's "addictive culture."[4]

These examples, and many more, were attempts to categorize different types of culture—usually descriptive in nature, they often proposed more and less effective cultures. This tradition focuses on values, beliefs, and climate. Both organizational culture and individual personality show a persistent set of behaviors which we link together as "traits" or qualities.

Organizational Culture as Capability

As important a perspective as it provides, the "culture-as-personality" definition is only half the story in that it focuses on qualitative and descriptive characteristics. The other half of our definition revolves around organizational capabilities. Dave Ulrich, from the University of Michigan, is one of this perspective's most prolific and eloquent spokespersons.[5] One might also include in this perspective the "good to great" paradigm of Jim Collins[6] and the "congruence" model of David Nadler,[7] or the "strong culture" thesis of Kotter and Heskett[8] from Harvard. These authors move away from a set of values-based variables to a set of organizational capabilities in defining organizational culture. Whereas the central premise of the culture typologies was a descriptive search for the "best culture," the central premise of the capabilities definition of organizational culture is that *strong cultures are correlative, and perhaps causal, to performance.* By the same token, weak cultures abound, and similarly correlate to poor performance. Therefore we can study which capabilities within a culture most often correlate with success and thereby establish a knowledge of which capabilities add most value. The important new premise of the "culture-as-capability" perspective is that numerous "organizational personalities" can be successful starting from many different value-premises. By the same token, many "successful" organizational cultures (for example, Peters's "excellent companies") did not create value, or even survive.[9]

The Human Capital Capabilities Definition of Organizational Culture

In an attempt to move human resources and organizational development away from subjective, soft data toward measurable phenomenon, several authors have developed yet another definition of organizational culture-as-capability. Ulrich[10] and Lawler, Mohrman, and Ledford[11] have developed a paradigm that treats culture as the net total of a set of organizational capabilities. Usually these capabilities begin with what most think about as traditional human resource processes: communication and involvement processes, performance management, development of talent, compensation, and other measurable processes that have traditionally resided in the human resource function.

A particularly well-developed definition of organizational culture in this capabilities tradition is found in the Denison culture assessment tool (Figure 2.1). This model starts with four dimensions—Internal Focus, External

Focus, Flexible, and Stable—and then expands them into twelve organizational capabilities that form the skeleton for a tool that links culture-as-capability with traditional measures of financial performance:

1. Mission: strategic direction and intent, goals and objective, vision
2. Consistency: coordination and integration, agreement, core values
3. Involvement: capability development, team orientation, empowerment
4. Adaptability: creating change, customer focus, organizational learning

The great accomplishment of the Denison Organizational Culture Survey is that the twelve dimensions are scored as standard score percentiles, against a normative sample of close to a thousand companies over twenty years. Using this database, its creators have been able to do what no other culture paradigm has ever done: make statistically valid correlations between Denison scores and measures of financial performance.[12]

If Handy's fourfold typology is at one end of the organizational culture continuum, the Denison model is at the opposite end. When the Denison tool refers to "core values," it is not measuring specific value positions or "organizational traits" but the capability of the organization to evidence clear and consistent core values *whatever those values might be.*

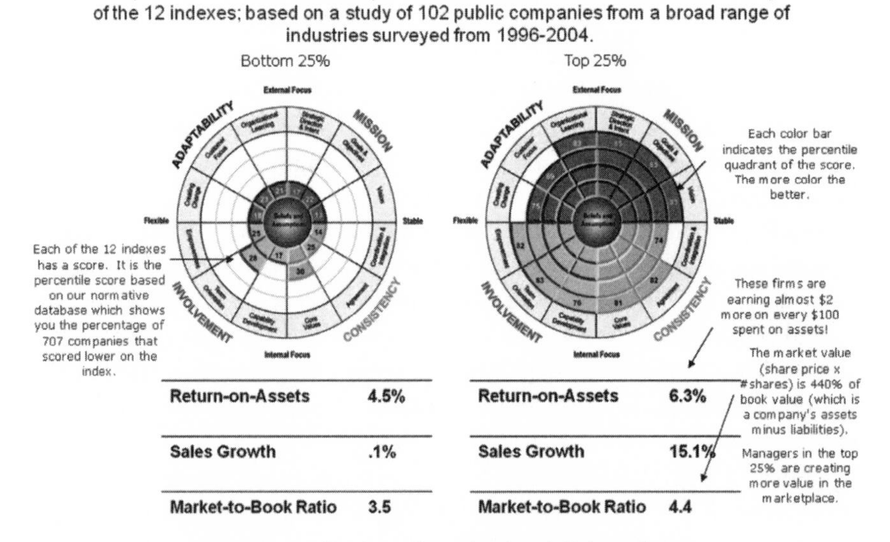

FIGURE 2.1. Denison Organizational Culture Survey
SOURCE: Used with permission of Daniel Denison.

Let us now return to our earlier question of why so many leaders seem so uninterested and uninformed about the enormous power for value creation of organizational culture. Consider the following "five fallacies" of perspective on organizational culture:

1. The "irrelevant" view: It's fluffy and subjective—it's unimportant, just ignore it.
2. The "fatalist" view: It's fixed DNA—live with it.
3. The "complexity" view: It can be influenced briefly and locally—it's too complex and random to ever really "shape"—it's a "living organism."
4. The "mechanistic" view: It's solely the result of human resource levers—compensation, benefits, and performance reviews.
5. The "personal influence" view: It's purely a reflection of leadership personality, of the founder or original leader; other influences are cosmetic.

This is the a priori challenge in defining organizational culture when you are a leader faced with altering your culture, a little or a lot. In this applied and practical context, all of these viewpoints are true—except the first—to one degree or another. I call these "the five fallacies" because they represent a collection of partial truths about organizational culture that have crept into our thinking about organizational culture in ways that ultimately destroy value, rather than creating it. The key take-away from the five fallacies is this: they are each partial truths that, if given credence, create a self-fulfilling prophecy that greatly reduces the leader's ability to shape culture in the service of value creation.

Conclusions

A useful working definition of organizational culture should include both the "culture-as-personality" *and* the "culture-as-capability" perspectives. My goal in the preceding has been to make this very simple point: organizational culture is a set of unique personality types in which none is better than another *and* organizational culture is a set of best practice capabilities that can be statistically arranged along a continuum of "better" and "worse." Both of these are necessary perspectives to incorporate into a robust working definition for leaders charged with the task of shaping or changing their organizational cultures. Stated as a prescription: to ignore one of the two definitions is to limit the effectiveness of your culture change effort before it has even started.

Here are the conclusions of the preceding stated as axioms:

1. Organizational culture is both a set of shared norms and values—a unique personality—*and* a portfolio of organizational capabilities.
2. There are no "best" organizational personalities when the criterion for "best" is financial performance and value creation. There are both some very flexible and some very structured organizations that evidence success and failure.
3. There are, however, clearly some "best" organizational capabilities: universal best practices that can be statistically linked to value creation—easily at the correlation level, and increasingly at the predictive level.
4. The well-informed leader charged with influencing culture is well advised to embrace both the personality and capability traditions in his or her working definition of organizational culture, realizing that there are many "right" ways to do this.
5. It is important to have a well-defined culture, as long as we remember that there are many "organizational personality types" that can be successful. This is precisely why both the "personality" and "capability" aspects are necessary elements for the practical goal of changing culture.

Chapter 2 Summary

In Chapter 2 I have created a working definition for organizational culture. This definition has two aspects, both of which are necessary for culture change, and neither of which can stand alone. Culture-as-personality calls out the qualitative, subjective, and experiential aspects of the "climate" of the organization. Culture-as-capability calls out the objective, more easily measurable aspects of culture often thought of as "levers" that can be pulled to shape distinctive value-creating capabilities.

In Chapter 3 I outline the Five Critical Success Factors for Culture Change.

3 Five Critical Success Factors for Culture Change

"Critical success factors" are just what the name suggests: activities that are critical for the success of a target outcome. The "Five Critical Success Factors for Culture Change" described in this chapter are a way for leaders to quickly determine whether they are focused on the correct priorities (Figure 3.1). A few of these critical success factors are time-honored, commonsense practices applied to the culture change paradigm; others are less obvious, though no less important. These five factors will certainly make good common sense to most readers, but they are also the result of observational and participatory research with more than a hundred culture initiatives over twenty-five years, in numerous different industries with companies

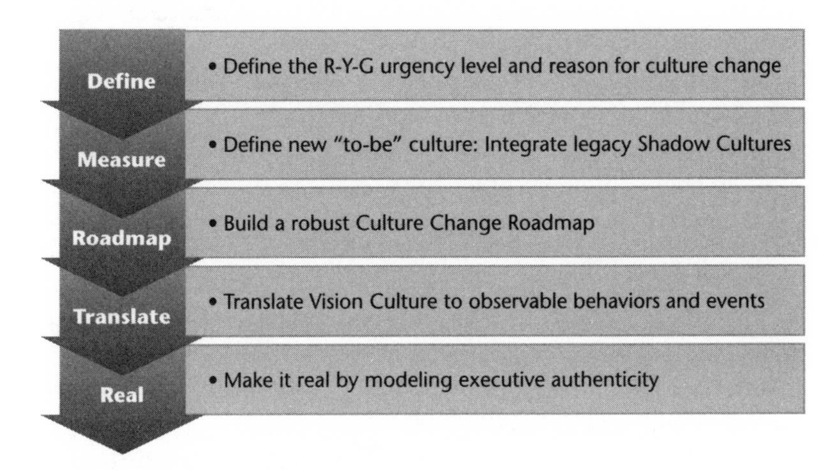

FIGURE 3.1. The Five Critical Success Factors for Culture Change

of varying sizes. When one or more of these five factors is missing, the intended transformation of the culture will not occur as quickly and may outright fail. Of course, organizational culture is evolving all the time in unintended and "organic" ways. My focus on these five critical success factors is to call out those intentional leadership activities that target and accelerate the movement of the culture in crucial ways.

Critical Success Factor 1: Define the Level of Urgency and the Reason for Culture Change

Anyone can change, but without a reason—why should they?

The top leader in the culture must define the "why" of the change and create the "motivating reason" for what no organization ever wants to initiate on its own: changing comfortable and familiar behavior patterns. The "legacy" culture is a powerful force that should never be underestimated as an obstacle to successful culture change. Think of it as a "life force" that wants to continue its existence and will fight any attempt to alter it. Even in a relatively new or young company, by the time the leadership is thinking about "our culture," something has come before, and that cultural footprint will have a momentum; perhaps less momentum than in a hundred-year-old company, but never "zero."

The second powerful force that must be addressed and offset in a successful culture change is the gravitational pull of daily operations—the day-to-day business of the organization. Obviously, running the business is important and not something that anyone thinks should "go away." I will address in Chapter 5 the very real danger of "internal preoccupation." Despite this danger, carving out space from the daily activity of the organization once culture change is deemed necessary, on the basis or rationale of a "motivating reason," is a critical success factor.

A third powerful force that opposes culture change is competing initiatives. These might be important initiatives related to building organizational capability in key functional areas deemed to be competitively, or otherwise, important. I will have a great deal more to say about this in later discussion of the "red-yellow-green" discrimination of level of urgency in Chapter 4. There will almost always be other enterprise-level initiatives that compete for organizational energy and attention. Part of the job of the top leader is to make this prioritization. Good leaders will prioritize clearly and decisively; poor leaders will fail to prioritize with conviction and clarity; and incompetent leaders will not prioritize. Great leaders will prioritize and inspire their lieutenants to inspire others.

The central point of culture change Critical Success Factor 1 can be stated as a logical proposition:

> If the top leader has determined that culture change is necessary, then success of that effort will hinge in significant measure on the degree to which a motivating reason has been clearly articulated for those who must change.

There are as many ways to do this as there are organizations and leaders, but there are several universal factors as well—which I will discuss in more detail in Chapter 5, on "Setup." For purposes of articulating critical success factors, suffice it to say for now that *if a compelling reason for culture change has not been convincingly communicated at the outset, culture change is unlikely to occur.*

Critical Success Factor 2: Define the "New" and "Legacy" Cultures

> *Culture change is always a journey—one made possible only when you know where you are starting and ending.*

There is always a gap between the "culture we think we need" and the "culture that we have." Defining this gap is a critical success factor, and I have seen many culture change efforts fail due to lack of awareness of and attention to this key success factor. In fact, it is more complicated than simply understanding the gap between the "as is" and the "to be" cultures: there are two "Shadow Cultures" hidden in every organizational culture (Figure 3.2). Understanding the Shadow Cultures and thoroughly resolving differences between them is an important step in the Culture Change Process, which we will explore thoroughly in Chapters 5 and 6.

The Shadow Cultures are not distinct subcultures so much as they are potential distortions or "mistakes" in conceiving the "to be" culture.

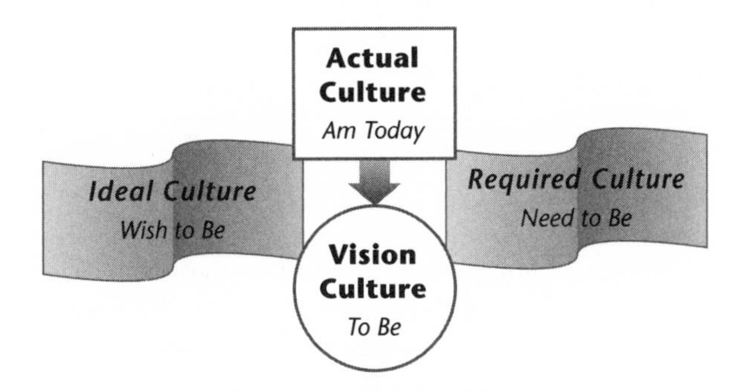

FIGURE 3.2. The Shadow Cultures

Though often overlapping, there are really four distinct aspects that should be considered in a culture change, two "real" cultures and two "shadow" cultures. We will have a great deal more to say about the Shadow Cultures and how to manage them in Chapters 5 and 6. For now, let us briefly define what all four aspects are:

1. The *Actual* Culture—*what we actually are*—is the combination of the legacy and current cultures *as they really are,* that is, as seen through objective eyes that are not biased by the distortion of "looking good" or "not looking bad." There are few leadership teams that truly see the Actual Culture—for the obvious reason that clear self-perception, especially of the cultural improvement areas, is always muddied by self-interest. This is one of the reasons why so many culture change efforts begin or end with the departure of executive leadership. It's not that they are bad leaders, as much as they cannot see clearly the culture that has been created by them in the course of their leadership.
2. The *Ideal* Culture—*what we would like to be*—is the first of the two Shadow Cultures. It is a projected image of values, behaviors, and capabilities that we *would like to see* in the organization. It is important to realize that this idealized image of what we would like to be is not a realistic or appropriate target for the culture change process—at least not by itself—and for this reason it is a "shadow," not a reality in the way that the Actual and Vision cultures are.
3. The *Required* Culture—*what the external environment needs us to be in order to produce value for stakeholders*—is the second Shadow Culture, a culture that is demanded by internal and external reality—or the stated business strategy of the company. This Required Culture is almost certainly different than the Ideal or Actual cultures, particularly when the strategy has recently changed.
4. The *Vision* Culture—*what we have committed to become*—is the integration of the three other cultures; a vision of the future that pulls together *who we actually are, who we would like to be, and who we are required to be* into a mature and realistic vision of what we are actually going to strive for.

Any of you that have spent some time in the modern American corporation will know that many organizations tackle the challenge of organizational culture with a one-day offsite in which the "new culture" is discussed by senior executives. This set of flip charts is then polished up into a communication package and ceremoniously distributed. What is badly overlooked in offsites such as these is the existence of the Shadow Cultures. The reason such efforts are doomed to failure before they begin is that neither the Actual Culture nor the Shadow Cultures have been adequately identified or vetted, and so remain cultures that will powerfully but invisibly influence the culture change effort in a number of predictable ways:

- When the truth of the historical and current Actual Culture has not been honestly recognized and discussed, it continues to exert powerful forces on any attempt to change.
- The Ideal Culture is most often an intellectual exercise in which some popular homilies ("We like to have fun" or "Customers come first") get slapped up onto a flip chart. These "noble aspirations" do not take into account the real constraints of the Actual Culture, or the necessary modifications of the Required Culture. They are a naïve or superficial academic exercise, when taken alone.
- The Required Culture may be very close to the future Vision Culture, but that depends greatly on the circumstance. In almost all cases, it is important to include some key elements of the Actual and Ideal cultures. This may be for simple practical reasons, for example, "We are an aggressive, sales-oriented culture that will never be a completely reflective and strategic culture." Or, there is almost always some "baby" that no one really wants to throw out with the "bathwater" in the legacy culture, for example, "It's okay that we think relationships are important, we just need to be more disciplined about accountability—not suddenly "heartless." To throw the "baby out with the bathwater" may be unrealistic, and also may be out of alignment with what the Required Culture demands.

I will explore the Shadow Cultures in more detail shortly. Critical Success Factor 2 might best be stated in this way: *the "to be" future vision of the organizational culture must seek to integrate and be informed by its Real Culture and its Shadow Cultures, or else the culture change effort is doomed to failure from the start.*

Critical Success Factor 3: Build a Culture Change Roadmap

Culture change is a big project that requires clarity about who does what, when, and where.

Though plenty of work, this third critical success factor should be familiar to anyone who has tried to coordinate enterprise activity in organizations large or small. The Culture Change Roadmap is the "master planning document" of the initiative. There are numerous variations, but a strong Culture Change Roadmap should always include the following:

- Delineation of the key activity tracks
- Observable, and when possible, measurable milestones and outcomes
- Clearly assigned responsibilities

Supporting this roadmap would be an Excel or Project document that lists target dates, milestones, and persons responsible for the many subtasks that are necessary to make this roadmap a robust project plan. There are many ways to organize the Culture Change Roadmap, and we will have more to say about this in Chapter 5.

There is a level of detail, documentation, and management that is not the CEO's job. As with the company budget, it is critical that the CEO know what's in it, how and where it is being executed, and who is responsible for which pieces. The Culture Change Roadmap is the organization's commitment to observable progress and should be a company confidential, but internally public, document that is reviewed by top leadership on a regular basis and communicated broadly within the organization.

As a tool of project management, the Culture Change Roadmap is really nothing new. It is essentially the "project management plan" for the culture change. It is one of the five critical success factors for the same reason that successful implementation of a new enterprise resource planning system or acquisition of another firm would also require a similar mechanism for master planning and coordination.

What is less obvious, and surprising, is that so few organizations take the trouble to properly invest in this simple tool. Unlike a budget—the ultimate "project plan"—the Culture Change Roadmap can be daunting to those uncomfortable in attempting measurement of non-numerical phenomenon. In part due to the challenge of measuring social, cultural, and behavioral outcomes, the tremendous value provided by the Culture Change Roadmap is missed. A central and recurrent tenet of this book revolves on this point: not knowing how to measure, and certainly not being comfortable, are poor excuses for treating culture change in passive or fatalistic ways. There are ways to objectively and reliably measure the important elements of culture change, and these must be coordinated into a master document that tracks progress.

Most leadership teams can forge a project plan, requiring first, careful identification and prioritization of the most important culture outcomes and second, creative problem solving about how to measure progress and success in these outcomes. The analogy to an enterprise-level initiative aimed at creating some key capability is very close. Migration to a new culture is really the same thing as creation of a new "meta-capability." Organizational culture is essentially a constellation of several capabilities linked together under one umbrella. Remember we defined organizational culture as *both* "company personality" and "organizational capability"? A well-conceived and constructed Culture Change Roadmap will include structural process improvement, human capital, reward, and individual behavioral capabilities that delineate where the "rainbow meets the road" in actually changing the culture.

One of the reasons it is so important to embrace the dual definition of organizational culture as both personality and set of capabilities is that this allows us to demystify and measure the what, how, who, when, and where of the culture change. The Culture Change Roadmap—though no more or less than a high-level enterprise project plan—is absolutely critical to the success of a culture change effort. Like any such tool, it can be well or poorly conceived and executed. There is some small danger of *overinvesting* in the Culture Change Roadmap by creating something overly elaborate, but this is the exception. By far the most common mistake is oversimplification and a lack of measurable outcomes and clear responsibility at the executive level. This is precisely why the Culture Change Roadmap must be owned and driven by the CEO, even though the majority of the content and execution will be completed by the leadership team and a cross-functional task force.

Critical Success Factor 4: Translate the Vision Culture into Behavioral Competencies and Measurable Events

The journey map from the ten-thousand-foot view is useless when you're on foot.

Translating the Vision Culture into behavioral competencies and measurable events is also important. There are many right ways to do this, and the final product varies considerably with the organization in terms of its format, level of detail, and other customized features. I will have a great deal more to say about this when I discuss "Launch" in Chapter 5. Like a number of elements that I will touch on, the actual translation from Vision Culture to behavioral competencies is not something that the CEO or top leader actually does him- or herself. This task is heavy lifting better done by someone with expertise in behavioral competencies. Because it is a critical success factor—in other words, culture change will not be successful without completion of this step—it is absolutely a work product that the CEO needs to own. As the following Bank of Hawaii example illustrates, the CEO and top team will need to become very familiar with the behavioral competencies end product—because they own the overall task, but, more important, because they need to live it (Critical Success Factor 5). We will dive into more depth on this point in Chapter 6. At present, an example is the best way to illustrate the benefits of translating vision into concrete and observable behaviors:

> In 2000 Bank of Hawaii set out to change its culture in response to the disruptive changes in the regulatory environment that completely transformed how a bank was defined—broadening these boundaries in such a way as to open up an entirely new competitive landscape that would now include brokerage, insurance, and numerous other financial services. Among many things that Bank of Hawaii did to adapt to this change in the environment—which really required a total transformation—it became clear to everyone that the legacy "support" culture needed to change dramatically in the direction of a "performance culture." This notion of the "performance culture" was articulated in a number of narrative documents that defined both the strategic business and cultural context. After this Critical Success Factor 3 was completed, the Managing Committee—the bank's top executive group of chairman, president, and three vice-chairmen—spent a half day teasing out what the "performance culture" actually meant in terms of observable behaviors. With some help from the author and the senior Human Resources executive, the committee agreed on five leadership competencies as the "critical few":
>
> 1. *Achievement:* Makes an internal push for stretch objectives. Accepts personal risk-taking and initiative. Has a sense of urgency.
> 2. *Information seeking:* Makes a systematic attempt to obtain needed data or feedback. Involves others in that information gathering.
> 3. *Customer service:* Seeks information about real underlying needs of client. Acts as a client advisor, advocate, and partner.
> 4. *Developing others:* Values and models coaching, training, and development. Delegates fully to subordinates as a vehicle for development. Rewards development with "coin of the realm."
> 5. *Teamwork and cooperation:* Empowers others. Promotes a positive, friendly climate. Facilitates a win-win resolution of team conflicts.
>
> These five leadership competencies—in addition to other structural, reward, and process targets—became the "kernel" that served as the master code for culture focus. Application of this "kernel" spanned the gamut from expectations the Managing Committee began placing on their own behavior to numerous human capital levers such as performance management, compensation, and talent development processes in the organization. Depending on the context, this "kernel" took on various forms; for example, in the talent management arena each of these five competencies was then further defined in greater detail that included four or more subcompetencies for each of the original five.

It goes without saying that the specific "target" or Vision Culture (the integration of the Actual Culture and the Shadow Cultures) and related competencies just illustrated were unique to that strategic time and place for Bank of Hawaii, and not every organization would execute in the same way. The point is this: if you are serious about creating true culture change, then you need to be serious about Critical Success Factor 4. Take that Vision Culture document and translate it into something that is observable and, ideally, measurable. The necessity and benefit of this critical success factor should be obvious: without such specificity of observable behavior, there is no way for well-intentioned members of the organization to focus on a common goal. Just as dangerous, those who cannot or will not focus on the new behaviors have an easy out when the target behaviors are not well-defined and linked clearly to the Vision Culture and business strategy.

This same principle of objective measurement should also apply to any initiatives that come to be included in the Culture Change Roadmap; these initiatives should be what is called "SMART":

- Specific
- Measurable
- Achievable
- Realistic
- Timeframed

For example, many Culture Change Roadmaps will include some change to the performance management system—ranging from "install it because we don't have one" to "align the content with the new Vision Culture behavioral competencies." The difference between a "roadmap" and a "list," and why this is a critical success factor, is that the roadmap will specify what the outcome is, how that outcome will be measured, and what the timeframe of that outcome will be. Larger roadmap outcomes will have subordinate milestones that demonstrate progress toward the final outcome to make them easier to track, as well as demonstrate how they are achievable and realistic.

Critical Success Factor 5: Model Executive Authenticity

Without authentic executive modeling of expected new behaviors, the culture will not change.

The well-intentioned CEO and top team could diligently and artfully achieve success in all four of the previous critical success factors yet ultimately fail in their overall objective to change the culture if the top leadership team does not consistently model the behaviors of the Vision Culture in word and deed, explicit and implicit behavior. It is a bit unlikely that the leadership team that has successfully met the specification of the four previous critical success factors would fail completely—but it is quite common for one or two members of the leadership team to behave in ways that are inconsistent with the new culture. It is absolutely critical that the CEO and leadership team hold themselves scrupulously accountable to key leadership behavior defined in Critical Success Factor 4 and, to the greatest extent possible, make decisions and communicate in ways that reflect the "kernel" of the Vision Culture.

This is important for the obvious reason that it is impossible to be credible with any version of "Do what I say, not what I do." Even more important than this observable behavior is the practical fact that these new leadership behaviors *are* the new culture. As decisions in all areas of the company are made under the new light of the Vision Culture, these actions begin to shift the current Actual Culture to the Vision Culture. When the leadership team does not fully articulate, embrace, and then model these new behaviors, yet continues to speak about them, failure will be quick and painful. There is a special kind of cynicism and disengagement that arises when members of the organization see their leaders as hypocritical. It is a widespread cancer in the modern business world and for leadership beyond the corporate world into the political sphere.

One of the several reasons why it is so important to understand and integrate the Shadow Cultures (the Ideal and Required cultures) into a realistic Vision Culture is to ensure that what is aspired to *is* a realistic set of behavioral changes for the leadership team. It is far better for a leadership team to acknowledge the realistic limitations of what it can change and incorporate that attenuated objective into the Vision Culture than for it to ratify an unrealistic set of idealized culture attributes that are unlikely to come about.

This is why spending the appropriate amount of time to clearly understand the Shadow Cultures is so important: what is decided in this phase of the initial framing of the culture change must be modeled first, and then consistently, by the top leadership team.

In summary, no CEO should undertake the process of organizational culture change without adhering closely to the steps outlined in the Five Critical Success Factors for Culture Change:

1. Define the level of urgency and the reason for culture change
2. Define the "new" and "legacy" cultures
3. Build a culture change roadmap

4. Translate the vision culture into behavioral competencies and measurable events
5. Model Executive Authenticity

Inadequate completion of any one of these five critical steps can lead to a slowdown or a complete halt in your efforts at culture change.

Chapter 3 Summary

In Chapter 3 I outlined those "critical few" success factors that should be present in any culture change effort that is serious about results. This ends Section I and leads us to Section II, where we will dive into the four stages of culture change execution: Setup, Launch, Propagating the Wave, and Celebrating Progress.

Section II

Implementing Culture Change

In these next four chapters I will outline the four sequential phases of the Culture Change Process. In the interest of creating a practical model that maps to reality, the Culture Change Process is laid out as a sequence of steps. Keep in mind that an actual culture change will never play out exactly as depicted in our "field guide." Indeed, it is unlikely that the culture change of any two organizations would look the same. The map is not the territory, but how valuable it is to have a good map when you have lost your way!

Not every organization and situation requires the same level of effort to align culture with strategy, so naturally, not all of these tools and methods are required in every circumstance. In the "real world" of organizational life, things are iterative and messy. As every CEO knows, the big secret is that you don't really control very much—though you may influence a great deal depending on your ability and the circumstance you are in.

Despite these uncontroversial truths about leading in real organizations, there is tremendous value for the CEO in realizing where truly "hard dependencies" exist in the Culture Change Process, in other words, what the first step is that you should always complete before going to step two, unless you want to come back from step three to redo step one.

Of equal value is to appreciate that short list of critical success factors without which a culture change will not occur. For example, given a moderate to high level of urgency for culture change, I can categorically assert that the effort will fail unless the five critical success factors have been met, in sequential order. For example, Critical Success Factor 5, Model Executive Authenticity, is always a good thing. As it relates to culture change, it is a wasteful investment of personal and organizational energy to focus on it before the Vision Culture has been well defined and translated into observable behaviors.

Similarly, efforts to define the "new culture" that have not taken into account the Shadow Cultures will always yield a suboptimized culture change initiative, often one that fails due to investment in something that is superficial, unmeasurable, and uninspiring, instead of "true" and "real."

The real world is complex, messy, and uncontrollable, but there are rules and predictable outcomes for those with eyes to see, and the wisdom to use them. The primary job of effective top leadership is to "define reality" for the organization by communicating organizational goals and the means to achieve these goals, and establishing the "rules of the game." The Culture Change Process we will now dive into is a map of that territory that includes basic rules you should not ignore, as well as numerous tools, suggestions, and ideas for a variety of situations with which you may find yourself confronted. The Five Critical Success Factors for Culture Change are those rules in the "culture change universe" that you should ignore only at your peril, if you are truly serious about changing your culture. Other suggested tools and methods in these next several chapters are just that: suggestions to draw from depending on your situation and preference.

The next several chapters will each respectively tackle one stage of the culture change process, from Setup to Launch to Propagating the Wave to Celebrating Progress (Figure II.1). A short preview of these chapters is provided here.

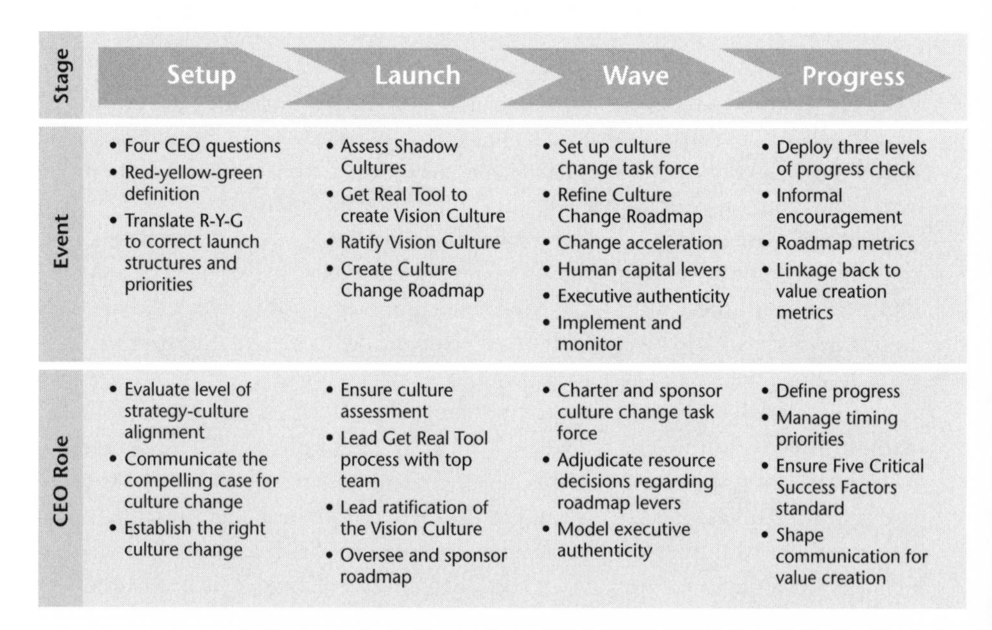

FIGURE II.1. Culture Change Process—master view

- *Setup:* Realizing the need for shift in the culture, making the case for the initiative, and establishing those initial structures that will be required to develop the new culture are necessary first steps. The CEO's decision to define the need for culture change as "Condition Red," "Condition Yellow," or "Condition Green" is what will drive Launch. In this chapter I will offer the "CEO's Level of Urgency Assessment Tool" and several case examples.
- *Launch:* Identifying the Shadow Cultures and integrating these into the Vision Culture, which then becomes the target, is at the heart of any culture change regardless of whether it is in "mild yellow" or "severe red" condition. The "Get Real Tool" and baseline measurement of culture are offered as key methods to create tangible, measurable impact. Linkage to value creation and development of the Culture Change Roadmap are the final outputs of the "Launch" step.
- *Propagating the Wave:* In Chapter 6 I identify the "big three," must-have levers of culture change for CEOs. First of these levers is best practices for change acceleration and change communication: a methodology for minimizing the natural resistance that we all have to any change. The second lever comprises key human capital and capability tools such as organizational design, competency definition, rewards and metrics, and talent-management processes—all essential initiatives on the roadmap to help make the Vision Culture real. And the third lever provides ways to model executive authenticity with a variety of tools and methods for the CEO and top team.
- *Celebrating Progress:* What has been accomplished? How, when, and where should the CEO and top team call out progress in the culture change? Linkage between value creation and the Culture Change Roadmap is the ideal metric to measure culture change success, but there must also be recognition and encouragement on an *ad hoc* basis. In Chapter 7 I explore the CEO's role in celebration and recommend best practices for tangible, intangible, and other means of celebrating success.

Role of the CEO in the Culture Change Process

Before moving on to the first stage of the Culture Change Process, role definition between the CEO and other culture change or human resource experts is worth mention. It is my strongly held view that culture must be owned by the CEO or top leader if it is to have any hope of success. This is a simple and, to anyone with practical experience of organizational change, self-evident truth. The complexity beneath this simple truth lies in the details of how, when, and where the CEO should be involved in which aspects of the Culture Change Process.

There is general agreement at the two extremes of this question. Few would disagree that the CEO must establish culture change as a priority. Few would disagree that the CEO should not be involved in translating behavioral competencies into items on the performance appraisal. Exactly who does what in the Culture Change Process also depends on available expertise and talent within and without the organization. In the delineation of the Culture Change Process that follows I have tried *not* to dive too deeply into the technical details of various tools, methods, and the extensive body of change management or human capital methodologies that are described by others and appropriately aimed at organizational effectiveness and human resource professionals.

The analogy used in Chapter 1 is worth repeating: the CEO needs to understand as much about the Culture Change Process as he or she would about any other important functional discipline, without being a technical expert. The delineation of the Culture Change Process that follows touches on numerous areas that CEOs need to know enough about to understand why that method or tool is important, what the outcomes look like, and what their direct involvement should be. I am absolutely *not* suggesting that CEOs should develop the technical expertise required to execute or manage all of these specific culture change steps, but that they open themselves to a different level of responsibility than they have perhaps felt before relative to their leadership of these "soft" areas.

Setup Launch Wave Progress

4 Setup

If creating value is the central mission of the CEO, establishing priorities is an essential tool for doing so. The first stage in the Culture Change Process is called "Setup" because the activities of this step are all related to setting up the correct structures and making the appropriate case for culture change. To do this effectively requires that the CEO first evaluate what level of threat and urgency is presented by the culture of the organization. This assessment, in turn, provides a rational foundation for what level of organizational attention and resources should be applied to the culture change effort.

In this chapter I will first provide a decision model to help the CEO establish the correct level of urgency for culture change, then will move on to a "red-yellow-green" catalogue that links a continuum of culture change urgency to appropriate levels of organizational attention.

A "first cause" set of questions facing every CEO is how he or she will "define reality": "What is expected of me?" "What is my agenda?" "How do I create more value than is already present by the time I move on?" "What is working and not working?" This is a set of questions that every new CEO should be answering. It is absolutely a set of questions that the board of directors should be asking to inform their choice of the CEO, and subsequently evaluate performance.

Given that the pace of change in the external environment has so greatly accelerated in recent years, it is not a stretch to assert that every CEO has a materially "new" set of challenges created by external changes at least every couple of years. At some level, every day, week, and quarter brings new challenges, but for our purposes relative to culture change, the periodicity is more appropriately set at twelve to twenty-four months. Culture simply cannot change in less than a year or two, and the impact of the answers to these questions is set in a similar timescale.

The Four Questions Every CEO Must Answer

There are four basic questions the CEO should be asking when beginning a new job, or on a periodic basis to ensure adaptation to external changes. These four questions are sequentially dependent, meaning that question 4 cannot really be answered without the answer to question 3, and so on. Naturally, in the real world there is iteration in the sense that leaders may have enough data about question 2 to move forward on question 3, but then make further refinements as new information surfaces.

1. What is expected of me to create value and keep my job? (Hopefully the same thing!)
2. Is the current company strategy a reasonable way to create that value?
3. Do I have the right organizational culture to execute that strategy?
4. Do I have the right team to mostly do all of the preceding?

Questions 1 and 2 are critical precursors that set the stage for question 3, which is central to our focus and the starting place to determine the need for culture change: "Given this strategy, is the existing culture that I see in front of me the *best*, or depending on other priorities, an *acceptable* vehicle through which to execute that strategy?"

The reader may be surprised to hear from this author that not every company should make culture change a top priority. Many companies have a culture in place that does not justify or require the kind of organizational attention demanded in the Culture Change Process described here. Without too much work, one can easily imagine some obvious examples:

- The company has just completed a three-year culture change effort, after which the CEO retired or left for health reasons.
- The answer to question 3 is, "Yes, the organizational culture is already a good, or good enough, culture to align with and execute the strategy."
- The answer to question 2 is, "There is no company strategy, or it has failed and that's why I, the CEO, am now here—to define the right strategy for value creation. Therefore the question of culture, though important, must follow resolution of the strategy question."

- The answer to question 1 is, "To keep my job will require me to substantially divest or downsize half of the company in the next twelve months. After that's done, we'll define a strategy and build the culture that can support it. Until then, it is a distraction and stranded investment of organizational time and attention."

Two Caveats

Having acknowledged that not every organization needs a robust culture change process, I would add two important qualifications to that assertion before going on to discuss in more depth when culture change is critical versus desirable.

The first of these qualifications is an observation based on my many years of culture change experience. In that final "lonely at the top" decision by the CEO about how important is culture at this time and place, it has been my observation that a "fatalistic" filter often colors the answer to this question of whether culture change is a high or low priority. In the language of "decision error," the probability of a "false negative" decision error ("The culture *is* strong, healthy, and well-aligned with the strategy, and therefore needs no attention") is much higher than the probability of the "false positive" decision error in which inappropriate or excessive attention is placed on shaping the culture relative to other priorities.

The reasons for this will vary with the particular CEO and circumstance but among common misconceptions about organizational culture, a tendency toward the "irrelevant," "fatalist," and "complexity" view is far more common than a proactive view based on a previous sense of mastery and success in shaping a culture.

The second qualification to the statement that not every organization requires a major culture change focus is that even the perfectly aligned strategy and culture is a delicate and temporary balance that requires some shaping and direction by the CEO and leadership to maintain. In what I will define, just ahead, as the "green" condition, there may indeed not be an urgent need for enterprise-level, public attention to be placed on changing or shaping the culture, but there will *always* be a need for some continuing attention to the culture, even if only a relatively modest investment.

Where Do You Stand When Trying to "Move the Earth" with Your Lever?

Keeping in mind our two caveats—first, that CEOs err on the side of underestimating the importance and feasibility of shaping culture and second, that there is never a justification for complete inattention to organizational culture—we move now to consider how the CEO or top leader can best determine actions going forward and answer question 3 above: "Do I have the right organizational culture to execute my strategy? If, not, how urgent a priority does that need to be?"

A useful analogy comes to mind in Archimedes' famous claim: "Give me a lever and a place to stand, and I will move the earth." If the "earth" is organizational culture, and the "lever" is the culture change process, the question before us is where to "stand." A key piece of the answer to that question lies in the CEO's *a priori* beliefs about organizational culture, that is, what the CEO's basic assumptions are about what organizational culture is and how or whether it can be influenced. In Chapter 2 I argued that organizational culture is absolutely susceptible to influence by a leader with the right set of understanding and tools. Though somewhat "invisible" in the question of "where to stand," accepting the malleability of organizational culture is quite important for obvious reasons. If the CEO comes to the question with an unconscious bias that culture is "fatalistic" or "irrelevant," the choice about where to stand has largely been made, irrespective of the actual reality of how well the strategy and culture are aligned. This is the most common cause for the frequent "false positive" decision error—organizational culture is erroneously dismissed with a "no action necessary" conclusion.

Let's assume for the moment that the reader is persuaded by the basic logic presented in Chapter 2 and that the "fatalistic" and "irrelevant" distortions are not present, that is, you believe that *organizational culture is changeable with the right tools and methods*. Even after that hurdle is passed, the second half of this "level of urgency" question will depend on how effectively the CEO assesses the current situational reality of strategy-culture alignment. It is to that question of urgency that I now turn: when is the misalignment between strategy and culture at a "red," "yellow," or "green" threat level?

Red-Yellow-Green Levels of Culture Change Urgency

We use a simple three-level model to help the CEO and top leadership determine levels of urgency for culture change: Condition Red, Condition Yellow, and Condition Green. The R-Y-G model is a decision tool that I have found useful over twenty-five years of field experience, and hope the reader does as well.

There is some well-conducted survey research that is confirmatory of both this R-Y-G model and broadly of several of the culture change critical success factors. The IBM Global CEO Study[1] is an excellent example; the authors concluded the following:

> Over a two-year period, the percentage of CEOs expecting substantial change climbed from 65 percent in 2006 to 83 percent in 2008, but those reporting they had successfully managed change in the past rose just 4 percentage points, up from 57 percent in 2006 to 61 percent in 2008. This disparity between expecting change and feeling able to manage it—the "Change Gap"—nearly tripled between 2006 and 2008.
>
> Most CEOs consider themselves and their organizations to be executing change poorly, but some practitioners have begun to learn how to improve their outcomes. For the practitioners themselves, we found that, on average, 41 percent of projects were considered successful in meeting project objectives within planned time, budget and quality constraints, compared to the remaining 59 percent of projects which missed at least one objective or failed entirely.
>
> Troubled or failed projects create cost overruns and, by definition, fall short of achieving the desired objectives. When nearly 60 percent of projects fail to meet objectives, significant expense is incurred in terms of wasted money, lost opportunity and lack of focus. Change Masters [professional change consultants with expertise in change management] understand that reducing the likelihood of troubled projects, even slightly, can have a clear and rapid payback.
>
> Our respondents identified several of the key barriers to change. Although tangible tasks like changing IT systems or addressing technology barriers may be expected to present difficulties, our practitioners did not report them among their greatest challenges.
>
> Instead, the main obstacles they identified were changing mindsets and attitudes (58%), corporate culture (49%) and underestimating project complexity (35%). Project professionals—who typically request more time, more people, more money—reported that these soft challenges are actually more problematic than shortage of resources (33%).
>
> Practitioners firmly place key responsibility for the fate of change projects in the executive suite—an overwhelming 92 percent named top management sponsorship as the most important factor for successful change. Rounding out the top four success factors were employee involvement (72%), honest and timely communication (70%), and corporate culture that motivates and promotes change (65%).

I take comfort in the empirical validation that this very recent study of fifteen hundred CEOs and change practitioners provides for my similar conclusions drawn from twenty-five years of applied practice. To briefly summarize the relevant conclusions:

- Culture-related variables are the single biggest obstacles to successful enterprise project implementation—by a significant margin

overshadowing the "hard" factors such as technology, functional expertise, and resources.
- By almost unanimous consensus (92 percent), top management must be actively involved and fully supportive for any change initiative to succeed.

Not every organizational culture is in such a state of strategic misalignment that it deserves the same level of organizational attention. The R-Y-G construct is a benchmark tool for the CEO and top leadership to evaluate how high a priority to place on the Culture Change Process. As the reader will see, that determination has widely varying implications for the level of organizational attention and resources that should be allocated to the activity. So it is more than an interesting categorization system—though certainly that. When properly used it will help the CEO avoid the "false positive" yet not go overboard to the "false negative" to over-invest precious executive attention on a less deserving activity. Let me now define what I mean by red, yellow and green conditions before I go on to outline in more detail the "Launch" actions necessary for the red and yellow conditions.

Condition Green

As the name implies, Condition Green is a circumstance in which there is good alignment between business strategy and culture reality (the Actual Culture). Depending on how comfortable one is generalizing key findings from the IBM Global Change Study, it is safe to say that not very many organizations find themselves in a Condition Green situation.

Without exception in my experience, Condition Green companies are that way because current or previous top leadership has invested heavily in shaping and aligning the culture. A practical definition of Condition Green is simply this: there is little variance between the Actual Culture and the two Shadow Cultures because they already line up well with the Vision Culture. The Green Condition is one in which the Vision Culture is "already here"—because the real work of identifying and integrating the other cultures has been done previously. The Actual, Required, and Ideal cultures are close to being the same, which by definition means they are well aligned with the strategy. As we have defined it, the Required Culture *is* that set of cultural traits and capabilities that are necessary for the strategy to be successful—usually not the same set of traits and capabilities that currently exist (Actual Culture) or are aspired to (Ideal Culture). A good example of the Condition Green situation is provided in Case 4.1.

Case 4.1. Don't Screw This Up

The case begins with the succession from General Electric's Jack Welch to Jeff Immelt in 2000. Welch had been CEO for many years and reached an age where both he and his board of directors felt it was time for him to hand over the reigns to a younger CEO. Immelt's primary mandate was some version of "Don't screw this up!" That mandate did not mean that Immelt should adopt a fatalistic view toward shaping the culture, nor did he. With hindsight, we now see that Immelt faced incredible challenges with the crash of the dot-com era and the recession of 2001. The task of keeping afloat in harsh times did mean that culture change was not his highest priority, nor was it anything pressing or broken. The challenge for Immelt is a good example of the "Condition Green" mandate. The culture was in proper alignment with the strategy but still required continued reinforcement and minor modifications based on changes in the environment that would require a shift in strategy.

Like individual human personality, there is no state of "not-behaving" for an organizational culture. Even seemingly quiescent or passive behavior is still behavior. "Lack of behaving" is still behaving. As CEO or top leader, you may consciously elect not to attend to the culture for a variety of legitimate reasons. Or, out of ignorance, you may not be aware of it—but in either case, all of your behaviors as a leader will continue to shape and influence that culture.

It is important to remember that organizational culture is never a static phenomenon but truly an open system that is constantly evolving. The great paradox is that despite this evolution over time, it is surprisingly stable and resistive to significant rapid change, even when this is literally a requirement for survival of the company.

In Condition Green the culture still needs attention, but there is no manifest misalignment with the strategy or between divisions of the company. This does not mean that "no action" is required or that the leadership should not be paying attention to how their behaviors continue to reinforce the well-aligned culture. For culture, once tuned up and aligned, is a fragile state that can be lost quickly through inattention.

In Condition Green, organizational culture should be on the radar of leadership in continuing management practices, but not necessarily one of the top five priorities for the company—perhaps not even one of the top ten. Like the boundary between "yellow" and "red," the boundary between "green" and "yellow" is a continuum of degrees, not a digital event. Unfortunately, it is also not really an empirically determinable event but one of relative degree across a continuum.

This one final point bears repetition in our discussion of Condition Green: it is a relatively infrequent state for a company to be in, and one that never persists indefinitely. As the external environment changes—a certainty—the strategy must change and the culture will need reshaping and refinement.

Condition Yellow

In between Condition Green and Condition Red is, of course, "Condition Yellow": the circumstance in which there are clear misalignments between strategy and culture, though not rising to the level of urgent survival. If we apply the R-Y-G level-of-urgency construct to the theoretical universe of "all organizations," we would see a normal distribution in which Conditions Red and Green are less frequent extremes, with Condition Yellow as the 67 percent that includes one standard deviation on either side of the mean. That is to say, *most* organizations have *some* misalignment between strategy and culture, and Shadow Cultures that are not fully integrated into a Vision Culture.

A good example of a Condition Yellow circumstance is offered in Case 4.2, about a small business that was a client of the author's for over ten years.

Case 4.2. Baby with the Bath Water

Myerson & Company, a small financial services firm, had built a reputation on personal relationships and "customer intimacy" with its clients, for whom it offered specialized trust and tax services. As the larger financial institutions received regulatory permission to offer trust services and began to move into Myerson's customer space, they put their well-developed transaction processing and systems capabilities to work trying to take business away from Myerson with a competitive claim of more reliable and efficient service at a greatly reduced cost. Myerson's leadership realized that they needed to invest substantially in better systems and processes, though made the strategic decision not to try to compete directly on cost with the larger institutions but maintain their "high value/high margin" position with a large portfolio of existing clients who truly valued that customer intimacy and attention on them. In roughly the same timeframe, the founder and president, Mr. Myerson, had been attempting to make the transition out of daily operations and into a chairman role, and to bring in a seasoned professional manager and operator to run the company as he moved out of daily operations and eventually into retirement.

As that transition unfolded, the new COO of Myerson began actively realizing that beyond an upgrade of systems and business processes, a culture change was necessary—one focused on creating greater managerial and process discipline throughout the company. The legacy culture had been one of a "family" in which processes were not always defined or documented; the professional competency of the staff, though dedicated, was not always best in class. They were able to make up for these deficits by just spending a lot of personal time and attention with their small portfolio of clients, who could see past the occasional clerical or filing error—and indeed these were rare because of an existing culture of customer service and excellence. The incursion of the larger financial institutions created a clarion call for Myerson to upgrade the quality of its technology, processes, and systems, as well as to professionalize the managerial culture, instilling greater discipline and a continuous process-improvement mentality—without throwing out the "baby" of the firm's long-standing commitment to personalized customer intimacy with the "bathwater" of lower managerial standards, accountability, and professionalism.

This is a typical example of Condition Yellow, in which the environment has changed in ways that threaten profitability and *could* threaten future value creation and even survival, though neither of these immediately. The "house is not burning down," yet there is a manifest, material misalignment between business strategy (better operational efficiency and managerial discipline to meet competitive pressure) and a legacy culture (lax, familial culture, yet intensely loyal to the founder and firm clients). The time dimension is always important, but dramatically so in this assessment of red-yellow-green threat level. For many years, Myerson & Company was in a mostly Condition Green situation—for the most part enjoying steady growth, stable profitability, and manifest value creation due to the appropriate attention placed on the strategy and related cultural alignment by the founder and his team. As the environment changed, that Condition Green moved quickly to Condition Yellow and was clearly going to continue moving from yellow to red as the competitive environment became more aggressive while Myerson's culture became further out of alignment with the strategy necessary to effectively compete.

Action was definitely required—but it was not the "number one" priority, nor something that would threaten the imminent survival of the firm if not done. Culture change was appropriately set into the firm's top five priorities for the coming eighteen months and became one of several primary focus points for senior leadership and the entire organization. Failure to attend to this situation would have meant that the strategic adaptation of developing more transactional-operational capability in response to a changing competitive environment would have been increasingly out of alignment with the Actual Culture—which contained both desirable cultural elements—loyalty to customers—and undesirable elements, such as poor managerial accountability that led to inconsistent results and incomplete initiatives.

Condition Red

At the far end of this continuum is the "no option" burning platform in which culture must truly change or the company will not survive. These are situations in which there are major misalignments between external environment, business strategy, and organizational culture. Strategy formulation based on realistic assessment of the external environment is unquestionably an essential responsibility of the CEO and top team. In the four CEO questions, it is the antecedent driver for question 3 related to cultural alignment. In my experience, the strategy question is often well attended to and there is good awareness of what likely threats are, and how the organization needs to adapt to meet them.

What is curious—and one of many reasons for this book—is that somehow this vivid awareness of strategic threat and misalignment with the environment does not translate into any culture focus. As a result of the CEO's failure to consider question 3—the strategy–culture alignment question—precious time is lost. Leadership teams faced with the realization of strategic threat turn to familiar levers: cost cutting, focus on sales, acquisition and merger, new marketing campaigns, new technologies. These measures are undoubtedly legitimate and often have a positive effect, but in the Condition Yellow going to Condition Red circumstance they are often too little too late. Culture change—even modest change—takes months and years, never weeks. It is truly critical for the CEO to be posing the culture alignment question because if the answer turns up "yellow" or "red," there is no time to be lost. Immediate action should begin. See Case 4.3 for an example of moderate Condition Red circumstances.

Case 4.3. Bank of Hawaii Moderate Condition Red Culture Change

Leaders of Bank of Hawaii, a medium-sized regional bank, realized in the late 1990s that their real competition was less First Hawaiian Bank across the street than Bank of America, CitiGroup, Merrill Lynch, and Schwab, all of which could reach the bank's customers via the Internet and ATMs. As in many companies that "wake up" to some competitive threat, this bank's managers quickly realized that the single biggest obstacle to successful competition was the attitude and competency of their four thousand employees, that is, their culture. The Actual Culture of this, and most regional banks, was a genteel form of "order taking." People needed checking accounts and loans, they came to the bank because there was no one else to go to, and the bank met their needs while making a tidy profit. The idea of selling and competitive practices used by brokers and mortgage firms was not only not aspired to, but truly anathema. Beyond this, the business culture in Hawaii stems from a wonderful, relationship-oriented, caring and supportive ethnic and national culture reflecting Polynesian and Japanese values that were dramatically out of alignment with the banking cultures of New York and San Francisco. The strategic imperative was both clear and well articulated. Suddenly it became very clear that if the culture of the organization did not become more sales-oriented, aggressive, and "efficient," they would likely blink out of existence—not in ten years, but in three or four.

Several other local competitor community banks had been acquired or had shut their doors, and clearly more were to follow as the industry "consolidated."

This is a moderate Condition Red circumstance in which a strong public commitment to culture change by the top leadership needed to be in the organization's top three priorities. Bank of Hawaii survived and is doing quite well, but this did not occur until 90 percent of the top leadership that initiated the culture change had left or been replaced by new leadership that was entirely a product of the large financial institutions that were the "competitive threat."

Like the extreme Condition Green circumstance in which little or no action is required, there are extreme Condition Red circumstances in which it is too late to make decisions about changing the culture, because external financial or business realities have overtaken the CEO's prerogative. Or, as in the infamous Enron case, the culture created by top leadership is, after a period of great success, a victim of moral cracks in the culture. These are the exceptions, but there are situations in which the culture change is simply not going to make a difference because the basic existence of the organization is going to fundamentally change in a timeframe that makes culture change irrelevant. This is also a circumstance that can arise in mergers and acquisitions when the strategy of the acquiring organization is to "absorb" the acquired's culture. This is generally not an advisable strategy because there is almost always something new and of value that the acquired company can bring into the merger.

A company in extreme Condition Red that the author worked with during an eighteen-month period was a titan in the bar-code scanning space—Scanning Technologies (Case 4.4).

Case 4.4. Scanning Technologies: Extreme Condition Red Culture Change

Scanning Technologies had exclusive rights on a portfolio of bar-code scanning patents registered in the 1980s. Through the early 1990s and up until 2002 or so it literally owned the market. The company was known for its highly aggressive sales tactics, which helped it win business but earned it fear and hatred amongst competitors, as well as some of its customers. Like many Internet-era technology companies in the 1990s it overstated revenue projections in ways that were alleged to be felonious—many of the executive team were later charged. But the immediate symptom in 2001–2002 was that revenues and profitability dropped off. This led initially to the ousting of the president/COO—after a career spent in the company. An internal "favorite son" who had been previously passed over was appointed to be the new CEO, and a fresh young outsider from Cisco's executive team was recruited to be the president, with a charter to "set a new course" in the model of that highly successful and well-run company.

The new president brought in his former Cisco strategy consultant, and there was an intense focus on creation of a new strategy during the fall of 2002. Toward the end of that exercise, it became clear that Scanning's organizational culture was completely out of alignment with the new "wireless and Internet" strategy forged by the new team. I was engaged to assist with a culture change process that included many aspects of the Condition Red level of urgency, including a thorough culture assessment, creation of new values, and a Vision Culture, followed by an enterprise Culture Change Roadmap that had the full support of the executive team. Key elements of the new Vision Culture revolved around integrity, paying attention to customers, and creating results-oriented accountability. Despite the highly aggressive salesforce, the majority of the organization, based in remote Long Island, an hour from Manhattan, was more supportive, loyalty-based, long tenured, and occasionally just mediocre, in some measure due to the "talent wars" that did create real obstacles to recruitment of the best and brightest technology talent. This organization had become complacent about its commanding market share, which kept growing without an insistence on hiring and developing the best talent. The culture roadmap that sought to address these and other human capital capability gaps was dutifully executed by the top leadership team, and there were authentic moments led by the new president in which it was made very clear that real change was afoot, the bus was leaving, and anybody not willing or able to get on it would be left behind. There were a number of departures and new executives brought into the top team by the new president, but things continued to stall in the business performance of the company.

What nobody fully realized at the time that this well-conceived and executed strategy and culture change effort were occurring was that criminal activity was alleged to have occurred and was under SEC investigation. This was a situation in which the solid strategy and culture change work were simply too little too late. What most thought was a garden variety turnaround Condition Red turned out to be, in fact, a terminal Condition Red in which unethical and illegal acts had occurred, been covered up for a brief period, and eventually discovered. Eventually, most of the top team was forced to leave under legal pressure or left as they discovered what some of the prior practices had been. In 2004 the SEC announced that eleven executives were being charged with securities fraud and that the company had agreed to pay $37 million in fines. In 2005, the recently arrived president, previously at West Coast Tech, left to head up medium-sized Mid-West Tech. In 2006, Scanning was acquired by large Mid-West Tech at a fire-sale price, and the company ceased to exist as Scanning Technologies.

This is a sad tale of a once-strong company that drove itself into the ground, destroying significant portions of its previous value, entirely as a result of toxic values. Despite new leadership, a new strategy, and earnest attempts to change the culture, these toxic values brought the company failure because the damage had already been done by the time the new strategy and culture were initiated.

The CEO's Level of Urgency Assessment Tool

One particularly thorny challenge for the CEO in determining whether the company's culture is in a Condition Red, Condition Yellow, or Condition Green circumstance is that some assessment of the culture is required before that determination can be made. If a yellow or red condition is present, then a more thorough assessment of the culture and strategy alignment will follow in the course of the formal process anyway. Clearly, it does not make sense to mount a significant public assessment of the culture without some clear reason.

Figure 4.1 presents simple questions that are intended to assist the CEO in making that initial determination. They are really just a "break out" of basic CEO question 3: "Do I have the right organizational culture to execute the strategy?"

	Working Well		Unclear		Working Poorly
1. Is the culture aligned well with the strategy?					
Individual and organizational competencies are consistent with stated strategic business objectives; for example, in an environment where dramatic innovation is required to succeed, there are new product development processes and related rewards for innovation in place.	1	2	3	4	5
Core values and social style of the company are well aligned with strategic objectives; for example, in a highly competitive environment there is an appropriate level of urgency and aggressiveness about getting results.	1	2	3	4	5
The Actual existing culture is a. An accelerator for the strategy (1 or 2) b. Neither barrier or accelerator (3) c. An active barrier (4 or 5)	1	2	3	4	5
2. What is the total business circumstance of the company? a. Dire—bankruptcy, acquisition, or significant loss of key stakeholders' confidence is imminent. (5) b. Turbulent—there is rapid growth or contraction, but financial value, customers, and market success metrics remain positive. (4 or 5) c. Steady state—the business is meeting stakeholder expectations for performance in a stable environment. (1 or 2)	1	2	3	4	5
3. What is the organizational climate? a. Views of the culture are generally positive throughout the company. Most are proud about the culture or see it as a key asset (1 or 2) b. There is misalignment—either between top, middle, or lower levels of the organization or horizontally across key functions or business units. (3 = moderate, 4 = severe) c. There is open discontent and dissatisfaction with the company's culture. Culture misalignment is an open topic. There are morale and retention symptoms. (5)	1	2	3	4	5

FIGURE 4.1. The CEO's Level of Urgency Assessment Tool

For each of the rating statements, select a number in the right-hand column along the range of 1 to 5, with 1 being "Working Well" or positive and 5 being "Working Poorly" or negative. Total the scores you have entered. If your score on this quick diagnostic is more than 10 you can be certain you are nowhere in Condition Green territory. Over 15, you are certainly in Condition Red. At 5, you are certainly in Condition Green.

Let us now turn to the practical application of this tool in setting up the Culture Change Process. At this point, the CEO has drawn an initial conclusion about Condition Red, Condition Yellow, or Condition Green status. The question now is, What actions should be taken to set the stage for the culture change?

The Unique Task of the CEO: Setting Up the Appropriate Structures for the Level of Urgency and Creating the Compelling Reason

Let us remember that we are covering quite a large universe of possibilities in the red-yellow-green model, attempting to simplify as much as possible what will always be a judgment call for the CEO in establishing priorities. In exploring this important challenge, I have tried to strike a balance between an artificially mechanical set of rules that are almost certain to be academic or oversimplified and a "trust your gut, you'll know" resignation to complete subjectivity without basis in distinctive observations. Though quite an important question for the CEO to ask and resolve, remember that red, yellow, and green are theoretical points along a continuum.

Our purpose in offering the R-Y-G model and tool is primarily to bring home the point that the degree of strategy-culture misalignment should drive a commensurate level of attention, urgency, and resource allocation. If these were always the same, there would be no value in making this determination, of course.

As we will see in the next three chapters, there are many aspects of the Culture Change Process that can and should be delegated to executive and senior leadership. Establishing the R-Y-G priority with an understanding of how that translates into a compelling case for change, organizational focus, and allocation of time and resources is decidedly *not* one of these tasks that should be delegated. It is certainly a determination that should not be made in isolation without discussion and iteration, but in the end, this determination of what priority culture change should have, based on a sound assessment of strategy-culture alignment, is a unique responsibility that *only* the CEO can assume.

Level of Urgency Equals Level of Attention

The determination of "level of urgency" translates directly into "level of attention." Figure 4.2 offers examples of what Conditions Red, Yellow, and Green look like when they are translated to organizational activity.

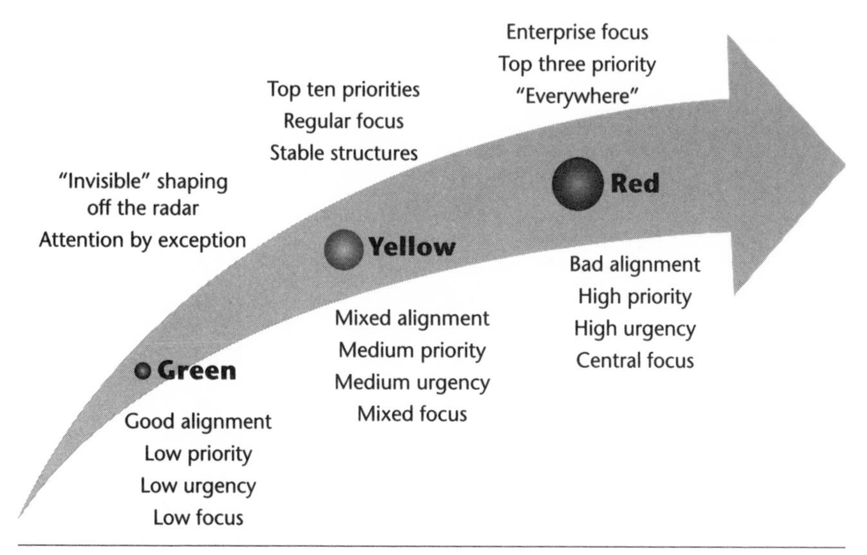

FIGURE 4.2. Red-yellow-green organization impact levels

Condition Green

In the Condition Green setting there is good alignment, or the culture has previously received considerable focus with good results. The level of attention for Condition Green should include behind-the-scenes, invisible shaping, and attention that might, by exception, not even include an "initiative" or any public focus. In the circumstance most likely to create Condition Green—a successfully completed culture shift initiative—appropriate actions would include the tail end of what we describe as the fourth stage of the process: Celebrating Progress. A strong and aligned culture is a relatively infrequent phenomenon, and it is certainly a reason to be proud, positive, and reinforcing of one's "great culture." Internal newsletters, marketing communications, and linkage to external branding are all things that one might expect in a Condition Green situation.

The challenge with Condition Green is "not losing what we have"—or assuming that the "journey has already been made." I will have more to say about this stage of the culture-shaping process in Chapter 7, "Celebrating

Progress." There are many "organizational hygiene" kinds of activities, such as quality on-boarding of new hires, linkage to brand, and continuous ameliorative finetuning, that we will discuss in more detail in that chapter.

In terms of Setup, the point is this: if you are lucky enough to have arrived at a Condition Green situation—enjoy it! Remember that this is a statistically infrequent circumstance, so make sure you're not talking yourself into something that is not truly there. But if you determine that you are indeed in Condition Green, clearly a "major public-focus initiative" would be overkill and unnecessary. Case 4.5 is an example of what Setup looks like in Condition Green.

Case 4.5. Orderly Succession at Pacific Hotels

A beloved and charismatic president retired after many years, passing the leadership to his hand-picked successor, who was well liked and competent, though not yet "revered" in the way the departing president was. The outgoing president had invested a great deal of his leadership attention to developing a uniquely branded culture that he modeled in his own personality and leadership actions. Though the succession was orderly and uneventful in that there was a well-planned overlap transition and never any question about who the successor would be or when it would happen, the new president was simply not the same "big heart" that his successor had been. The well-established, well-aligned culture that the outgoing president had worked to create and then maintain over fifteen years was not in any jeopardy of disappearing suddenly, yet there was nervousness in the organization about whether the new president would really carry the same "torch" for this proud and successful culture. The new president proactively reassured his own staff and the larger organization that he was committed to continuing the culture tradition that had allowed the company to be successful. Going even a step further, he asked the HR department to do an informal "alignment audit" of various HR levers just to make sure that there were, indeed, no unintentional, minor misalignments. In his first leadership offsite as president, he spent a half day out of three in a facilitated discussion with his team on what the core values really were and how this new team was going to behave in ways consistent with those values. A "refreshed" list of key competencies reflecting the established culture was created, and baked into a variety of HR promotion and performance management criteria. The new president suggested that he and all members of his team do a "360-degree" assessment as a reality check, and budgeted for this. The focus on organizational culture was mostly a rousing and collective pat on the back.

Conditions Yellow and Red

In the Condition Yellow and Condition Red circumstances the CEO has made a determination that the culture will not be an accelerator for the strategy, but a barrier or gate. Public focus and explicit communication are required, as are dedicated temporary structures with a primary focus on the culture change. The best way to think about this is as a continuum that varies along several dimensions from "mild yellow" to "severe red."

What do red, and yellow mean in terms of how the CEO should communicate to the rest of the organization? There are three key variables to pay attention to:

1. Level of urgency
2. Impact or footprint of the culture change
3. Degree of engagement required

Let us look closer at what it means for the CEO to conclude the company is in a red, yellow, or green condition, in each of these three dimensions.

Level of Urgency. At the "yellow" end of this dimension, the CEO is publicly communicating messages such as, "I am concerned (struggling, worried, or so on depending on severity) about what I see as elements of our culture that will not accelerate and even block the execution of our strategy."

- *Yellow:* In this, my first "state of the company" address, I would prioritize a focus on aligning that handful of elements as one of our company goals in the next year (but clearly along with other goals, and clearly not number one, two, or three). The timeframe is "soon," and the level of urgency is moderate, but not burning-platform.
- *Red:* At the "red" end of this dimension, the CEO is sounding the clarion alarm: This company is based on what I can see are some strong values, but it is also clear to me that much (or most, or the majority depending on severity) of our existing culture is totally out of alignment with our strategy—which I think is the right one. If we do not change our culture in these areas, I think our survival is at stake. Now that we have a clear, good strategy defined, changing our culture should be our top priority, along with these other two. The timeframe is "now," or we won't be here to have a culture.

Structures. This dimension refers to those changes in the organization that provide the appropriate level of focus and attention on the culture change initiative.

- *Yellow:* On the "yellow" end of this dimension, the CEO should appoint a cross-functional task force that has overlapping membership with the executive team and charter that task force to execute a culture change process with the full support of the CEO and executive team (much more on this in Chapter 6).

- *Red:* On the "red" end of this dimension, there may need to be a task force to handle execution details of the Culture Change Roadmap, but the culture change task force *is* the executive team, led by the CEO. If the organization does not have these capabilities available internally, this is a time for a legitimate and logical use of expert consultancies that can quickly import a methodology, tools, and perhaps additional pairs of leadership hands when these are in short supply.

Engagement Level. This dimension refers to the scope of the culture change initiative, from "green," where the visibility is small because there are already the appropriate levers in place, to "red," where there should be enterprise-wide awareness and impact.

- *Yellow:* Eventually, even the mildest Condition Yellow culture change needs to have an impact on every member of the organization. Realistically, particularly in a large organization, this takes time, as we will see shortly in the following chapters on Launch and Propagating the Wave. It could be as much as a year or two while the "wave propagates." The level of urgency will drive the extent of new structures that are created to implement the change. The footprint of the new structures will, in turn, drive the size and pace of engagement.
- *Red:* In Condition Red, there is a compelling case for more directive "push" methodologies. The Condition Red initial setup is aimed at getting the attention of the entire organization and is bundled with a "mandatory" message. The classic CEO communication "the bus is leaving—we hope you're on it" comes to mind. Restructuring of performance expectations, compensation, terminations and hires, and so on are a few of the very powerful tools that CEOs can set in motion to engage the organization and get attention in a Condition Red circumstance in which "pull" and persuasion are simply not options allowed by the "burning platform."

Chapter 4 Summary

In this chapter, on Setup, I have described the critical task of the CEO in establishing the priority of culture change on the basis of degree of alignment to the overall company strategy. Subsequent to that unique CEO responsibility to assess the level of threat and urgency for a Culture Change Process, I illustrated a model of urgency that spans a condition of green (minimal "maintenance" action required), yellow (moderate action, top five priorities), and red (urgent, enterprise-wide, top one or two priorities). Finally, I described what Setup entails in each of these R-Y-G conditions.

Remember that the steps taken during the Launch stage are entirely dependent on the conclusions drawn in Setup. Determining the R-Y-G condition is an *antecedent dependency for a broad range of culture change variables in Launch.* The erroneous, false positive Condition Green assessment by the CEO could lead to inadequate attention on culture change, and to dire consequences. The erroneous false positive Condition Yellow or Condition Red could lead to excessive attention and resources being placed on culture change, robbing other priorities at times when those attentions and resources are badly needed elsewhere.

Of equal importance, how this R-Y-G assessment is translated to CEO decisions and communications to frame the Setup phase will play a large role in determining the success of the culture change. The CEO who realizes he or she has a Condition Yellow strategy-culture misalignment, but then behaves in ways more appropriate for Condition Green, is failing just as much as though he or she had mistakenly diagnosed a Condition Green.

We will now move to the second of our four phases of executing culture change. In the following chapter, "Launch," I outline specific steps, tools, and methods for beginning the Culture Change Process once Setup is complete.

Setup | **Launch** | Wave | Progress

5 Launch

The table is set and now we move to the first course. At this point, we know that the culture is at Condition Red, Condition Yellow, or Condition Green—and why. The CEO has done a thorough job of answering the "four questions" and used the CEO's Level of Urgency Assessment Tool to drill down on question 3: "Do I have the right organizational culture to execute the strategy?" Finally, the CEO has translated this assessment into concrete actions for communicating the level of urgency, chartering the appropriate structures, and defining the right level of engagement along the continuum from extreme Condition Red to extreme Condition Green.

Launch and *Propagating the Wave* phases are what many would likely call "culture change" in that they are more visible public activities. We cannot emphasize enough the importance of the less visible Setup activities of the CEO that precede these next two phases. People need a "reason" to do what they do—especially in their organizational lives in which there are always multiple competing reasons ranging from expectations of superiors to parochial departmental and personal agendas. The Setup phase is partially about conducting an objective initial assessment of strategy-culture alignment. It serves the critically important purpose of helping the CEO determine his or her own "reason," so that he or she can, in turn, create a compelling reason for the rest of the organization related to culture change. The need for such initial steps might seem obvious, and it is, but my experience is that it is often treated haphazardly, or overlooked entirely by CEOs who are otherwise thoughtful and disciplined leaders.

We turn first to an important—and original—way to think about organizational culture. The idea of the Shadow Cultures is key to creation of a "to be" target culture—what we established in Chapter 3 as the Vision Culture.

The Shadow Cultures

There are two Shadow Cultures—the "Ideal" and the "Required." These are not so much distinctive subcultures as they are imperfect approximations on the way to creating the "to be" or Vision Culture. They may also be thought of as potential mistakes that organizations make in their attempt to create the "to be" or Vision Culture. Before we move into a more thorough understanding of the Shadow Cultures, it is valuable to understand the idea of the Johari Window.

The Johari Window of Organizational Culture

This question of Shadow Cultures is neither academic nor theoretical. There is good reason why understanding and clearly articulating the Shadow Cultures is one of the Five Critical Success Factors for Culture Change. Perhaps one of the most compelling metaphors ever invented to describe a fundamental truth of social interaction is the Johari Window (Figure 5.1).[1] This timeless metaphor illustrates one of the reasons that the Shadow Cultures come to be and persist.

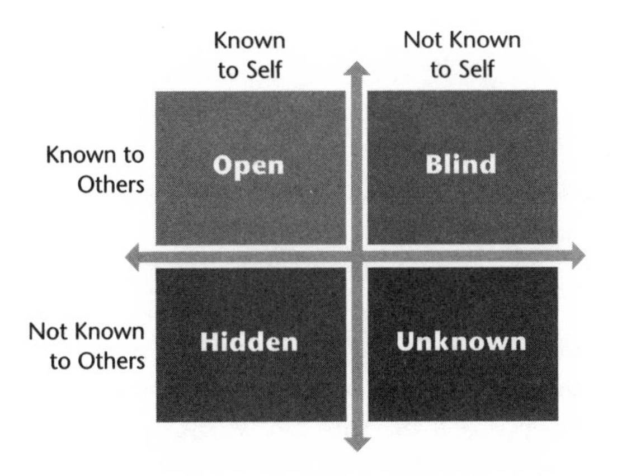

FIGURE 5.1. The Johari Window

The simple premise underlying the Johari Window is this: human social interaction—whether individual, group, or national—is *always* colored by limitations on the degree of awareness as a function of stance or perspective to a referent point. In the realm of social interaction, there are four possibilities:

1. The organization clearly sees some aspects of its culture in the same ways that outsiders do.

2. The organization sees some aspects of its culture in ways that others do not see.
3. The organization is blind or unaware to some aspects that outsiders see.
4. The organization is blind, along with outsiders, to some elements of the culture that are unknowable by all observers, inside and outside the organization.

Understanding the Johari Window is key to our understanding of the Shadow Cultures. The self-evident point that bears regular repetition is this: there is no social institution that can see itself with total clarity. The reason the Ideal Culture exists is due, in part, to the propensity of individuals and groups to strive and achieve in the future. The reason the Ideal Culture is always out of synch with the Actual Culture is because the organization can never see itself with complete clarity—as an outsider would.

The actionable implication of the Johari Window concept is this: if the CEO's goal is to create value by aligning strategy with culture, then a realistic appraisal of the culture—and all its parts—is important. Let us now explore in more detail the four dimensions of every organizational culture: The two Shadow Cultures, Ideal and Required, and the Actual and Vision cultures.

The Ideal Culture

As the name suggests, the Ideal Culture is aspired to and idealized. There are many ways in which the Ideal Culture is articulated. It can be expressed as a set of aspirational values—the familiar plaque and laminated card that are found in conference rooms and key chains. It can sometimes come about in the course of a strategy session, team building, or other activity of the leadership team focused on mission, values, or vision. In some cases this set of values or principles comes forth when a new CEO comes to the organization. And finally, it may come forth as a response to events in the organization that underscore what the values are *not*.

Whatever the mechanism that has articulated the Ideal Culture, what makes it a Shadow Culture is not the content but the relationship to the Actual Culture, in other words, how accurately it reflects prior and current actual values, behaviors, and capabilities. The uniquely defining characteristic of the Ideal Culture is that it is what we want to be, not what we are or should be—the defining characteristics of the Actual and Required cultures. An example of the Ideal Culture will help illustrate the point (Case 5.1).

Case 5.1. The Ideal Culture as Meaningful Voice:
Case of the Silicon Valley Internet Startup

The leadership team of a successful and growing Internet company in Silicon Valley decided that it was time for a "real" executive offsite in which a number of important strategy and culture topics would go onto the agenda. The company, roughly three hundred employees and $30 million in revenues, was growing explosively—and had doubled in both revenue and staff over the past fifteen months. Everyone agreed that "our culture" should be a topic on the agenda. Prior to this event, there had been discussion about "our values" and how these should be the basis for both the internal culture and the external brand of the company. The founder and chairman was a believer in "mission driven" strategy and espoused a set of value principles that he communicated clearly and frequently. The VP of Marketing also had a strongly held and well-articulated list of value premises that he had generated based on his beliefs about the brand promise and his own observations of what the company aspired to be.

The VP of Marketing's list of values was brought forth in a series of discussions prior to, and at, the executive retreat. The list included "be authentic," "be accountable," "be humble," "be powerful," and "be clear"—each accompanied by a handful of defining substatements. These were discussed by the executive team and key representatives at the next level of management, codified as "our values," and finally communicated to all employees in a number of communications over the ensuing month.

This is a great example of the voice of the Ideal Culture coming forth in a way that was meaningful and well-intended. What makes it a manifestation of the Ideal Culture is that it had very little to do with the Actual Culture, which was anything but humble, clear in setting priorities, or effective in establishing accountability. In fact, an objective assessment of the existing culture called out the precise opposite of several of these value points. The company was struggling mightily to narrow priorities that were both numerous and unmeasured, as well as to establish some simple management discipline around evaluating performance. Because the founders had spawned a truly good idea that had taken off in the marketplace, they were anything but "humble." Indeed, one of the key findings in the objective survey performed by the external consultant was that the founder and key product-development staff assumed that customers did not know enough about the service to provide meaningful input and should largely be ignored so that "our bright engineers" could build cool new products that would "delight" customers who were too ignorant to know what the engineers did not.

There is nothing wrong with generating substance to the Ideal Culture as this company did—in fact we recommend some time on it. The key point is this: *don't mistake what you think you should be with who you actually are.* The Ideal Culture is, by definition, a set of attributes that is sometimes mistaken for the Actual Culture or the Required Culture. This real example of a company I worked with briefly is a good one to illustrate this all-important point. For a variety of reasons—most of them related to the founder's strong belief system and inspiring communication style—this set of values was largely adopted as "our values" without full acknowledgment of the many actual behaviors that were completely incongruent with those values.

On the surface there is nothing inherently wrong with this—there is always some discrepancy between the Actual and Ideal cultures; indeed, there is value in the exercise of articulating "who we would like to be."

The danger is one of suboptimized value creation arising from two common misconceptions: first, the mistaken belief that articulating the Ideal Culture is a picture of the "to be" or Vision Culture. And second, and much worse, the failure to fully reconcile the Ideal and Actual cultures with meaningful commitment for change. This failure to fully acknowledge the Actual Culture has a variety of causes that we will discuss more fully when we come to the Actual Culture. In this "Silicon Valley" case example just described, it was a simple case of "founder's syndrome," in which the founder was not ready to fully acknowledge his own major role in shaping the Actual Culture and believed fervently in his own original value premises. Again, there is nothing terribly wrong with this, but if the path to value creation is to align culture with strategy, a persisting belief that our culture is "what we would like to be," without sufficient attention to "what we actually are," is not an efficient means of creating that value. Despite this generally applicable rule, there are exceptions, for example, when the fervent and inspiring leader shapes a culture over time around a set of value principles that are well aligned with both strategy and execution. Steve Jobs's mercurial leadership of Apple Computer comes to mind.

Another brief example will help define what we mean by the Ideal Culture (Case 5.2).

Case 5.2. The Workplace We Would Like to Have

Myerson & Company—described in an earlier chapter as an example of a moderate "Condition Yellow" situation—launched a well-conceived culture change process that was fully supported by executive leadership and launched in an effective manner. In the course of applying the "Get Real Tool" (which we'll describe shortly—essentially a methodology to integrate the Shadow Cultures), it became clear that most of the executive team, and many of the employees, wanted to work in an environment in which there was a minimum of bureaucratic processes. (As you'll remember, this was a company beset with the strategic realization that future value creation, indeed survival, was dependent largely on a culture shift that required a more disciplined and professional management environment.) When the executive team articulated the attributes of the Ideal Culture, it was similar to the Actual Culture: a supportive, familial environment in which valuing of employees and customers was a much higher priority than process and management discipline. When this team described the culture-they-would-like-to-have, it included continuing value on customer responsiveness and that very rewarding sense of family-friendly job security that included policies which allowed telecommuting, flexible schedules, and heroic individual efforts to bypass established processes in the service of solving a customer problem.

The Myerson case is a clear illustration of how the Ideal Culture is not the "target culture" that we must aspire to in the service of value creation. This mature and capable leadership team was fully aware of the legacy culture, which lacked rigorous discipline, and the strategic business reality that demanded a change. As equity owners, they looked at the road ahead and said, "Even for a lot of money, is this the environment that I want to work in?" It's a good example of an earnest articulation of the Ideal Culture, alongside a sober assessment of the Actual and Required cultures. It also illustrates an important point, that the Shadow Cultures are rarely the same despite some degree of overlap.

Finally, Case 5.3 is a third example of the Ideal Culture, defined in relative lack of awareness or dishonesty.

Case 5.3. Our New Values

Scanning Technologies was alleged to have overstated revenue, leading the SEC to initiate a formal investigation into the company's accounting practices. After the CEO and CFO left and new executives were brought in to replace them, the leadership team launched a culture change process. At a well-conceived all-day executive retreat, five "core values" were defined: "achieve customer success," "pursue excellence," "foster innovation," "perform with integrity," and "deliver on commitments." These value anchors for the new culture were extensively discussed and debated by the leadership team, and then translated into high-quality behavioral competencies.

To the organization's great dismay, further irregularities were discovered, and it became painfully clear that at least one of the core values—"perform with integrity"—was simply some words on paper, and far out of alignment with the Actual Culture, in which clearly there was not "performance with integrity" but continuation of the same behaviors and further coverup.

This is another clear example of the Ideal Culture—that which we wish to be—yet not all that we actually are.

The Ideal Culture is not always *completely* out of alignment with the Actual and Required cultures. The culture change that followed these initial Launch activities at Scanning included much that was well aligned with both the Actual Culture and the Required Culture, but the "integrity" piece was little more than wishful words that had not been historically demonstrated and, as it later came forth, was not manifest in some quarters, even after the commitment to newly minted, ideal values was publicly communicated as the foundation for "our new culture."

The Actual Culture

In the language of individual personality, the Actual Culture is "who we are"—the familiar and everyday self that we label "me." The Actual Culture is what most people are describing when they refer to "the culture" or "our culture." The typologies that I touched on briefly in the definition usually refer to the Actual Culture.

Understanding the Actual Culture has everything to do with the perceived need for culture change. *In a perfect Condition Green circumstance, the Actual, Required, Ideal, and Vision cultures are all the same.* This is a statistically infrequent event, in my experience. In the majority of circumstances—mild yellow to extreme red—there is some problematic degree of change between the Actual Culture and the other three.

Even when the Actual Culture is not terribly misaligned with the Shadow Cultures, there are almost always aspects of it that are not clearly seen by top leadership. This is one reason why I define the Actual Culture as the "objective" and "multi-stakeholder" view of the culture. Using a "reasonable person" standard, I start with the premise that no individual or culture can fully know itself—the basic point of the Johari Window.

Attempting to understand the Actual Culture from multiple perspectives invariably creates a more complete and accurate snapshot of what it truly is. I will have more to say shortly about the measurement of culture and the importance of multiple perspectives. For the moment, suffice it to say that top leadership, employees, and outside observers often view an organizational culture quite differently. It is not that any of these perspectives is "untrue," but simply that they are always incomplete.

The Required Culture

Different than the Ideal and Actual cultures is the Required Culture: that set of cultural attributes that is most capable of executing the strategy. On the surface, the Required Culture may appear to be similar to the Ideal Culture, and depending on the leadership team, the two may share features. Like the difference between the Ideal and Actual Cultures, the size of their difference will vary as a function of the clarity, competence, and honesty of the leadership team describing the culture.

A good example of the Required Culture can be seen in the Myerson & Company example cited earlier. The company had a wonderful, familial, supportive culture that employees found motivating and positive. They understood that the external competitive environment and the strategy *required* them to have a culture that was going to offer less personal freedom, longer hours, and greater results. This was most definitely *not* their Ideal Culture. It is largely a continuation of the Actual Culture with a dash more accountability and discipline.

The Required Culture is "what we *must* be to succeed or survive" as defined by a view of external reality translated into the firm's business strategy.

The Vision Culture

The Vision Culture is the truthful integration of the Actual Culture and the Shadow Cultures into a well-defined future target. The Vision Culture blends the aspirational quality of the Ideal Culture along with the pragmatic quality of the Required Culture and grounds these in the reality of the Actual Culture. In the language of individual "selves," the Vision Culture is the mature integration of what we strive to be, with what we have to be, grounded in what we actually are.

The Vision Culture is the end result of a process in which the other three cultures are understood in context of each other (Figure 5.2).

- The Ideal Culture must be held up to the light of the Required Culture—yet not simply replaced by it.
- The Required Culture must be revised in context of the Actual Culture.

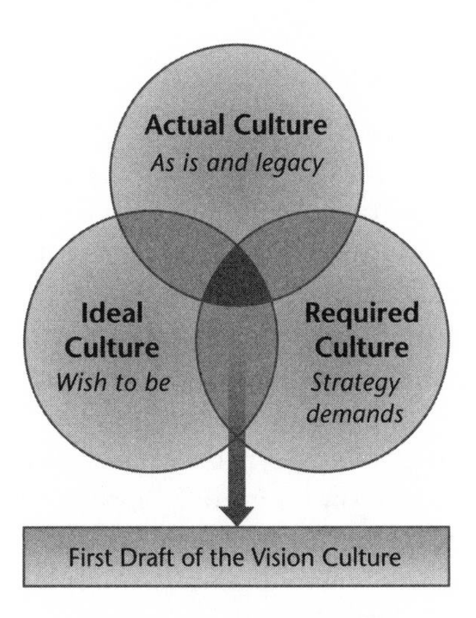

FIGURE 5.2. Overlapping Shadow Cultures point to the Vision Culture

Why Do We Need to Understand the Shadow Cultures?

One might ask, Why not just focus organizational change attention on the Required Culture, since by definition that is what the strategy requires for value creation? Why waste time understanding the Actual and Ideal cultures? The answer is that the Required Culture must be tempered by the practical limitation of the Actual Culture—"who we are past and present." Taken alone, without grounding in the Actual Culture, the Required Culture becomes just an idealized image with the same deficiencies as the Ideal Culture: "what we want to be." Stated in the language of the individual, what external circumstance demands of us is always constrained by the reality of our actual capabilities. Having understood that the best strategy for value creation requires transformation to targeted organizational traits and capabilities, the organization will actualize that change only within the context and constraints of its legacy capabilities and values (the Actual Culture). To make the Required Culture a feasible goal, it must be understood and modified by those traits and qualities of the Actual Culture that cannot or will not change.

This is a great deal more than simply an interesting theoretical point. There are easily as many organizational culture change initiatives that fail reaching for the Required Culture as fail believing that the Ideal Culture is the target. The Required Culture that has not been tempered by the real constraints of the Actual Culture is as likely to fail as the Ideal Culture that is not grounded by the Required Culture. The importance of the Shadow Cultures is that they reflect "impractical" or "incomplete" perspectives that, if taken by themselves to be the goal of the culture change, are doomed to failure.

As with individuals, the fate of companies vacillates interactively with the environment. There are few companies in business today that were in existence two hundred years ago—because most have all "died" or become something so different as to be a new entity. Even the "giants" such as General Electric, General Motors, and ATT that can lay claim to their early 20th century pedigree by name could not be called the "same company" one hundred years later, though they may have the same name.

Here is the key point about the Shadow Cultures: it is rare for a company's culture to be in complete synch with the strategy. It is rare for the Actual Culture to be in complete synch with what leadership aspires to. As with individuals, there is always some difference between these various perspectives. For the CEO who takes seriously his or her charge to create value, the smaller the differences among the Actual Culture and the Shadow Cultures, the greater the likelihood of value creation.

Measuring Culture

The CEO is not the person to conduct the annual survey of customer satisfaction; nor does he or she need to execute measurement of the culture at the tactical level. The CEO's role is to set the expectation that there *will* be a rigorous and professional assessment of the Actual Culture. With the goal of providing the executive overview or "short course," I will first describe different approaches to measurement of culture and then suggest basic best practices.

Why Is Measuring Culture Important?

Measurement of individual and social phenomena is a large and complex field with well-developed traditions in anthropology, sociology, and psychology. The basic tenet of this tradition can be summarized in the following: social behaviors can be quantified using a combination of experimental design, statistical methods, and structured observational techniques. Can we measure and predict social phenomena with the precision of chemistry or physics? No. Is it possible to objectively quantify behavioral phenomena so they can be reliably and validly measured over time and across organizations? Yes.

The aggregation of many subjective views becomes objective as those views converge. Stated in commonsense terms, this simply means that one individual's view of a culture is just that—an opinion. But when you take hundreds or thousands of individual views, areas of consistent convergence become reliable objective fact. This oversimplifies a sophisticated and scientific set of statistical methods, but will do for our purpose, which is to establish that culture, like all social phenomena, can be reliably measured. How and why that is true is not something CEOs need to drill down into, anymore than they might wish to understand how conjoint analysis techniques allow the marketing staff to reliably measure customer opinions of service and products.

Why is it important to measure organizational culture in the Culture Change Process? For all the same reasons that it is important to measure any organizational phenomena that have material impact on sources of value creation—from customers to finances to operational performance. To expand on this self-evident point:

- Measurement of organizational culture provides a baseline against which progress can be assessed at future measurement points. Clearly, if you have decided it is worth the effort to initiate a culture change effort, you want to know whether progress has been made by that effort.

- For all the reasons described in our discussion of the Shadow Cultures, it is both necessary and valuable to accurately define the Actual, Ideal, and Required cultures.
- Finally, measurement of the culture defines a common language that is the basis for any and all change initiatives related to the culture that may follow.

This third point is perhaps of greater importance in the culture space than in other areas of organizational measurement. Unlike financial and operational performance disciplines, which both have a well-developed language and measurement tradition, measurement of organizational culture is primitive by comparison.

Four Basic Approaches to Measuring Culture

There are four basic approaches to the measurement of organizational culture. These approaches reflect traditions in the discipline of social sciences measurement, and include a spectrum of survey, interview, and consensus-building interactive events.

1. Statistically valid and reliable tools
2. Checklists and informal tools
3. Qualitative interviewing
4. Large-group dialogue

Let me describe in a bit more detail each of these four approaches. As with our review of the organizational culture concept, our goal is not to provide a methodical and scholarly review of measurement of organizational culture. Our review of these four approaches has the sole objective of informing CEOs of what they need to know about this topic. The CEO is not the person who is going to pick the tools, or conduct the data collection—anymore than he or she would pick the accounting software. The CEO and top team *do* need to understand the difference between the four approaches, and what minimum best-practice standards are in the overall task of measuring the culture.

Statistically Valid and Informal Tools. Statistically valid tools are those that have been developed using psychometric techniques to ensure some level of validity and reliability. Validity and reliability are technical psychometric terms, but in layman's terms the principles underneath them are common sense. The validity of a tool refers to the accurateness with which it measures what it claims to. Anybody can make up a good list of questions to better understand organizational culture. The statistically valid tool begins as just such a "list," but then over repeated administrations to many organizations, along with statistical comparison to existing objective criteria, this "list" of questions is gradually refined to achieve a predictable and reliable capability that an unvalidated "list" of questions will never have.

This is the layman's short rendering of a complex, multistage process. Suffice it to say that when this psychometric process is conducted with the goal of creating a valid and reliable assessment tool, the user of that tool is assured of a statistically determined level of accuracy—both in *what* the tool measures and in its *reliability* to accurately measure over time and in diverse settings.

Not surprisingly, such statistically valid tools are not in great abundance—primarily due to the significant obstacle presented by acquiring fifty to one hundred companies to develop such a tool. A well-known and widely used culture assessment tool is the Denison Organizational Culture Survey.[2] This tool, developed over fifteen years with a sample of over a thousand companies, can lay claim to what few other culture assessment tools can: statistical correlation with financial and other independent criteria such as return on equity and customer satisfaction.

Because the Denison survey has this statistical power, it is a tool, not just a checklist. There are others with statistical power, but none with as a large a database, and many of these are proprietary consulting tools meant to incentivize use of other consulting services and not generally available to the public without an existing consultative engagement.

Hofstede has also developed an excellent suite of tools that calls out cultural differences across nationalities using his five-dimensional typology.[3] Hofstede's "5-D" tool is based on the culture-as-personality model, unlike the Denison tool, which takes a culture-as-capability perspective. Both are useful, but as I will suggest further on, there are important practical limits to how much surveying any organization can tolerate—choices need to be made.

A third example of a statistically validated assessment tool is the Organizational Culture Assessment Instrument,[4] based on the Competing Values Framework and described by Cameron and Quinn. Like the Hofstede five-dimensional model, this tool is based on a culture-as-personality view.

Checklists and Informal Tools. There are many informal checklists and survey instruments that have not been validated statistically. These can be useful adjuncts, even though they lack statistical rigor, because they can be quickly and flexibly created and administered. Such tools include the Harrison & Stokes Culture Assessment[5] and the Dawson Culture Lexicon. There are numerous others—often created ad hoc by the organization or experts in the field. Though this approach does not provide statistical rigor, it does provide far greater flexibility and customization because individual items can be changed to suit particular requirements of the assessment. These more informal "lists" are particularly useful when describing subcultures and the Shadow Cultures in focus groups or with a leadership team that needs help "priming the pump" with descriptive language. The statistically validated tools don't have the same flexibility because they can only retain their power if their item pool remains constant.

Qualitative Interviewing. This approach includes a variety of group and individual interviewing formats. It is really the only way to access and define the narrative and descriptive view of the culture. Unlike the previous two methods, it makes no pretense of statistical validity. The group version of this is essentially the "focus group" format in which small numbers of employees are asked to discuss a series of prompting questions but allowed considerable latitude to explore and digress.

The individual interview has the advantage of being completely confidential, allowing discussion of more sensitive topics related to historical events and leadership behaviors. These are far less likely to come up in group settings and even less likely in the fixed-survey-question format of the statistically validated tools. For these reasons, it is absolutely invaluable, though limited by the obvious subjectivity of the methodology. That limitation is greatly reduced when multiple interviews and focus groups are administered as recurrent themes come to the surface over the course of the data collection.

Large-Group Dialogue. This last approach encompasses a variety of setups but can include as many as a hundred or more participants. The basic format begins with a framing of key issues to the large group and is followed by small-group discussions that can be structured to achieve a variety of hoped-for outcomes. The event ends with some kind of report-out from the small groups to the large group on their conclusions. In some versions of this approach voting methods may be used to reinforce consensus. The primary value and utility of this approach is to surface issues and build consensus about shared views, or solutions. It is unique in that it produces real-time shared awareness in a much larger group than is possible with the qualitative interviewing approach.

Culture Measurement Summary: What the CEO Needs to Know

As I noted, finding and administering the right culture assessment tool is not the job of the CEO. However, the CEO should be knowledgeable about what different approaches can produce, and what minimum basic best practices are required.

There are various "right" techniques to approach culture assessment but also some minimum basic guidelines to stay within and some "wrong" ways to avoid. The CEO needs to ensure that the culture assessment process is objective and balances minimum intrusion with stakeholder involvement, criteria that both external consultants and internal HR staff may lose sight of.

Culture Measurement Basic Criteria

Criterion 1: Measure the Actual Culture Objectively. To accurately define the Actual Culture, there should be one objective tool, such as the Denison tool, and a blend of the other three approaches to capture the narrative and stylistic attributes of the Ideal and Required cultures.

As part of Criterion 1, include measurement of significant subcultures in measurement of the Actual Culture.

Criterion 2: Balance Involvement and Intrusion to Create a Minimum Footprint. Minimize the impact of the assessment on people's time. Filling out surveys is nobody's idea of a good time. Insult is often added to injury when that investment of time by respondents is followed by inaction. Part of the CEO's responsibility in sponsoring the Culture Change Process is to ensure that the specialists that are engaged in some of the execution details do not use up more time than is necessary to fulfill the relative priority of the task in the larger context of changing the culture. Once an organizational process is unleashed, it can take on a life of its own. The culture assessment is a means to an end—the CEO must ensure that it does not become an end in itself.

On the other side of this issue, assessment of the culture is a crucial first step toward its modification and requires active participation by all representative constituencies of the organization. This total involvement ensures that the final view of the Actual Culture will not be biased by a single constituency and helps to create investment and ownership in the process beyond the top level.

It is a mistake to think that "measuring the Actual Culture" is somehow a neutral event "before the real initiative begins." Nothing could be farther from the truth. Yes, the culture assessment is a means to an end, but in raising the question "What is our culture?" expectations have been raised and the process has really begun.

Having reviewed what the CEO needs to know about culture measurement, let's move on to the "Get Real Tool"—an applied methodology to create the Vision Culture out of the Shadow Cultures. Before we dive into the Get Real Tool, we will briefly explore the problem of subcultures.

The Problem of Subcultures

Anyone who has worked inside a large organization will attest to the fact of subcultures within the greater organizational culture. The question of subcultures jumps out in context of measuring organizational culture and the integration that is accomplished in the Get Real Tool process. As a purely practical problem, should subcultures be measured? And, if so, how many subcultures, and where should one draw the line in what constitutes a subculture? There is certainly no "standard" or widely accepted definition for subculture. Nevertheless, anyone who identifies with a subculture existing within a larger organizational culture will claim resolutely that "we" are not the same as "them." In many cases, there is some structural, geographic, or historical explanation for the existence of a subculture.

At one far pole of subculture definition, there is a credible argument for calling many functional departments or geographies a "subculture": "The engineering department is a different world—they have their own building and way of doing things that is different from everyone else in the company. Their basic belief is that they are really smart engineers designing cutting-edge cool stuff that customers will discover they need after seeing how cool they are."

At the other end of this subculture continuum is the postmerger environment of two companies that were previously distinct but are now "one company" and technically one organizational culture. A dramatic, but all-too-common example of this can be seen in the case of an acquisition of a smaller competitor on the West Coast by an East Coast electronics manufacturer (Case 5.4). After the purchase, the acquired company became the "San Jose business unit" but never lived up to corporate expectations for profitability. Ten years after the acquisition was completed there was still considerable tension and bad blood, manifest in a thousand ways from budget decisions to sales coordination to basic communication.

Case 5.4. California Country Club

Ubiquitous Electronic Devices, Inc. acquired ITC almost ten years ago. Now the San Jose–based business unit is the largest profit-and-loss center in the company, with the most people, most products, and greatest number of patents. It is also currently the least profitable. According to the Boston headquarters executive team this is in large part due to the "country club" lifestyle culture of the San Jose business unit.

"They overpay everyone because of San Jose market salaries, and yet the place is empty at 5 P.M. It's that same group of senior engineers and executives that came over from ITC and, despite four new GMs in the last six years, we just can't seem to change the culture out there that operates without a sense of urgency and with an entitled work ethic that doesn't care about what customers think or need. They seem to think that all they have to do is invent exotic engineering marvels and customers will flock to their doors. Well—it hasn't happened. It is not the way we do things at this company, and their financial results in California reflect that old culture that led them to be acquired by us."

The San Jose business unit employees, almost two thousand strong, describe their culture as "innovative" and "creative"—though "Boston headquarters is slowly beating that out of us with their one-dimensional focus on short-term profits. We have lost much of our best engineering talent to National Semiconductor and other competitors who pay better and, more important, value the innovative talent that is the only thing creating competitive value in this increasingly commoditized business we have become. Yet they treat us like second-hand citizens, refusing to promote our best people, cutting our research budgets by 50 percent—what do they think is going to come out of San Jose if they keep skimming all the profit off the top and never investing? When they acquired us ten years ago, they made it clear that we had "lost" against them in the marketplace and were now "owned" by us because they were financially well managed. That culture has gradually eroded the innovative dynamism that used to exist here, and with it most of the value that they paid for in that acquisition. Shareholder value has systematically been destroyed—and entirely due to mismanagement of our culture, and failure to integrate some of what we do best into their existing culture. They have created a San Jose island that is looked on by Boston with disdain—most of the good people have left, and we are now on our fourth GM in six years!"

Though there are many interesting questions about subcultures that bear further investigation, for our purpose of using culture as an engine of value creation, there are only two key questions that need clarification.

First, when and how do you *measure* a subculture? And second, how do you *integrate* that subculture into the practical "culture-to-be," or the Vision Culture?

Let's take both of these questions in turn—though I will defer a more complete discussion of how to integrate the "subculture" of an acquired or merged company to Chapter 8, "Three Culture Change Scenarios."

Measuring Subcultures

Subcultures are "real" and, if large or different enough from the broad organizational culture, must be distinguished during the assessment of the Actual Culture. Objective, survey-based tools such as the Denison and the Hofstede make this easily possible, as respondents complete the survey simply through identification as members of those subcultures. Even relatively low-impact subcultures such as might exist in a functional department or geographic unit can be unobtrusively differentiated with simple survey methodology.

In the merger situation, the culture change focus may be as much on constructively blending the two cultures as on creating the Vision Culture. As I will discuss in more detail in Chapter 8, it is my view that subcultures should be treated as parts of the Shadow Cultures to be understood and integrated. In some cases this may mean a gradual diminishing of the "acquired" culture. In other cases, it may mean adopting large portions of the "acquired" culture into a truly fresh Vision Culture for the newly combined entity. There are reasonable arguments for both approaches, though much depends on the business strategy and wisdom of the leadership. The potential for value destruction as a direct result of unintegrated postmerger cultures that continue to operate in conflict is statistically high.

The Get Real Tool

Integrating the partially true views of the Shadow Cultures into the Vision Culture is a crucial step that requires practical tools. The Get Real Tool is a simple methodology that takes what is real from the Shadow Cultures to create the focus point for the organization going forward.

As the name implies, the goal of the Get Real Tool is to drive out distortion and wishful thinking from the organization's image of the Vision Culture. The Get Real Tool is the process that produces the Vision Culture, which in turn is the basis for the Culture Change Roadmap.

The Get Real process must be led by the CEO and owned by the top team. The culture assessment inputs that are necessary to complete the Get Real process will typically be completed by internal staff or external consultants with the expertise to objectively measure the Shadow Cultures. The Get Real process can *only* be completed by the CEO and top team because material decisions related to the strategy and culture can only be framed and finalized by that top team.

Here is an overview of the sequential steps in the Get Real process. In what follows I will outline the practical actions and deliverables for each of these steps (Figure 5.3).

Step 1: Objectively assess the Actual Culture
Step 2: Qualitatively describe the Required and Ideal Cultures
Step 3: Compare and contrast summarized shadow cultures
Step 4: Create the "to be" Vision Culture informed by the shadow cultures

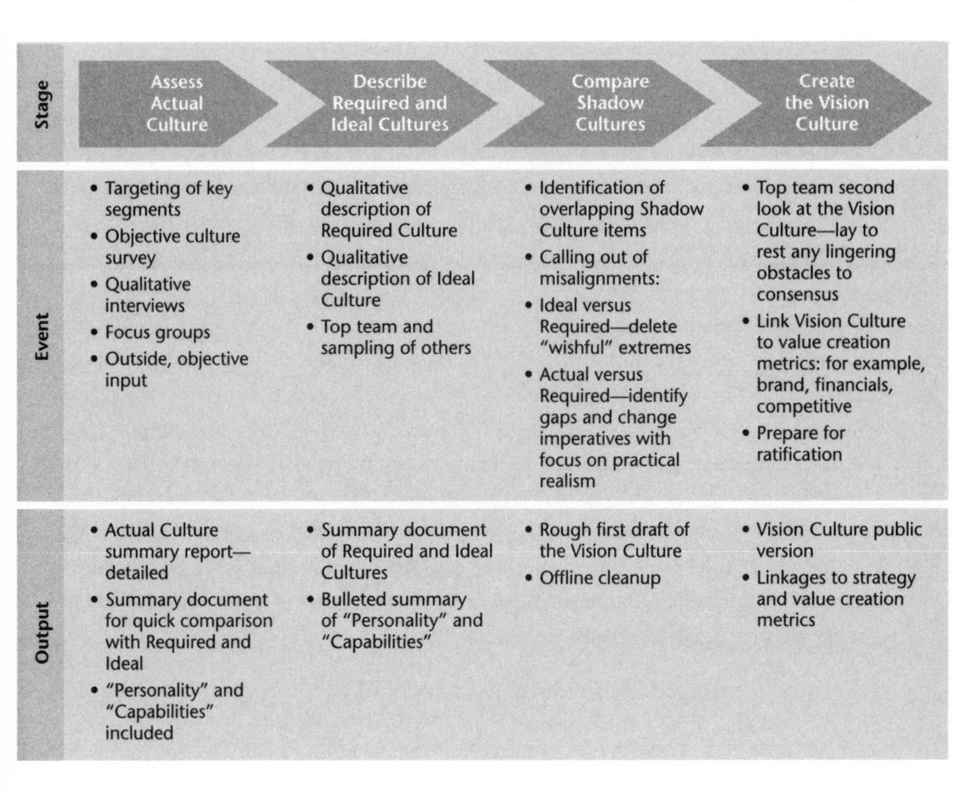

FIGURE 5.3. Get Real Tool process steps

The final output of the Get Real process is a work product of the top team. Typically this is a document that outlines major attributes of the Vision Culture—in the language of both organizational capabilities and organizational personality.

Get Real Step 1: Objectively Assess the Actual Culture

As we discussed in the earlier chapter on assessment of culture, it is essential to capture as objective and complete a snapshot of the Actual Culture as possible, and there are multiple techniques for accomplishing this. In the extreme Condition Green or Condition Red circumstances, a complete culture assessment may be unnecessary or moot. In that majority of Condition Yellow circumstances that populate the largest portion of the bell curve, Case 5.5 would be a typical Get Real Step 1 assessment of the Actual Culture.

Case 5.5. Scanning Technologies Culture Assessment

After Scanning Technologies had created its new "wireless strategy" and its leadership realized that they had a Condition Yellow culture misalignment, I was engaged to coach the executive team in conducting a culture change process. The assessment phase included administration of the Denison Organizational Culture Survey to the entire organization—about four thousand employees worldwide. This presented significant language, administrative, and logistical challenges, but a 78 percent response rate was achieved with excellent representation up, down, and across all major organizational segments. Parallel to the administration of the Denison tool, roughly twenty-five individual interviews were conducted with selected board members, all of the executive team, and key next-level staff. Finally, eighteen focus groups were conducted, after being designed with a global business unit and functional representative sampling principle. Both the individual interviews and the focus groups had a structured set of questions to ensure consistency, while giving wide berth for participants to say whatever they felt was relevant to the stated task of understanding the legacy and current culture. This entire process took about a month in terms of public footprint time, excluding the initial planning and the offline data analysis, which entailed a couple of weeks on either side of that thirty-day public footprint.

This three-pronged approach to assessment of the Actual Culture should stand as a model. The Denison tool provides benchmarked, objective assessment of any culture, regardless of size or shape. Like any modern survey, it allows "slicing and dicing" of respondent demographic information to assess subunits within the larger organization. The top-team-level interviews and focus groups provided the qualitative, values-based narrative and historical perspective that is inaccessible through an objective tool such as the Denison. Interviews and focus groups also provided a very real opportunity for a significant portion of the organization to be involved in meaningful ways. Focus group participants were asked to serve as "collection points" for their co-workers in advance of the focus group they were assigned to attend, so as to create as wide, yet minimally intrusive, a net of information gathering as possible.

These several sets of results were analyzed and distilled by a team of internal and external experts into a summary report that focused on high consistent themes that recurred across all three data sets. There was little disagreement—really by anyone—that this analysis represented an accurate and objective assessment of the Actual Culture. This snapshot of the Actual Culture was summarized in a short presentation document, but backed up with a large quantity of interview and statistical data.

Get Real Step 2: Qualitatively Describe the Required and Ideal Cultures

The Ideal Culture, as you will remember, is that set of values and qualities that exist in the form of wishful aspiration. Unlike objective assessment of the Actual Culture, the task here is really more one of articulating and describing this set of ideals than it is objectively assessing something. As always, there are several approaches to a figuration of the Ideal Culture, depending on the red-yellow-green urgency level and on what may have been previously articulated.

As long as the Actual Culture is objectively and thoroughly measured, it is my view that descriptions of the Ideal and Required cultures can be generated quickly and without anything approaching the same public footprint or level of effort. They are essentially the answer to the following two questions, obtained informally by the leadership team.

1. What do we wish the culture to be in the future?
2. What does our business strategy demand that the culture be in the future?

We have found the informal checklists tool used by a team in brainstorm mode to be the best way to describe these two "future" cultures. The Actual Culture—though a complex living organism—needs to be measured, precisely because it "is," and not "to be." The deliverable for both Ideal and Required culture assessment is an uncomplicated "list" of attributes that include both "personality" and "capability." These two lists—one each for Ideal Culture and Required Culture—should be developed through a team process that begins with open brainstorm but ends with a definitive final list of descriptive attributes.

The end goal for both is a short executive summary list in the same format of the summary for the Actual Culture, but without all the objective detail beneath it. Here are some guidelines for assessment of the Ideal and Required cultures:

1. *Who*. Involve a representative panel of voices—especially for the Ideal Culture. It can be energizing and rewarding for participants to include a few cross-sectional focus groups in the process of creating the Ideal Culture. The Required Culture calls for a smaller group—perhaps no more than the top team and a handpicked additional few who can help make the link between existing strategy and Required Culture.

2. *How.* The key design principle for description of the Ideal and Required cultures is *keep it short and simple.* Unlike measurement of the Actual Culture, which requires a thorough process, meaningful descriptions of the Ideal and Required cultures can be accomplished in an afternoon of executive team time, followed by ratification after initial descriptions have been polished. A prompt such as the Dawson Culture Lexicon or any of the values-based tools can be useful to stimulate ideas through a framework and language. We have also seen the well-designed town hall approach be very effective in creating a vibrant and useful description of the Ideal Culture.
3. *What.* There are two content deliverables: lists of Ideal Culture and Required Culture attributes. The quick, easy, and entirely sufficient way to create this result is to frame a dialogue around the following two separate questions:

   For the Ideal Culture: "What do we wish the culture to be in the future?" Ask participants to think about this prior to the discussion, upload an open brainstorm to flip charts, engage in some brief explanatory discussion, and end with a final list that includes both personality and capability attributes. Remember that the tone of this discussion is aspirational—there are no "wrong" answers, though the consensus of the group may determine that there are "low priority" answers that do not make it to the final list.

   For the Required Culture: "What does our business strategy demand that the culture be in the future?" This is a more complex question that may include considerable overlap with the Ideal Culture discussion. It is important to ground every attribute, whether organizational personality or capability, with the criterion "Why is this necessary for execution of our strategy?" Unlike in the Ideal Culture list, there *are* "wrong" answers to this question—or more likely items on the initial draft list that do not survive the scrutiny of the team against the test of strategic alignment.

Sometimes the Ideal Culture is lofty and aspirational without any solid grounding from the reality of the Required and Actual cultures. In a more self-aware and mature organization, it is "wishful" with an awareness that it can never be. The Myerson & Company Ideal Culture cited earlier is a good illustration of this. In full awareness they wished that the Ideal Culture could come to pass, and were insistent that some elements of the Actual Culture, which were very positive yet out of alignment with the Required Culture, persisted. These were attributes related to flexible and family-friendly work hours—and ideal and core value—that they were reluctant to give up, even though the top team realized that greater accountability combined with lower tolerance for incompetence were attributes of the Required Culture that were directly linked to future value creation in a tougher competitive environment. This created an effective solution—though not pleasing to everyone—that allowed the Myerson top team to craft a more balanced integration of what was required with what they aspired to. This is precisely the goal of the Get Real exercise, and why it can never be "automated" without executive dialogue and judgment. It requires trade-offs like this one cited from Myerson, that essentially concluded, "We accept that increased competitive pressure requires us to be more disciplined, but that Required Culture "sacrifice" must be tempered by some continuing commitment to our Ideal Culture which includes respect for continuation of our family-friendly workplace. These are not, at their core, diametrically opposed."

In the Condition Red scenario, it is common for the Required Culture to play a prominent role. Case 5.6 illustrates why the Required Culture cannot stand as the final set of specifications for the Vision Culture but must be tempered by inescapable realities of the Actual and Ideal Cultures.

Case 5.6. Required Culture at Scanning

The Required Culture at Scanning Technologies was generated to a large degree in context of the business strategy. As the leadership team took stock of the rapidly dawning "wireless world" and conducted a business assessment of organizational structure and human capital practices, key attributes of the Required Culture came into sharp focus. A good example of one of these Required Culture attributes that ended up being mitigated by the Actual Culture was a perception of newly arrived outsiders about the overall quality of the workforce. The company was headquartered in Long Island—about an hour's commute from Manhattan—and in a somewhat remote area. The workforce they were trying to attract—especially in the 1990s during the "war for talent" in Silicon Valley and other urban centers—was unenthusiastic about living in what many technology urbanites perceived to be a less exciting and stimulating small town. When they had to, they constructed compensation packages to attract key talent, but over the years on a company-wide basis many local residents were hired into the company and stayed. Average tenure of the overall workforce at headquarters was ten-plus years. One attribute that received considerable focus in the Required Culture was institution of "modern human capital" practices in the GE/Jack Welch fashion of the day: get rid of the C players, hire only A players, raise the bar on talent acquisition. This is a perfect example of a Required Culture attribute that came right off the page of the business strategy. Stated briefly, the gist of it was this: we have too long rested on our intellectual property laurels of ten years ago and need to energize the company with new outside talent and innovation, and "raise the bar" so that we can compete with Cisco, Motorola, and so on in this "next big thing" tidal wave of wireless information acquisition in our traditional bar-code scanning space.

This Required Culture attribute, though grounded in the necessity of competitive strategy and value creation, was simply not fully implementable given the enormous gravitational pull of the legacy workforce and the many deterrent obstacles presented by the physical location of the company in a remote area that was fundamentally unappealing to the targeted talent pool.

This is a good example of why the Required Culture cannot simply stand "as is" without pressure testing from the Actual Culture. This example also illustrates why it is important to fully assess the Actual Culture, and at least snapshot the Required and Ideal cultures. It is only in teasing out the distinctions between the Shadow Cultures that a robust, feasible, and therefore implementable future "to be" culture target can be defined.

Get Real Step 3: Compare and Contrast Summarized Shadow Cultures

At this point, three culture description documents have been created in summary format: one for the Actual Culture and one each for the two Shadow Cultures. Were it not for the fact that there are important material decisions to be made by the top leadership team, this might otherwise be a more mechanical task of reconciling the three cultures to a final distillation: the Vision Culture. There will always be low-hanging fruit across the three lists that can safely be put onto the Vision Culture final. Remember, by definition, a cultural attribute appearing on the Actual, Ideal, and Required culture lists is an attribute of the Vision Culture.

The heavier lifting will involve identifying the significant differences across the three lists. This is uncomplicated at the clerical level, but can evoke strong emotions around including and excluding culture attributes that are held dear to key stakeholders. There are many ways to accomplish this in terms of team facilitation mechanics, but the essence of the task boils down to this: "What are the differences between the Actual and the two Shadow Cultures?" Procedurally, this involves some offline staff work to tee up differences and the framing of a conversation in Get Real Step 4 by the top leadership team.

Get Real Step 4: Create the "To Be" Vision Culture Informed by the Shadow Cultures

The fourth and final step of the Get Real process is to shed the "unnecessary" attributes of the Shadow Cultures. What emerges is a Vision Culture that is consistent with the enduring "identity" of the organization (its Actual Culture and its Ideal Culture) and the requirements of strategic adaptation to external reality to create shareholder value (the Required Culture).

The Get Real process is based on three simple axioms:

1. The Ideal Culture, though motivating, ignores practical constraints of the Actual Culture and strategic demands of the Required Culture.
2. The Actual Culture is always out of alignment with the Required Culture, except in the rare Condition Green circumstance.
3. The Required Culture, if taken in pure form as a "to be" culture target, does not incorporate the practical constraints of "what we currently are" or the motivational fuel of "what we aspire to be"—which may be quite different from what the strategy demands.

It would be nice if there were an "automated" set of steps to turn the Shadow Cultures into the Vision Culture; however there is no such thing. In what follows I will lay out some decision guides and an example of what this series of process steps looks like. Needless to say, because every organization culture and circumstance is unique, there are many right ways to execute Step 4 of the Get Real process. The only "wrong" way to proceed is to completely omit this, or any other, step. Our general best-practice guidelines for the entire tool are all applicable to Step 4. Presuming the Shadow Cultures have previously been well defined and summarized succinctly, keep it simple, on track, and short. In many cases, in just laying out the three Shadow Cultures next to each other a self-evident Vision Culture begins to emerge. Less frequently, there are material and real conflicts that need to be resolved. Here are three simple questions that when answered represent substeps for Step 4:

Substep 4a: What is the list of Shadow Culture duplicate or overlap attributes? The answer is the first draft of the Vision Culture. These uncontroversial attributes can often be pulled together in advance of the Step 4 Vision Culture discussion.

Substep 4b: Is there anything in the Ideal Culture that is out of alignment with the Required and Actual cultures? If so, why is it there? If there is not a compelling reason for it—delete it.

Substep 4c: Is there anything in the Required Culture that appears to be an unrealistic execution stretch relative to the Actual Culture? After discussion on how big a stretch it may be, mitigate or modify it so that it is an achievable change target by the top leadership team.

After substeps 4b and 4c are completed there should be no items in the Ideal and Required culture lists, for they should have been added to the Vision Culture draft or eliminated as unrealistic or unnecessary.

The overview of Get Real Step 4 can be summarized simply in this way: starting with the default Vision Culture list (overlapping, uncontroversial items from the Ideal and Required cultures), vet the small number of remaining items. The Ideal and Required cultures are the "to be" cultures. One is wishful yet unmindful of external reality, the other is completely aligned with external reality, but unmindful of existing constraints of the Actual Culture. The task is to reconcile the Required and Ideal cultures into the "necessary but achievable" future target for the organization culture: the Vision Culture.

Why make this so complicated? The answer is: Don't! Make it as simple and uncomplicated as possible, as long as you have met these three inviolate, best-practice guidelines:

1. The three Shadow Cultures are defined in the minimum best-practice ways just described.
2. The CEO and top team discuss and reconcile any material differences between the Ideal, Required, and Actual cultures.
3. There is a net output in the form of a draft version of the Vision Culture that includes both values-personality and capability attributes. There is no hard and fast rule about "how many" personality values versus capability attributes—it should roughly balance. Whether this is 50-50 or 65-35 is immaterial. It should not be 90-10.

The less meeting time and process required to create this outcome, the better. However, shortcuts that do not rise to these three minimum success criteria are doomed to failure, and may actually make matters worse than had no effort been attempted in the first place.

The Ideal Culture masquerading as the Vision Culture is the most common error. Because it is not tempered by the realities of the Required Culture, it is little more than a wishful fantasy. Less common, though equally likely to end in failure, the Required Culture masquerading as the Vision Culture may not realistically take into account the practical limitations of existing personality and capabilities.

The Role of the CEO in the Get Real Tool

Get Real Step 4 absolutely requires the active involvement and leadership of the CEO. There are many offline staff- or consultant-related tasks in the Get Real process: conducting the Actual Culture assessment, facilitating the top team sessions on Ideal and Required cultures, summarizing and formatting the Shadow Cultures so that they can be effectively discussed by the top team. The CEO should know about these steps and what the deliverables are, and assign competent staff expertise to make sure it all happens.

What the CEO absolutely should *not* delegate is the leadership role related to driving the process with deliverables that meet the best practices described earlier. An even more crucial role for the CEO is the team leadership during the content discussions that emerge out of the Shadow Culture vetting and final resolution to a committed Vision Culture.

The Ideal Culture discussion needs process facilitation to make sure that all views get a chance to surface. Any skilled facilitator can do this. What only the CEO can do in this discussion is summarize and close the discussion. The same is true for the Required Culture. In the early phase of this executive discussion about what the strategy demands, the task is to ensure that the team is focused and realistic, that all reasonable views are voiced. Any good facilitator can accomplish this, and the CEO may elect to actively participate or hang back. There is a rationale for both. After a few hours the CEO needs to use his or her "soft power" to close the discussion in a way that only the CEO can make a final call on. If there is a significant difference in the team about whether this or that culture attribute belongs in the Required Culture list—only the CEO can resolve that.

There are many effective ways to resolve conflict in a top team discussion of material matters that require a unified decision. The variety of ways in which the CEO may create consensus is an important topic, but not within the scope of this book. What is essential is that first, the CEO must know enough about the Shadow Cultures and the basic goals of the Get Real methodology to step in and move the process forward to a close. Second, because the content of these top team decisions is sometimes high impact and material, the CEO *is* responsible for the outcome—whether there is an "active" King Solomon cutting-the-baby-in-half decision or a "passive" nondecision in which there is remaining ambiguity about the final Vision Culture.

To recap: the Get Real Tool is a straightforward four-step process that takes the three Shadow Cultures and translates them into a Vision Culture description. This Vision Culture may then serve as the "to be" target of the Culture Change Roadmap, and of all organizational time and energy devoted to making the culture an engine of value creation.

Linking the Vision Culture to Value Creation

It is important that the Vision Culture be linked to value creation. Without this linkage to value creation, culture is not harnessed as a force to optimize the company strategy. A thorough discussion of what constitutes value creation is far beyond the scope of this book, but a few points are worth calling out in the narrow context of the interdependency of value creation with organizational culture.

First, company value is ultimately a values-driven determination. In the public company, value creation is measured in market capitalization, share price, and the multitude of subordinate financial measures that reflect components of this overall value as defined by the marketplace.

Defining the value of an organization is a measurable but complex phenomenon, and creating such value requires a Vision Culture that is closely linked—the Required Culture takes on a new importance. In defining the Required Culture, it is important to first define how value will be created, and to link ways in which value will be created to attributes of that Required Culture. Not all, but hopefully most, of these Required Culture attributes will find their way to the Vision Culture final list, which becomes the focal goal of the company and the "to be" bookend for the Culture Change Roadmap.

A helpful way to think about this linkage is as a series of "if . . . then" contingencies that link value creation with the Required Culture. Here are a couple of examples:

- If the strategy to create value demands faster product-development cycles, then what will this require in terms of organizational values, attitudes, and capabilities—in other words, the culture? Perhaps a shift to greater innovation, cycle time efficiency, and a revamped product-development cycle. Perhaps a different set of competencies and standards in the product-development group.
- If the strategy to create value demands real-time customer access to accounts, then what will this require in terms of values, attitudes, and capabilities? Perhaps a new kind of IT capability combined with a shift in attitude about who the customer is and how to create positive attitudes. Perhaps a reordering of who the most- and least-valued customers are.

In context of the Get Real Tool and final definition of the Vision Culture, it is important to make this linkage between value creation factors demanded by the strategy and attributes of the Vision Culture. Aside from the compelling logic that underlies the premise, linkage of the two creates a powerful additional benefit. *A propos* our earlier discussion of the Setup phase, after the CEO has drawn his or her own conclusion regarding the "four questions," this explicit linkage between the Vision Culture and value creation metrics is arguably the most powerful communication tool to articulate the logic behind the red-yellow-green condition designation. It is also a good argument against the wrongheaded separation between strategy, value creation, and organizational culture. The quip "culture eats strategy for breakfast" is very true. A great strategy will never succeed in a misaligned culture. Linking both to value creation is a powerful communication tool based on impeccable logic that goes to the very foundation of why the organization is in existence.

Culture and Company Brand

We usually think of company "brand" in association with the famous consumer names: Pepsi, Coca Cola, Crest, Dell, Lexus, Google, to name a few. More and more the concept of brand has been recognized as an important building block of organizational strategy. It is something to be carefully created and nurtured because it is also an important means for creating value. To greatly oversimplify a vibrant and growing literature, the concept comes down basically to this: *To the extent that customers believe in, and then act on, our "brand promise," we have created new economic value, in that this leads the market to pay something over and above the exact same product with no brand, and to select our product over competitors for "emotional" reasons such as loyalty, affinity, and other subjective beliefs and attitudes that elevate the brand in the mind of the buyer.*

Brand is a complex and multidimensional concept that we will not explore in any depth here, other than to emphasize the critical importance of explicit linkage between company brand and organizational culture. The logic for this linkage is compelling and self-evident. Whatever "brand promise" we make to our customers can only be kept to the extent that the organizational culture reflects and supports those attitudes and behaviors that are necessary to sustain that promise. If the external brand centers on a theme of reliability and quality, but the Actual Culture is one of carelessness and customer disrespect, this brand will not likely create much value. If the rationale for investment in expensive marketing campaigns aimed at building brand awareness and loyalty is that there is a value creation return on investment, then it stands to reason that there must be more than just "marketing" of the brand. It must also be *delivery* of what has been promised in the brand, otherwise value creation will be short-lived, if even present.

The purpose for this digression into brand is twofold: first, the brand promise cannot be kept without a culture that supports it. Indeed, the Actual Culture defines the practical limits on what the brand promise can truly deliver. Second, there is great power for the CEO in explicit linkage of the Required Culture and then the final Vision Culture, insofar as there is visible, explicit point-to-point correspondence between descriptive attributes of the brand, and descriptive attributes of the Vision Culture. One can apply the same Shadow Cultures paradigm to brand thinking. There is an "actual brand," the experience customers report having. An "ideal brand" would be the wishful thinking of the company about what customers are experiencing. And a "required brand" is what the company needs to do to close the gap between the ideal and actual brands.

As with the Required Culture, this may not always be possible, for a variety of reasons from cost to competitive landscape to internal capabilities. The principle still stands strong: the danger of "shadow brands" destroying value due to an unrecognized gap between "real" and "ideal" brand is no less than that for organizational culture.

Ratification of the Vision Culture: The Delicate Balance Between Involvement and Direction

The Get Real Tool process is largely a task for the top leadership team—actively led by the CEO. The output of that work—the Vision Culture—now becomes the centerpiece of effort aimed at changing or shaping the culture. It is important to ratify the Vision Culture—especially in the Condition Yellow and Condition Red situations, when a change effort of some magnitude is about to be undertaken. There are many things to consider in deciding how best to ratify the Vision Culture, some of them commonsense extensions of the R-Y-G level of urgency and impact principle.

If the Vision Culture represents a substantial and dramatic change from the Actual Culture, this presumes an extreme yellow or red condition and raises the importance of broader ratification. Similarly, the opposite is true in the milder yellow and green conditions. This follows one of our basic principles: when value creation is the standard, not every culture change is of equal importance and magnitude. In broad strokes, virtually every decision and activity related to culture change flows from this initial key determination by the CEO.

A less straightforward question is, How directive should we be in conveying the Vision Culture to the rest of the organization? If the CEO and top team are excessively directive by simply "announcing" the Vision Culture, they risk failed adoption and anemic engagement. If they are overly democratic, framing the communication about the Vision Culture as a work in progress, ratification may never come. The answer, as always with these kinds of false dichotomies, lies somewhere in the middle, depending on the specific organization and circumstance.

True ratification of the Vision Culture is an important milestone to end the Get Real Tool process. The top team has put much effort into crafting the Vision Culture during the Get Real Tool process. After all this effort, it feels "finished"—but of course, the real work is just beginning. The all-too-frequent impulse is to make an "announcement," thinking that this will accelerate acceptance of the Vision Culture. Wrong! This seems obvious, yet it is surprising how often it happens! This kind of unilateral announcement creates the illusion that the complication of challenge and dialogue will be avoided. It also guarantees that there will be much greater delay at a later point in the Culture Change Process. This "Change Management 101" principle is never more true than with something as important as culture change. The more dramatic the distance between the Actual Culture and the Vision Culture, the more involvement in the ratification process there should be. There are many ways that ratification can actually occur, depending on key elements of the Vision Culture that the leadership team wishes to reinforce, material subculture dynamics, and practical matters related to the size and footprint of the organization.

The reader will find these principles and best-practice recommendations useful in striking the right balance for ratification of the Vision Culture:

1. *Stakeholder Representation.* Make sure that all major constituencies of the organization are involved in the ratification process—in one way or another. Even a chance to change a few words and some punctuation can have a significant positive net effect. From an execution perspective, it is wise to mirror the ratification process with the recently completed Actual Culture assessment. Think of the entire Launch phase of the Culture Change Process as an ongoing conversation between the top team and the organization that begins at the end of Setup with communication of the rationale behind the R-Y-G determination, is followed by the Get Real Tool process, continues with the Vision Culture ratification, and ends finally with a first draft of the Culture Change Roadmap.
2. *Constituency Representation.* In the smaller organization, the logistics of this ratification conversation are less complex structurally, but may be even more complex in terms of adherence to key cultural norms. In a smaller organization, familiarity creates more of an

expectation for involvement—and influence—than in the larger organization where it is simply impractical.

Add to this basic principle special attention to important subcultures that may have emerged in the assessment phase, or are already well-known. For example, in many technology organizations, some of the key engineering staff may have small groups or even be individual contributors who might not otherwise be included in a ratification discussion. Clearly, in a merger situation, it would be critical to ensure full representation in the ratification discussion.

3. *Many Designs for the Ratification Event.* Not everyone in the organization necessarily needs to be actively involved in the ratification process. In larger organizations this is simply infeasible, and in smaller organizations undesirable or unnecessary. Having identified representative constituencies, there are several good ways to choreograph the ratification event(s).

   One is to take a sampling of opinion leaders from each of these constituencies and invite them to attend a Vision Culture ratification event. This might be a town-hall-style meeting or any number of other designs with the objective of creating a sense of ownership for the Vision Culture, while not setting the expectation that the entire document is open for radical editing.

   A less social, but sometimes more efficient, way to approach ratification is to kick off a very brief cycle with explanation and rationale for the Vision Culture, then ask participants to go offline privately, or in small groups, and answer a set of targeted questions that do not open the door to wholesale change:

   A. Is there anything we may have missed?

   B. Is it clear what we mean?

   C. What are some of the implementation challenges going to be?

   D. How big a change from the Actual Culture is this really?

   Ask participants to e-mail in their responses. Collate them and then close the process with a second brief, large-group meeting that brings closure to the Vision Culture following discussion of any differences.

4. *Validation of the Vision Culture.* Ratification is a first expression of the new Vision Culture. Remember that the ratification process is one of the first opportunities the top team has to exhibit key communication, decision making, and other primary attributes of the Vision Culture. A best-practice example looks something like Case 5.7.

Case 5.7. Vision Culture Ratification

The top team at a large midwestern electronics manufacturing firm had grown accustomed over the years to issuing one-way edicts on pretty much everything they decided. Interactive dialogue, even with the senior level below the top team, was relatively rare. Important issues were decided by a small inner circle and then allowed to trickle down as best they could. When the CEO and several of the top team were replaced by the board after the eighth straight quarterly decline in profits, a new CEO determined the organizational culture to be in an extreme Condition Yellow situation. A well-designed and executed Culture Change Process was undertaken. After the Vision Culture had emerged from the Get Real process, the CEO made it a point to ratify this document in a new and different way that the company had never experienced before, but which was prominently called out as one of the Vision Culture attributes: he personally conducted a series of town hall meetings—ten in all, with groups of twenty-five or so each. Meetings were an hour long with a relatively open design. The town hall meetings began with a brief explanation of the Vision Culture, including the linkage to value creation via the business strategy and priority attributes that were significant departures from the Actual Cultures. These meetings were hailed as a great success and evidence that this new CEO and his team were going to actually "walk the talk" of the words on paper in the Vision Culture.

5. *Timing the Vision Culture Ratification.* When is the Vision Culture ratified? This is not an empirical question, and there are many ways to arrive at this important milestone. Despite the challenges created by the subjective nature of the ratification milestone, here are three "tests", using observable data to help determine whether the Vision Culture has been ratified:

   A. Key constituency stakeholders (senior managers, functional and business unit leadership) have had a chance to review and comment on the Vision Culture. Though not all of their views may be incorporated, there is a forum in which key stakeholders may raise dissenting views and receive a reasonable response as to why their points have not been added to the final version.

   B. There is a clearly delineated time window after which the expectation is that the Vision Culture will be ratified. This can vary from a week or two in smaller organizations to a month in global multinationals. Assuming no major distractions or other unusual circumstances, it is hard to imagine ratification of the Vision Culture to require more than thirty days. This is not entirely "new" material, but has been in the awareness of the organization since Setup framing by the CEO and the assessment.

C. The process of ratification reflects key attributes called out in the Vision Culture. If inclusion and consensus building are key elements of the Vision Culture, then the ratification process should be designed to reflect these. If rapid-cycle decisiveness is the focal attribute, then the ratification process should be short, with crisp deadlines for closure. Within the reasonable standards described earlier, there are truly many right ways to accomplish this.

Ratification of the Vision Culture is an important milestone because it serves to firmly anchor the goal of the organization relative to the culture it needs in order to create value. It is the second-to-last planning-and-designing activity before the focus becomes execution and implementation. The last planning activity is creation of the Culture Change Roadmap, to which we now turn.

Creating the Culture Change Roadmap

The Culture Change Roadmap (CCR) marks the end of the Launch phase. Completion of a well-designed and *working* Culture Change Roadmap is also the third of five critical success factors for translating culture into an engine of value creation. The CCR is no more nor less than a well-designed "project plan" to focus and organize the culture change. A roadmap is simply a robust list of actions to be completed, meaning that it includes timeframes, roles, and outcomes (Figure 5.4). Like a project plan for moving to a new facility or implementing a new accounting system, it should include these minimum variables and dimensions:

1. A listing of key tasks or activity categories down the left column mapped against a timeline from left to right across the top of the roadmap
2. Timelined milestones to designate measurable—or at least observable—completion outcomes
3. Delineation of key roles and responsibilities
4. Identification of required resources
5. Delineation of key dependencies and contingencies across resources and timeframes

As is true for almost all aspects of shaping or changing culture, there are many effective ways to meet minimum best-practice specs of a CCR, so long as they include a reasonable level of detail in each of the five dimensions listed earlier. Some companies invest an enormous amount of time and energy into a highly detailed CCR—other companies include less detail,

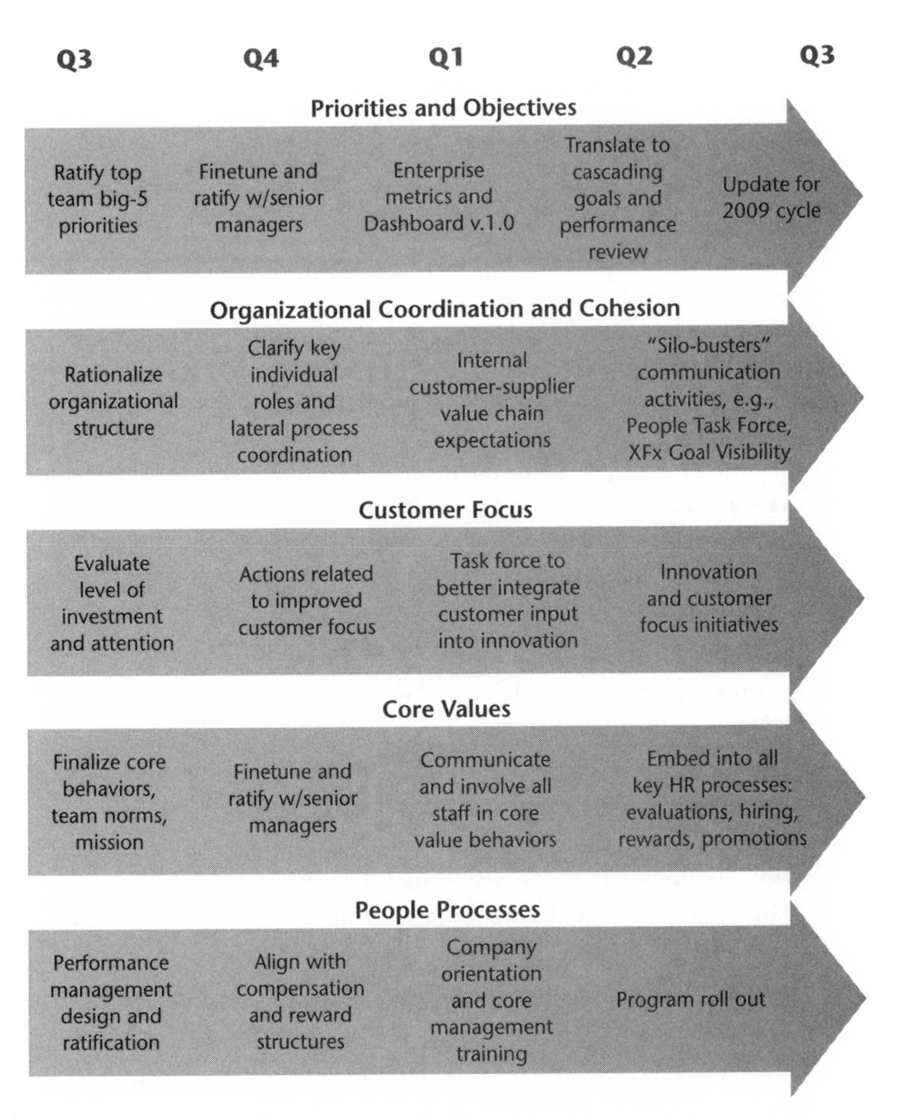

FIGURE 5.4. Culture Change Roadmap example

leaving execution to individuals who are responsible. Both can work, though as is the case with project plans in general, too much or too little detail each have the ability to suboptimize.

As with other concrete deliverables of the Culture Change Process, the role of the CEO for the CCR is to know that such a document is essential and to understand enough about what its purpose is to conduct general quality control. Like the documents of the Get Real Tool, this document is not one to which the CEO needs to put his or her own pen. The CEO should charter qualified expert staff, and consultants as needed, to generate the initial draft of this document. This first draft must then be reviewed and ratified by the CEO and the top team—both in the interest of editorial quality and to ensure full sponsorship of the document. If there is a culture change task force, finalization and administrative overview of the CCR is one of its primary duties. In a larger organization with geographic and stakeholder complexity, the roadmap will serve as an enterprise-coordination tool not unlike the project plan for any other kind of large-scale change. In these more complex settings, having a detail-focused "project manager" type and an intuitive "marketing communications" type are essential capabilities to ensure that the CCR has the metrics beneath it to be trackable and measurable, and the outbound communication focus to ensure it is a living document that sponsors and agents of the culture change are fully apprised of. These project management execution details are *not* the job of the CEO, and are often delegated to top team members in the larger culture change.

The role of the CEO regarding the CCR is as follows:

- Ensure that it is created to a minimum set of best-practice specifications as outlined earlier.
- Make execution of the CCR a top team priority—unless the company is in Condition Green, in which case a CCR is not necessary.
- Ensure that the appropriate amount of continuing top team attention and resources is devoted to CCR execution.
- Solve high-level conflicts that may arise in the course of the CCR execution.

As with any "living document" that commits an enterprise's organizational time and resources, the CCR must be reviewed on some periodic basis to maintain attention, create accountability, and make course corrections as events unfold.

The CCR is a robust action plan that documents actions to address the gaps that exist between the Actual Culture and the Vision Culture. After the Vision Culture has been ratified, the arc of the journey is clearly visible: we are "here" in the Actual Culture, and we want to be "there" in the Vision Culture. The CCR is the actionable commitments made to remedy priority gaps between the here and there. I can safely say that those gaps will always be unique to the organization, in the same way the company's balance sheet and cash flow statements would be. There are some likely recurring categories and some "must haves" that are analogous to basic principles of the balance sheet, such as "liabilities will always equal assets." For example, there are several "human capital levers" that I will discuss in Chapter 6 that should always be present because they are such powerful channels through which to shape or change the culture—performance review and reward mechanisms, for example.

The process of identifying and then prioritizing the gaps between the Vision Culture and the Actual Culture that will populate the CCR can be accomplished in a number of ways—but obviously is a necessary step prior to creation of the CCR. Some gaps are enormous and high priority—for example a change in organizational structure or compensation—other gaps are minor, or actually subsets of the larger gap—for example, revision of the performance management document or submission procedure.

- Many companies combine Vision Culture ratification with a "decision accelerator" large-group prioritization process that accomplishes both the ratification goal and the gaps prioritization into a single event. This is a powerful and highly efficient way to produce multiple culture change outcomes while creating a motivating sense of involvement in a larger sample of up to seventy-five top leaders. This approach takes careful design, preparation, and expert facilitation, but has a high return on investment relative to the face time required of participants.
- Another approach is to have a one-time task force of internal expert staff and consultants generate a draft of the priority gaps and incorporate these into the CCR for top team ratification.
- Finally, in the situation in which the top team is fully engaged, either by motivation or necessity of a Condition Red situation, it is a relatively uncomplicated process to surface and prioritize key gaps into a rough draft of the CCR. With this level of top team involvement, the entire work product can be accomplished quickly and efficiently—though without the sense of participatory involvement of the expanded top leadership.

What Should Go into the Culture Change Roadmap?

The content that should populate the CCR will always be quite individual to the organization and its situational challenges. I have provided a few high-level examples, but every organization will have its own set of challenges it is trying to address in moving to a Vision Culture. Even when CCR items are similar or identical, they may be labeled with different language.

Here are some common examples of the content that can go into a CCR:

- "Big splash" structural changes that have high impact on a large portion of the organization: for example, changes in reporting roles and organizational structure, implementation of a new compensation structure, layoffs, consolidation of physically separate departments to shared location
- New capability or infrastructure creation that has not existed previously and is in the critical path to the culture change: for example, implementation of a performance management system, remote site communications, corporate university or training programs to develop Vision Culture–specific competencies
- Recalibration of existing systems to better align with the Vision Culture: for example, better alignment of incentive compensation to reinforce new and different behaviors
- Small but important symbolic changes that are intended to reflect culture shifts: for example, removal of "executive parking spaces" or other special privileges, or movement to open cubes from closed private offices
- Internal communication and decision-making procedures: for example, a quarterly town hall meeting or revised spending authorities

The creation of the Culture Change Roadmap marks the invisible end to the Launch phase of the Culture Change Process. "Invisible" because to all stakeholders—leadership, employees, or outside observers—the Culture Change Process is simply proceeding. Nevertheless, completion of a strong CCR is a critical success factor for any effective culture change—whether mild Condition Yellow or extreme Condition Red. It is the "plan to succeed" that makes a commitment to all about the intention of the CEO, top team, key leadership, and managers throughout the organization.

Chapter 5 Summary

In "Launch" I have outlined those initial actions that are necessary to get the culture change off and running: the Get Real Tool and the Culture Change Roadmap, which link the Vision Culture to key value creation metrics. We come next to the phase that I call "Propagating the Wave." Like many of the earlier culture change activities I have described, Propagating the Wave entails a series of activities that the CEO and top team must be knowledgeable about and take full ownership of. Much of the actual execution for Propagating the Wave will be done by others: human resource staff, cross-functional change teams, and perhaps outside experts, depending on the size and capability of the organization.

6 Propagating the Wave

The Culture Change Process up to this point has been directed largely toward creation of a Culture Change Roadmap. That roadmap captures the various initiatives that will move the organization to a Vision Culture. Whereas Setup and Launch are primarily readiness and planning activities, *Propagating the Wave* is more about "doing," or execution of the Culture Change Roadmap.

Unlike some of the unique culture change concepts, methods, and tools we have discussed in earlier chapters, the activities of Propagating the Wave are mostly well-known best practices from the fields of organizational effectiveness, human resources, change management, and leadership development. Continuing in my previous vein, this discussion will be aimed at "what the CEO needs to know" rather than being a more technical discourse for the expert or a review of the literature for academics.

The activities in this phase are central to making culture an engine of value creation, yet their execution will be delegated largely to others with formal responsibility or technical expertise. The culture change levers we are about to discuss are rarely the subject of graduate business education, if they are touched on at all. Many CEOs would consider these culture change levers the "arcane" responsibility of the senior HR executive and something they need not be bothered with. Irrespective of this viewpoint—which will vary with the sophistication of the CEO and top team—these are activities that are critical to the success of the culture change and that cannot be handed wholesale over to consultants or the human resource function. As we will see, there is absolutely some "technical detail," akin to Generally Accepted Accounting Principles (GAAP) rules or business continuity plans, that the CEO should know about but never lay hands on.

The three big levers of culture change that CEOs must appreciate at a level where they understand best practices and recognize critical outcomes are as follows (see also Figure 6.1):

1. Change acceleration and communication levers
2. Human capital levers
   A. Behavioral competencies
   B. Organizational design
   C. Performance management, rewards, and metrics
   D. Talent management
   E. Process improvement
3. Authentic executive leadership

The first of these, change acceleration and communication levers, are some of the necessary capabilities that any organization initiating any change will need to master. These are not new methods, and our discussion is aimed at CEO education. The second, human capital levers, is a large and growing field of "people technologies" that can be quite technical. Both of these areas are absolutely critical levers in the Culture Change Process, and the "behavioral competencies" portion of the human capitals levers is a

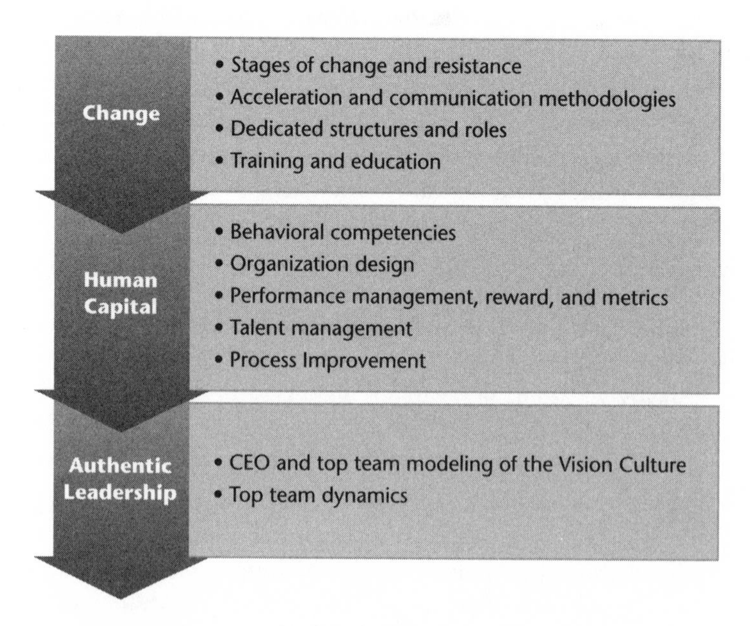

FIGURE 6.1. The three big levers of culture change

key element of Critical Success Factor 4. The third lever, authentic executive leadership, is also one of the five success factors and, arguably, the single most important implementation lever of the entire culture change initiative.

I enter into this discussion of the culture change levers with two strongly held views. First, these methodologies and processes are "best practices" that I will endeavor to outline, but never should they become more than a means to the end of culture change leading to value creation. Second, a direct result of the first view, these organizational processes should be kept to a minimum. I have coined the term *minimum best practice* to capture this idea: using the best available tools and methods, how can we get the job done with the smallest footprint and allocation of resources possible for the red-yellow-green level of urgency?

Best Practice for Change Acceleration and Communication

Change leadership has evolved over the past twenty-five years into an important basic organizational capability that every successful company must have in order to compete in a turbulent business environment. Like finance, marketing, information technology, and supply chain best practices, "change acceleration methodology" has moved from a differentiating competitive advantage to a basic organizational capability. It is a topic exhaustively and well-addressed in the literature, going back to William Bridges[1] and John Kotter,[2] enjoying a great surge in the 1990s as companies realized that business processes of any kind failed to successfully take root without adequate attention to change management. There are literally hundreds of books on the subject, and broad consensus about what the basic tenets are. What follows is a summary of key concepts and best practices for the CEO who is sponsoring a culture change.

The basic premise of change management can be summarized in this short set of assumptions:

1. *Stages of change and resistance.* Organizations and individuals (that is, "social organisms" of any kind) are naturally resistive to change, insofar as their "instinct" is to maintain stable homeostasis.
2. *Acceleration and communication methodologies.* When leadership realizes—either through skillful anticipation or reactive necessity—that change must occur, there is a body of tools, techniques, methods, and structures that can dramatically accelerate and facilitate both the pace and quality of change.
3. *Dedicated structures and roles.* Very much as with a movie or theatrical production, it is useful to think about a constellation of roles and

responsibilities that exist within the overall structure of "the change," whatever that might be: culture transformation, Enterprise Resource Planning implementation, reduction in force, acquisition, facilities move, and so on. Whether "sponsoring leadership" or "expediting agent," there are distinct roles to be played in any such change.

4. *Training and education.* The many tools, methods, and approaches just described need to be bundled into training modules that can be efficiently delivered to those responsible for making the change happen. Training events are primarily aimed at building skill for managers who are responsible for implementing the change, but in a larger organization must also carry the actual content messages of the Vision Culture across the enterprise.

Let us now consider each of these as levers to be applied in the Culture Change Roadmap.

Stages of Change and Resistance

There are few more powerful forces in a culture than the resistance to change exerted by the legacy Actual Culture. Indeed, we have characterized this earlier as something akin to a force of nature with its own powerful gravitational pull. Anyone who has worked in an organization with a strong culture will attest to this incredible force that resists alteration to "the way we do things." This is a dynamic that operates without regard for company size, industry, or geography; a characteristic of social organizations that seeks to perpetuate the status quo even in the face of compelling data that threaten that logic. And this is precisely the issue—it has little to do with logic and reason, and mostly to do with emotion.

The "change management" field has gone far beyond its humble original roots, but few experts would challenge the observation that it all started with a simple idea borrowed from the medical field. In 1969, Elizabeth Kübler-Ross[3] published her now famous "five stages of grief" (denial, anger, bargaining, depression, acceptance). Shortly after, her concept was adapted by a number of management psychologists—notably William Bridges—and translated into the managerial setting. This one simple paradigm has spawned a rich and highly practical tradition that continues to evolve today. The basic premise can be simply stated in these logical propositions:

1. Premise 1: *Loss produces a predictable cycle of emotional reaction.* Though certainly not as intense as physical death, loss of any kind reliably produces some version of these five stages in most people.

2. Premise 2: *Well-applied tools, methods, and techniques can accelerate this predictable cycle.* From management"s perspective, if there is the intention to initiate a change—especially a material change that will affect people's jobs, competence, future, income, and so on—it is desirable to have those experiencing the change *avoid* getting "stuck" in any of the earlier phases that precede "acceptance."
3. Premise 3: *The cost of not applying these methods is very high.* These "negative emotional states of denial, anger, bargaining, and depression lead directly to reduced productivity and, more to the point, reduce the likelihood that the intended change will occur. In different ways, they are all versions of "resistance" to successful change, and therefore countervailing forces to those responsible for creating successful change outcomes.

At the end of the day, change management is about reducing "drag" on the velocity of the change effort, by finding ways to accelerate emotional acceptance and even embrace the change.

As a general rule, the more extreme the R-Y-G level of urgency, the greater the resistance to change. When you think about it, this is a predictable causal relationship. The more extreme red and yellow culture change urgency conditions mean that the organization has been ignoring the incoming *rational* data from the external environment and "indulging" in a kind of self-deception that perpetuates some version of "we do not need to change." When the crisis comes—whether a drop in market share, profitability, or stock price—it is more likely to be in context of an Actual Culture that has resisted new attitudes and change in the face of a changing external reality (the definition of the Condition Red and Condition Yellow circumstances).

The central premise of the entire change management field is that management cannot "force" change onto an organization but should use the tools and methods that we are about to discuss as ways to influence the change. This is never truer than with culture change in which the ultimate target of change is human behavior. Is it possible to mandate a new policy for reporting accidents? *Yes.* Will this necessarily change the rate of accidents or the behaviors that precede them? *No.* Change management is about motivating others to do something that leadership believes is necessary for them to do. Even a relatively minor change, such as a facility change, will entail some disruptive discomfort; thus it stands to reason that a larger cultural change will be met with firm resistance. "Ordering" the change—especially in culture change—is a silly waste of time that can actually create further resistance than if nothing were done at all. We can see a simple example of resistance to change in Case 6.1.

Case 6.1. Do What I Say, Not What I Do

A new CEO was brought in to replace a highly autocratic and sometimes abusive CEO at a defense contractor after a sudden heart attack left the latter dead at sixty-one. He had been talking about possible retirement, and the board of directors had begun pressing him for succession plans when he turned sixty, but nothing had really been accomplished. This individual, a long-time senior engineer of the company, had worked his way up to the CEO position and was opinionated, decisive, and discouraging of dissenting views. Over the years he had shaped a culture in which the executive team was powerfully influenced by his management style, which demanded compliance—even though his stated management philosophy, and the company's "value statements," espoused an open environment in which constructive conflict was encouraged. The company had developed a mandatory "new employee orientation" that emphasized the importance of leaders taking initiative and expressing constructive dissent with superiors.

When the new CEO had been in place for thirty days or so, he started to realize that the many wall plaques and laminated cards he saw everywhere about "constructive differences" and "innovation" were about as far as those values went. His direct staff were "B-players" whose primary aspiration was job security—none of them had thrown their hat in the ring to take the vacant CEO job.

This new CEO thought he understood the problem and pronounced in his own words what was more or less a "Condition Yellow" culture circumstance on the basis of his assessment that the company had not produced new patents or really done anything but ride a wave of prior innovation using aggressive sales techniques. He saw a passive, security-oriented culture that had been beaten into submission by the now-deceased former CEO.

He thought his top team would be delighted and relieved to hear that his management style was the complete opposite of his predecessor, and he made this clear in a series of directive communications at a top team offsite: "I expect all of you to step up and take the lead. I don't have all the answers, and I want you to challenge me if you think I'm off track or on the wrong page. I want to change the culture, and central to that is a change in this pattern that I now see stemming from the previous CEO."

It is not too hard to guess what happened in this situation: nothing. The CEO's top team individually and collectively expressed their appreciation for this message and great relief at this change. The CEO left the meeting with a great sense of optimism and excitement about the change that was soon to come, but that change never actually materialized. He gradually realized that his team was now just dancing to a different tune—his tune—but that the basic dynamic of utter compliance, lack of dissent, and risk-aversion was still fully present.

This principle—that people will cling to the reality they know, resisting change to a new state—leads directly to a toolkit of methods for moving "targets" of change through this predictable set of emotional states more quickly than they might otherwise do so. This toolkit has expanded over the years but basically consists of various assessment and influencing tactics to move people through this series of emotional and mental phases to "acceptance."

Acceleration and Communication Methodologies

In the Condition Red and Condition Yellow culture change situations, some basic change acceleration capability is critical, and the culture change will not occur without it. In "yellow" going to "green," the other two big levers—human capital and executive authenticity—may be more appropriate. The Condition Red company that does not have some basic change management capability will need to quickly build or acquire it. There are numerous consultancies and training courses that specialize in delivering or building this capability.

Though using different labels to describe them, almost all approaches to change management rely on the same small set of principles—outlined briefly as follows:

Segmented Differentiation of the Change Impact. Understand how segmented subsets of the larger organization are differentially affected along a continuum from "very ready" to "very resistive" to change. This approach draws heavily from the basic toolkit of marketing research—using survey tools and focus groups to map the degree of resistance to company segment. In the culture change context, this change impact assessment tool divides the entire employee population into subgroups based on change issues, such as "degree of resistance" or "change impact." It helps the top team understand where, and to what degree, various segments of the organization are more or less *aware of, affected by,* and *resistive to* the Vision Culture. Here is an example:

> A recent acquisition of a New York company by a San Francisco financial services firm raised an interesting challenge for the acquiring company as it went through a Condition Yellow culture change. One of the key gaps on the Culture Change Roadmap focused on the need for shorter decision-making time, less consensus, and generally crisper meetings. As the "impact" and "resistance" change maps emerged, it was clear that the New York team of about two hundred people was going to have little resistance to this change; indeed, they were largely already "there." This information was used to tailor the local message—by reinforcing the subculture that was already there—and to indicate that fewer resources should be allocated to the change process in New York.

The goal of this particular acceleration tool is to accurately identify who, when, and where the culture change will most influence. This is an important step in the larger organization that has multiple geographies and business units. Even in the smaller organization, departmental and other subcultures can have very different levels of resistance. A common segment in the culture change arena has to do with newer and older tenure employees. For obvious reasons, the older tenure employees are often more attached to the Actual Culture than newer employees who more easily and fully embrace the new Vision Culture.

It would be important to treat these two populations differently in terms of customization of the message, amount of time and energy invested in change acceleration, and more direct and forceful dealing with severe resistance.

Communication and Influencing Strategies. These tools and techniques are mostly adaptations from the advertising and marketing communication techniques developed on Madison Avenue in the 1950s to sell consumer products. They use different media to strategically persuade specific target audiences with both general and customized messages. There are two key variables in this equation:

1. What *type* of communication is best suited to achieve the change objective?
2. How can the *content* of the communication be constructed in such a way as to minimize resistance to change and motivate acceptance?

Questions such as "What are the right communication media for certain kinds of targeted messages?" should be delegated to communications experts that do this for a living. It is important for the CEO to understand that there is a continuum from "cool one-way" media (the webinar, e-mail blast, or video presentation) to "warm two-way" media (the one-to-one dialogue or interactive group meeting).

The "cool one-way" media are ideally suited to creation of a broad, shared understanding about why the Vision Culture is so important and what its linkage is to the strategy and value creation. The Culture Change Roadmap would typically have some regular communication events aimed at updating about progress on the culture change. Timing, frequency, and repetition are all important variables that need to be taken into consideration for these "cool one-way" media. This is a very different kind of communication from "warm two-way" media, in which the objective is to involve and allow two-way influence. In the early stages of a culture change, the CEO will be having a number of conversations with the top team, board of directors, and perhaps external partners on the subject of Condition Red, Yellow, or Green and the importance of culture change. Obviously, these are not one-way announcements but dialogues in which the CEO's views may shift, and the experience of the parties will be one of shared consensus through mutual understanding of various issues.

The question of content is, of course, always somewhat unique to the individual circumstance, but there are some important general principles and techniques to be applied to those specific settings. Regarding content, there is a fundamental principle that is broadly applicable to a wide variety of settings and messages.

This is the "magnet" and the "wedge" principle: what are the "looking forward positively" and the "existing burning platform" reasons to believe in the necessity of the change? In the culture change setting, when Setup and Launch have been well executed, the "magnet" and the "wedge" will be apparent in the form of the R-Y-G condition rationale and the Vision Culture. The messaging principle is simple common sense: *give people who are being asked to change the most persuasive reason you can come up with*. Speaking generally to the culture change challenge, the "wedge" will always be some version of "we will perish or fail to create value without the culture change." The "magnet" is always at least the opposite ("we will create more value—and therefore be more secure, wealthier, happier, etc.—with the Vision Culture"), but often also presents other communication opportunities related to specific content in the Vision Culture. For example, in the Actual Culture that has been mired in negative silo politics, there may be a specific opportunity to call out the collaborative, positive environment of a culture with reduced parochial barriers.

After assessment of the differential degree of resistance in varying segments of the company, the rationale for customizing particular messages to various target audiences is self-evident. A magnet-and-wedge message that is too general may actually increase resistance and cynicism if it is directed to an audience with heightened sensitivity to a particular issue. Case 6.2 illustrates the importance of customizing messages to targeted constituencies.

Case 6.2. Engineering Group Acquisition

The engineering group of a small acquired company was very concerned that their highly innovative, low-structure, minimal formality subculture would be ravaged by the acquiring company's very process-oriented engineering culture, so much so that there were already rumblings from several of the acquired engineers about "taking headhunter calls that they had declined for years." The two CEOs and VPs of engineering got together to problem solve about what the best messaging was to reassure the acquired engineers that their innovation was highly valued and an impetus for the acquisition. Because they were in a different location, all agreed there was no reason to enforce new work hours or dress codes, but that some elements of the Vision Culture—such as accountability for hours spent on key projects to increase value-add of engineering expense—was an important cultural shift that all engineers were expected to make. This customized messaging, and the ensuing give-and-take between the engineering groups in the two sites, produced an invaluable business result: they began working more productively together on their actual engineering work, as the cultural clash faded into the background.

Dedicated Structures and Roles

Depending on the R-Y-G condition and the scope of the culture change initiative, a variety of temporary teams, change roles, and structures may be necessary to create the right level of attention and focus. Irrespective of this contingency, the concept of change roles is an important one in the change management tradition. Like most of these change concepts, this one is simple and common sense—but powerful when correctly applied.

The idea of change-specific roles was first introduced by Daryl Connor[4] and has earned a place in the canon of change management. Simply stated, the idea is this: any successful change initiative has four key roles.

- *Sponsors* may be initiating or sustaining. The initiating sponsor—often the CEO—first identifies the need for change and initiates the change process. The sustaining sponsor—often a member of the top management team reporting to the CEO—is responsible for strategic and executive decisions at the more tactical level. It is this individual who might charter some of the change methodologies we are discussing.
- *Agents* are charged with the tactical execution of the change.
- *Targets* are those individuals affected by the change.
- *Advocates* are internal or external consultants to the change, providing expertise of one kind or another to sponsors and agents.

This is a static view of change roles. This change roles concept also includes a dynamic quality in which sponsors become agents, agents become targets, and then the cycle repeats itself. Implied as the objective of any change effort, those who start out in the target role are successfully influenced and become sponsors or agents to influence other "new" targets. Even the initiating sponsor or the CEO begins the change journey as a "target"—they realize there is some external threat that requires them to change and they raise all the questions that any target would: "Do we really have to change?" "Is it really that bad?" "Will it go away if I ignore it?" Depending on the CEO's ability to accurately assess the true nature of the need for change, he or she will go through an internal transformation process to become the first initiating sponsor. The CEO might then go to the board and top team to persuade them of the need to address the threat. In those first discussions of the new threat, the board and the top team will also be targets of the CEO or initiating sponsor: they did not see the threat at all or view it seriously enough to have become initiating sponsors themselves. Some may resist more than others, but in that first contact with the need for change everyone is a target. If the initiating sponsor successfully persuades these first targets, they then become sponsors whose primary task is to make those that report to them agents and then sponsors.

One of several key success metrics for any change effort is the number of targets who are persuaded to become sponsors or agents. By definition, targets are those in the role in which something is being "done to them." When targets accept the need for the change, they become allies—as sponsors for those that they influence or agents to execute the change.

This principal holds true for any change, but especially so in a culture change in which the primary change focus is on attitudes and behaviors. The number of targets who remain at any point in the culture change is an excellent success metric—or "reverse" success metric, if you will. An organizational culture in which the CEO and all employees are targets is, in fact, a very apt assessment: they are targets of the external change that is headed straight their way, an external threat that is unseen or denied. The organization in which all or most of the employees have become sponsors or agents, with few targets remaining, is an organization that has succeeded in the first and most important step of culture change: committed motivation to create the Vision Culture.

Change Teams and Other Leadership Structures. In the yellow or red culture change conditions it is important to establish dedicated teams and leadership structures whose purpose is to focus on execution of the Culture Change Roadmap. There are several reasons why this is an important lever in the Culture Change Process, though, as always, the R-Y-G condition will determine the scope and size of these structures.

To one degree or another, implementation of the Culture Change Roadmap requires unbudgeted time for some managers. Except perhaps in Condition Green, when focused new activity is minimal, in all other conditions some new resource is required to implement the Culture Change Roadmap. Even a relatively mild Condition Yellow roadmap will describe actions that are more tactical than the CEO and top team have expertise or time to implement themselves. It is a poor use of executives' time and precludes an important opportunity for middle-management involvement and "evangelism" for the Vision Culture. Remember, the more targets-turned-sponsors, the more successful the culture change. This task force creates an opportunity for managers who are in closer direct contact with their constituencies to exert personal influence. It is a powerful expression of the CEO and top team's commitment to get others involved, further reducing any misperception that the culture change is solely an "executive," top-down initiative. Finally, when well-designed, staffed, and led, this kind of task force greatly improves the quality of problem identification and solutions as multiple views are surfaced and resolved or escalated to the top team.

The Cross-Functional Culture Change Task Force. For most culture change efforts, it is important to create a cross-functional team whose primary charter is to manage the tactical details of roadmap implementation. These teams are temporary structures that may require more time at the beginning of the culture change and diminish gradually as milestones on the Culture Change Roadmap are achieved. This "culture change task force" must be chartered by the CEO and top team.

Setting Up the Task Force. The following are common best practices in establishing the culture change task force:

- Team members should be capable and respected leaders—somewhere between six and twelve total members is ideal, depending on the size of the organization and scope of the Culture Change Roadmap.
- Task force members' existing responsibilities must be realistically modified to accommodate their role on the team. This adjustment might range from a small percentage to full-time, depending on the specific role for that individual. In a large culture change effort, a full-time team leader is almost always necessary. That individual is sometimes a member of the top team, but should certainly be a senior "high potential," well-regarded leader with a track record of cultural leadership and project management. The task force team leader is in a high-impact role—essentially reporting to the CEO in a new "cabinet-level" position focused on the culture change.
- There should be representation of the major organizational segments.
- It is helpful to include a marketing or communications task force member since communication is a primary task. Any of these more specialized skills can be "occasional" or "consultative," of course, depending on the size and scope of the change task.

- There should be one or two top team members on the culture change task force. In Condition Red circumstances, this might include the CEO, though generally the senior Human Resources executive and one other executive are sufficient to create a direct linkage to the top team. This overlap ensures that the task force will never get out too far in front of the top team, while also having a continuous line to the top team for full support.
- If change management capability does not exist inside the organization, the top team and culture change task force should receive training in change principals and methodologies at the outset of the culture change, for several reasons:
    - First, so that they are knowledgeable about how to proceed in all the areas I am describing here.
    - Second, so that they can customize the kinds of change management best practices being described here as a canon of principles and methods that become accepted practice.
    - Third, so that this seed group of top team and task force has the critical mass to be educators of others over whom they have influence.

Job of the Culture Change Task Force. Once chartered, up, and running, the culture change task force has several important responsibilities that are critical to the success of the overall culture change effort:

- Although the CEO and top team are ultimately responsible for initial creation and longer-term monitoring of the Culture Change Roadmap, it is the culture change task force that is filling in the tactical execution, monitoring, making course corrections, and problem solving.
- Informed by strategic guidelines of the CEO and top team, the culture change task force is the group that will conduct the readiness or resistance segmenting and will tailor messaging and communicating events to those target audiences.
- Particularly in a larger organization with a broader scope of its Culture Change Roadmap, members of the task force will play an active role as educators and as advocates of the Vision Culture. Whatever external consulting expertise may be necessary to get started, it is important that targets hear about the culture change from people they know and respect—ideally someone directly up their chain of command, or at least a senior leader who is able to make the case for change and answer questions knowledgeably about the organization.

Although this is sometimes a necessity due to lack of expertise or bandwidth, culture change should not be "led" by consultants. Whatever "shadow" role consultants may play as coaches, providers of material, or facilitators, the most successful culture change initiatives are those led in perception and reality by the leadership. The culture change task force has a primary responsibility to educate others about whatever the organizational canon of change management might be.

- The culture change task force also plays a critically important role in challenging the top team to remain authentic, as well as challenging their organizational constituents to move past resistance to embrace the Vision Culture, becoming sponsors or agents instead of targets.
- Both research and common sense tell us that people hearing for the first time about the need for change—targets—are far more receptive when they hear this message from a known and trusted superior in real-time dialogue.[5] When initial communications about the culture change are first disseminated, most targets will have a number of reactions and questions:
  - How does this affect me?
  - Why are we doing this?
  - How serious is the top team about walking the talk of the Vision Culture?
  - What is my role in the change?
  - Why aren't we doing "X" or "Y" instead of "Z"?
- The longer these natural questions go unanswered, the higher the probability of distortion, anxiety, and ultimately resistance. The most effective culture change initiatives are rolled out in such a way that the message is customized to the audience and delivered by someone in a position of authority who is credible and capable of answering basic questions. To achieve even these few simple outcomes means that they have intimate knowledge of the culture change rationale and objectives, yet sufficient familiarity with the local setting to allow informed flexible responses.
- The CEO still has a critical enterprise-level communication role to play, but even in the mid-size organization, employees may not know the CEO and suspect his motives as colored by the distortion that always accompanies being many levels away from the actual work.

Training and Education

It happens too often, unfortunately, that training and education are the primary, or sole, components of a culture change initiative. Simplistic reliance on training and education without other critical success change actions is one of the main reasons culture change fails, and why many are skeptical about whether culture can change. That being said, a thoughtfully designed training process is an essential component of any successful culture change effort. It is the "legs" that must carry the strategic communication "head." Training and education programs fall into two general categories—not all are necessary in every circumstance:

- Skill development is almost always required in a Condition Red or Condition Yellow culture change initiative. These typically are newly identified behavioral competencies or technical skills—often called out in a performance review process as an "organization-wide" development area.
- Education about the new culture can serve the useful purpose of broadly disseminating a consistent message about key values, competencies, or new processes.

Quite often these two are bundled into a single event—often with a more tangible work product. For example, a Vision Culture focused on becoming more innovative might create a customized two-day workshop that included

- Some general education about why innovation was so critical to the strategy and a vision of how the firm will do things differently
- A customized introduction to best practices that would speak to the firm's unique definition of innovation
- Skill development aimed at building specific innovation-related competencies, which might be more specific or technical for the R&D and Marketing function but more general for all employees
- Detailed descriptions of newly created structures and processes and their direct impact on selected employee roles and responsibilities
- Some fine-tuning application of these more general initiatives by workshop participants, customizing general corporate initiatives into specific local action-commitments

Training and education minimum best practice requires that these "legs" be well attached to the "heart" and "head" of the culture change. Too many companies address the training and education challenge by hiring an outside firm to deliver "education" about innovation, which means showing a couple of videos and having participants discuss their reactions. Useful, best-practice training and education should be interactive, practically applicable, and well-connected to the strategic rationale of the culture change.

Human Capital Levers

Like many of the topics that we have taken up to describe the activities required in Propagating the Wave, human capital levers is a large field with extensive literature, tools, and methodologies. I am cherry-picking those critical concepts and methods that the CEO needs to understand from a rich tradition drawn from human resources, organizational development, and industrial psychology. Like other functional disciplines the CEO is responsible for, this is a vast and often technical territory, but important for the CEO to appreciate as levers in the Culture Change Process.

We will explore five human capital levers that are crucial to the culture change process:

1. Behavioral competencies
2. Organizational design
3. Performance management, rewards, and metrics
4. Talent management
5. Process improvement

Behavioral Competencies: Creating the Common Language of the Vision Culture

The competency model begins with the premise that explicit descriptive detail, validated by consensus, can approach a level of objectivity and reliability that is useful in measuring what might otherwise be subjective and immeasurable. This is precisely why translating the Vision Culture into behavioral competencies is a large part of Critical Success Factor 4: it allows culture-as-personality to be stated in ways that are objective and measurable, and therefore usable as tools, baseline starting points, and future success outcomes. The Vision Culture—as a document—should not be cluttered with this detail, but without these more precise descriptions as an "appendix," the Vision Culture will remain ethereal and vague.

This is a particularly important tool to transform the "soft" stylistic and value elements of the Vision Culture into something concrete, observable, and therefore commonly shared. The competency model is about reliably observable behavior—an essential first step to *changing behavior.* It is also the basis for a new "common language" that is present in all successful culture changes. Though this new "common language" also typically includes stories and urban legends, these are more natural outgrowths of these first deliberate levers in the Culture Change Roadmap.

An example will illustrate this overlap between behavioral competencies and the "new common language" of the Vision Culture. Suppose a key element of the Vision Culture is to create a more "team-oriented" environment that is directly linked to an improved capability for greater innovation, faster product cycles, and less departmental parochialism. The Culture Change Roadmap has a specific deliverable, which is to translate "team oriented" into a cluster of leadership competencies that can then be used as the basis for assessment, skill building, performance management, and various rewards. In addition to some organizational structure changes, three "team competencies" are determined to be essential implementation actions to move toward this "team oriented" culture: *team leadership, team member effectiveness,* and *cross-functional awareness.*

In my experience it is not uncommon for the implementation to end at this point with the simplistic assumption that everyone knows what "team leadership" actually means. This is what we call the "headline" in search of "behavioral indicators"—an overly vague one-liner with no definition. It is a mistake to move on without having fully and concretely specified just what the "headline" indicates. An example of a "real" competency description for "team leadership" might look something like this:

Team Leadership
To get direct reports to work together efficiently toward common goals, a leader does the following:

- *Informs people:* shares information and ensures that team members are kept up to date on matters related to group needs, issues, or programs
- *Selects complementary team members:* purposefully assembles a team by selecting complementary abilities and styles for more effective team-performance
- *Establishes team direction and accountability:* establishes team accountability for a common mission, purpose, and set of goals
- *Resolves team conflicts:* intervenes, as necessary, to identify and resolve conflict among team members in a manner that reinforces teamwork values and a focus on common goals
- *Consciously builds team spirit and identity:* provides recognition, fair treatment, feedback, and opportunities for interaction and celebration aimed at enhancing group identity and "esprit de corps."

Obviously there is expertise required to construct from a blank page a real competency definition like this example for "team leadership." There are numerous formats and guidelines for creating real competencies, and clearly this is a task done by a consultant or someone in Human Resources with specialized expertise, not the CEO or any member of the top team. The key points are that it needs to be done correctly, there are no GAAP or Financial and Accounting Standards Board benchmarks for competencies, and the CEO should understand what the difference between a headline and a real competency is. *Building* the competencies is not the job of the CEO, but *using* them in hiring of new executives, evaluation of current direct reports, succession planning, or any other people-evaluation task certainly is. Rendering a decision on issues of fit to the Vision Culture or achievement of individual change targets can always benefit from the improved objectivity and accuracy that behavioral competencies bring.

It is also important to note that behavioral competencies are only one aspect of Critical Success Factor 4, which sets a standard for translating the Vision Culture and Culture Change Roadmap into measurable "observables" that minimize ambiguity at the implementation level. It rises to the level of a critical success factor because it moves culture change out of a subjective realm into an objective realm. "Objective" means that there is a clear common view of otherwise vague social events, thus allowing greater clarity about when change has occurred.

Organizational Design

It is hard to overstate the importance and impact of the formal structure on how people behave. It is the "architectural space" in which all events occur and therefore defines, like the walls and light that characterize any room, the constraints of what will happen in that "room." This is a big topic that is well treated in more detail by writers such as Jay Galbraith.[6] However, a note of caution: unlike the other human capital levers that are almost always required to one degree or another in culture change, changing the organizational structure is a major lever that may or may not be a necessary action.

A good example of how organizational structure does indeed shape the culture can be found in Case 6.3, in which the Vision Culture required transition from a product-principle structure to a solutions-principle structure.

Case 6.3. Moving from a Product to Solutions Organization Structure

A West Coast communications company had achieved great success in the conference room speakerphone field. As a strategy to fuel continued growth, it acquired first a video conference company and then an Internet transmission company. After the acquisitions were completed, for several years the company was structured into three distinct business units—each with an executive-level general manager. As broadband Internet raised the quality and availability of video conferences, the salesforce kept returning with requests from customers for a truly integrated platform that offered a "solution" from the three divisions in a single, integrated product. Customers were unhappy about having to deal with three separate divisions, only to discover after this ordeal that the company's own products did not always work reliably with each other! The marketing and sales functions identified four distinct vertical markets that were high potential growth areas: a military solution for battlefield communication, an educational solution for communication with remote locations, a medical solution for service of rural areas by large medical centers, and the business conference room solution for global companies.

This need for change was combined with the CEO and top team's vision to grow from $500 million to $1 billion in annual income, and a culture change was undertaken. The Vision Culture included a number of objectives, including better coordination and collaboration between the three business units on product roadmaps, and less parochial focus by the three business units. A critical piece of the Culture Change Roadmap included a redesign of the organizational structure to create new areas of responsibility in marketing and sales dedicated to the four vertical markets. Rewards for the business unit GMs were shifted to provide incentives for "solutions-focused" leadership behaviors. A newly empowered marketing function was redefined and filled with a more senior-level "chief marketing officer." There had been three unsuccessful incumbents in that VP of marketing position in the past three years—all attempting to persuade the business unit GMs that they should coordinate and collaborate to serve these vertical markets. It was only after the structure, responsibilities, and incentives had changed that proper attention to the vertical markets was possible.

Organizational structure changes may also take on a more modest form to bolster a Vision Culture attribute, along with other human capital levers. For example, creation of a new role reporting directly to the CEO in the quality area was a way that many companies made their initial effort to embrace a quality-improvement culture. The creation of the culture change task force, with leadership by a senior executive now reporting to the CEO (though perhaps not a permanent role), is another good example of how the CEO's commitment to culture change is made manifest. The proliferation in the "chief *something* (learning, innovation) officer" category is also exemplary of more modest structure changes that fall short of broad enterprise organizational structure changes.

Performance Management, Rewards, and Metrics

This is an area that *always* requires retooling in a culture change—sometimes a little, sometimes a lot, but always some adjustment is necessary. After modeling executive authenticity it is perhaps the most powerful set of human capital levers. It is also important to note that the seemingly tedious behavioral competency lever is an essential antecedent step to any meaningful application of these levers. Why? Because performance management and the rewards that will reinforce these new expectations are without an objective target until key attributes of the Vision Culture are translated into a measurable, common language of observable behavior.

Performance management, metrics, and rewards are each large and technical fields in their own right that we will not attempt to cover in depth. The tactical construction and implementation of the content and process of performance management is the job of the HR executive and his or her team. What does the CEO need to know about these human capital levers as a culture change tool?

The Performance Management Lever. Performance management systems are management control mechanisms to align strategic enterprise priorities with individual activity. Without question there is a top-down, and sometimes "coercive," quality to this practice. This may be one of the reasons why it is so common to have them incompletely implemented or missing altogether!

A recent *Wall Street Journal* article goes so far as to suggest that we need to "get rid of the performance review" and start over with a different model.[7] As the article unfolds, the author primarily objects to the fact that performance reviews are subjective, one-way evaluations by the manager, with insufficient opportunity for the direct report to weigh in.

There are as many different ways to ensure activity alignment from the top down as there are different organizational cultures. Some are more top-down and coercive, others are more cooperative mutual evaluations. Many organizations bolster the one-way evaluation with multi-rater data (usually referred to as "360-degree" data because they sample superiors, peers, and subordinates) that reduces the subjectivity of the manager's evaluation. Some organizations impose a "forced curve" on the evaluations in an attempt to ensure that some percentage of low performers are put on probation or otherwise penalized through withdrawal of rewards.

The key point is this: *in addition to being a powerful and necessary mechanism to propagate the new Vision Culture, the existing performance management system is also a powerful reflection of the Actual Culture.* Said another way: the performance management system is both a "delivery mechanism" and also a potential "target" for change in the Culture Change Roadmap.

To further complicate this multiple-cause problem, many organizations confuse the annual performance review system with talent development and succession systems, suboptimizing the value that could be produced by these two human capital management practices. Finally, add to this the practice of "forced calibration" made popular by Jack Welch at GE, in which performance management serves double duty as a tool to weed out "B" and "C" players, and you have mass confusion. Needless to say, all these human resource practices that we include as culture change levers are powerful reflections of the culture that must be considered as potential targets in the Vision Culture. The performance management system and related rewards to reinforce it are on a short list, along with executive modeling of desired behavior, of the most powerful mechanisms to reinforce and maintain the Vision Culture.

Some kind of mechanism to create alignment around behavioral competencies emerging from the Vision Culture is necessary. On the basis of the large number of possibilities and permutations just described, three scenarios emerge, though these are points along a continuum.

Scenario 1: Straightforward delivery mechanism. If the performance management system is in place, being used, and not a target for material change in the Vision Culture, then the action is fairly straightforward. The Culture Change Roadmap should reflect a sequence of linked actions to incorporate key behavioral competencies from the Vision Culture into the performance management system—and probably the talent management systems as well, (but more on that in the section on talent management). This is probably a Condition Green: the culture change has been recently undertaken, or human resources practices singled out for improvement.

Scenario 2: "Good enough" system—not in practice. This is a circumstance in which the performance management system is not in practice, but *not* a change target called out in the Vision Culture. This gray middle zone between the "straightforward" and "full target" scenarios is the most common, and spans the full gamut across the two extremes. In many cases, this scenario masks the underlying problem, which is really Scenario 3—there is something fundamentally broken in the performance management system, leading to disuse. If the issue is more that managers are avoidant of conducting a "good enough" performance management process, then the solution must come from the top in the form of better modeling and accountability.

Scenario 3: Clear change target of the Vision Culture. In many cases, the performance management system is a lifeless administrative ritual in which managers "check the box" to avoid conflict or "slam the box" in a misuse of their authority to impose their personal values. The process of accountability, the content of the actual tool, and linkage to strategic or cultural goals may be seriously out of alignment with the Vision Culture. In a surprising number of smaller companies, there is no real process in place. Particularly in family run businesses, or family-like medium-sized businesses where the founder is still involved, the work "just gets done" and there is a subjective distribution of rewards by the leader or leadership team at the end of the year. In this case, the remedy requires more attention and resources, but may actually be better in the culture change context since there are fewer "bad habits" to unlearn. The action in Scenario 3 is an overhaul (or *de novo* creation) of performance management practices, with new content reflecting key behavioral competencies from the Vision Culture.

The Rewards Lever. Rewards come in many forms and must be thoughtfully tied to expectations for performance and managerial behavior. Rewards and punishments reinforce cultural attributes all the time—sometimes deliberately, often as the result of unintended consequences. Formal rewards—fixed and incentive pay practices, benefits, and so on—must absolutely be forced into alignment with the Vision Culture and almost always have a legitimate place somewhere in the Culture Change Roadmap. Like performance management, this is an important lever of change to shape the culture, and it is often misaligned with expected behaviors described in the Vision Culture. The "three scenarios" of performance management that I just described are essentially the same for formal rewards and do not bear repeating. Performance expectations are largely "theoretical" without strong linkage to compensation practices. Perhaps the major difference between the two is that compensation practices are *always* present in some form or another—employees tend not to work for free. Executives expect, and usually get, some kind of incentive rewards linked to specific performance outcomes. Clearly, these formal rewards must be evaluated against a standard of alignment informed by the Vision Culture.

It is surprisingly common for the Vision Culture to be unveiled with great fanfare, but then for poor performers to continue to receive the same rewards that stellar performers receive. There is no quicker way to neutralize progress in a culture change than for those who have embraced the new culture to go unrewarded. Though there is a commonsense component to formal compensation, it is a highly technical field that requires specialized expertise. The job of the CEO is to understand the importance of this human capital lever, raise the issue, and ensure that an expert assessment of compensation alignment with the Vision Culture is completed. After this is done, the action will fall into one of the three scenarios described previously: no action, alignment and refinement of existing systems, or complete overhaul.

It is the informal rewards that bear further discussion. There is a considerable amount of research to validate the commonsense intuition that people are motivated by many more things than money. There is no better example of this than in the "brand name" companies such as Disney and LucasFilms, where employees sometimes work for less than "market rate" for the "privilege" of possibly catching a glimpse of Harrison Ford or being assigned to the iPhone development team. One of several powerful drivers in any culture is the collective unspoken motivators that create "value currency" in the environment. This may not always be rewarded with formal compensation (though clearly employees always get paid), yet operates as a powerful motivator nonetheless. In the "glamour" industries, informal rewards may be things as intangible as a meeting with a famous celebrity. In the technology industries, it may be the opportunity to work on a "cool" new technology like the iPod.

In almost all cultures, recognition in the form of public praise, advancement in the hierarchy, and internal reputation are powerful motivators. Increasingly for the "X" and "Y" generations, enjoying the work you do, or deriving some genuine satisfaction, are not only powerful incentives but necessary conditions to attract new employees. Although the popularized "best places to work" are not always actually the best places to work, it is a distinction that many companies consider an important competitive differentiator to attract the best new talent.

The point is this: the Vision Culture must translate into unique formal and informal rewards. When the Actual Culture rewards are missing or seriously out of alignment with the Vision Culture, they must be called out in the Culture Change Roadmap as action items. The CEO must appreciate what some of these informal and intangible rewards might be and set the expectation with compensation specialists and his or her own top team that such rewards will be created, or aligned to the Vision Culture. Not all of these will be simple linear linkages between "performance" and "compensation." Some of the most powerful incentives to behave in alignment with the Vision Culture will require creativity and innovation that can only come from those who are doing the work.

The Metrics Lever. By "metrics," I mean those many measurements that the organization uses to track success. Metrics are an important lever in the Culture Change Process because they bring focus to the scarce resource of organizational attention and energy. The CEO and top team have considerable latitude in selecting which organizational metrics they deem most important. The famous quip "What you measure is what changes" is certainly true and is the central reason why organizational metrics are a powerful lever in any culture change.

Performance management is one kind of organizational metric, but consider all the other metrics that "roll up" to determine whether one individual has "done a good job":

- Operational efficiency
- Customer satisfaction
- Employee satisfaction
- Financial metrics
- Departmental efficiency
- Business unit profit and loss

The list is virtually endless and the topic is vast with a long tradition. One high point—perhaps a pinnacle—in this tradition is the Balanced Scorecard model created by Kaplan and Norton in 1996,[8] which opened a universe of metrics beyond the narrow financial metrics that had been "king of all metrics" for decades. Instead of relying solely on financial metrics such as "return on investment," the Balanced Scorecard model suggests that we consider metrics in areas such as customer satisfaction (percentage of satisfied customers), operations (percentage of unused inventory), and organizational learning (time required to complete a process relative to industry standard). Like all value-add business paradigms, "The Balanced Scorecard Collective" has withstood the test of time, continuing to grow into a worldwide community of practitioners and devotees. One Balanced Scorecard metaphor that is particularly applicable to culture change is the "pilot dashboard" image.

> The CEO is a pilot flying a plane. There is a dashboard in front of the pilot that has many dials—big and little. There is a fuel gauge, an altimeter, an oil gauge, a directional gauge. What is the likely outcome if the pilot were to focus on only one of these gauges—as many CEOs focus only on the financial gauge? Answer: they could find themselves going the wrong direction, with plenty of fuel, only to run out over the ocean because they had paid insufficient attention to the directional gauge. They could find themselves crashed into a mountain—with plenty of fuel—because they did not pay attention to the altimeter's warning that they were flying at too low an altitude.

The point is a simple but extremely powerful one: the CEO that does not pay attention to a full dashboard of the right metrics runs the risk of crashing. This is never truer than in considering which metrics need modification to accelerate progress toward the Vision Culture. As with all the human capital levers, there are the "three scenarios" to consider when evaluating how to address organizational metrics. Are the right metrics in place, but the calibration of a metric needs refinement? Are there important metrics missing altogether? Are most of the right metrics in place, but the process to use them is broken?

From one perspective, the Culture Change Roadmap is one of a handful of CEO-level dials on the "big dashboard" for the organization. It is the "dial" for the culture change that must accompany other "big dials" that roll up to the "ultimate dial" of shareholder value. Another extremely useful set of concepts to apply to culture change from the Balanced Scorecard model is its notion of the causal inter-relationship between four major dashboard categories: financial, learning and organizational, customer, and operational. The authors emphasize that some metrics are "leading" indicators and some "lagging"; many metrics are both leading and lagging, though in different contexts.

For example, most of the financial metrics are "lagging indicators." When sales revenue is counted at the end of the quarter, the activity that produced that revenue metric is completed—the metric "lags" behind the organizational activity that created that outcome. For those with eyes to see, there are many "leading" metrics that faithfully predict the "lagging" indicator of "sales revenue": perhaps number of sales leads, ration of opportunities to close, and so on. To finish out the example, even the quarterly sales revenue "lagging indicator" may serve double duty as a "leading indicator" for other metrics: annual profitability, job satisfaction, and attrition rate in the salesforce.

Case 6.4 illustrates how important a full appreciation of metrics is to the culture change effort. Some of the milestones on the Culture Change Roadmap may directly involve a shift in which metrics are assembled and how they are used. The example emphasizes this important point.

Case 6.4. Profitable Lines of Business at Bank of Hawaii

Bank of Hawaii, like almost all regional banks, was organized around product lines such as credit cards, small business loans, residential mortgages, private banking, trusts, and so on. There were some thirty-two in all—bundled into larger portfolios that were organized into two separate business units: the "retail bank" and the "wholesale" bank. After the culture change was well under way, it became clear in the course of the organizational analysis that no one really knew what the profitability of each of these product lines was and, to make a long and complicated story very short, these thirty-two products were reorganized into a smaller handful of "lines of business" that were complete profit-and-loss business units measured by a metric of net profitability. In context of the bank's Vision Culture around increased accountability, this was a critical piece of the Culture Change Roadmap. The previous organizational structure was one in which associated metrics *and* the rewards that went to those responsible for the product lines did not always line up with performance of that product—in part because the leader of that product line was not responsible for the costs associated with production that were allocated to centralized, internal functional departments.

Changing the organizational structure to allow a metric focused on overall profitability was a necessary step that created direct line of sight between the Vision Culture "accountability focus" and the organizational structure, role, metric, and finally rewards for specific performance in those new lines of business. Without those changes, the "accountability focus" would have been an "empty suit" sham.

This change of organizational structure quickly clarified areas of responsibility, thus creating a kind of accountability that was impossible in the previous structure. The example also provides the perfect segue to the fourth of the culture change human capital levers: talent management.

Talent Management: What the CEO Needs to Know

The individual leaders of your company are like the cells of a larger organism in that every one shapes the whole. The more deliberate you can be about selecting and developing your individual leadership talent, the stronger your culture will be. Talent management, the fourth of the culture change human capital levers, is one that should usually be an action added to the Culture Change Roadmap. Like the other levers, how talent management is positioned on the Culture Change Roadmap will depend on the state of this capability and the gap between it and the Vision Culture. Even in the company that has outstanding talent management practices, the Vision Culture will be translated into behavioral competencies that become the "DNA kernel" for a wide range of talent management activities, from selection, development, and career and succession planning to compensation and promotion. All of these are potential targets for change in the Culture Change Roadmap, but also ongoing "delivery systems" for key elements of the culture.

There are numerous accelerators in the talent management area. In the context of culture change we have grouped these into two key areas: selection and development.

Selection, On-Boarding, and Orientation. Whenever there is an open position at the senior level, there is an opportunity and a risk. The opportunity, of course, is to reshape the area with a different kind of leadership, one more in alignment with the Vision Culture. The risk is that a flawed decision will make matters worse. It is always surprising to see companies taking too casually this important opportunity to shape the culture. When the Vision Culture has been translated into behavioral competencies, these should be used as a screening tool to ensure the new executive is a good fit with the Vision Culture. Sometimes the best candidate is internal but lacks domain experience or technical expertise. There are never quick answers to these questions, but especially in the consensus-oriented culture, it is important for the CEO to take a firm stand in shaping these decisions toward the Vision Culture.

After the executive has been hired, it is important that he or she be integrated into the organization with an on-boarding process that actively identifies risk areas that could derail the new hire. The team that the new hire comes into will also need to adapt; this is never *only* about the new executive "assimilating." At the same time, even in an active culture change, if a new executive hire arrives with a dramatically different leadership style, the proverbial "white blood cells" of the culture will delay at best, and derail, at worst, that executive's ability to be a change agent, and ultimately, to add value.

In the on-boarding example in Case 6.5, the hiring company had a strong and well-entrenched culture that most executives felt was "who we are" and "something that new hires needed to adapt to first, and consider changing second—after they had understood how the culture works and gained credibility."

Case 6.5. On-Boarding at a Global Industrial Company

A Fortune 100 global industrial and manufacturing company headquartered in the midwest realized it was at the eye of a perfect storm with the potential to prevent or reverse value creation if these key gaps were not addressed:

- Their executive workforce had an average age of fifty-plus with an average tenure of twenty-five-plus years, and there was an insufficient supply of next generation leadership to meet necessary demand
- A new CEO and radically new strategy sought to "change the rules of the game" in a highly commoditized and cyclic business
- There was an increasing recognition of the need to import new viewpoints and leadership styles to a strong, successful, but insular culture

It was not long before several executives connected these dots and took aggressive action by proactively recruiting very senior executive talent over a two-year period. The best search firms were engaged and did a fine job in placing the best talent.

Five of the six new incoming executives left within the first eighteen months of being hired! Some were "spit out," and others realized they could not tolerate such a different culture and left in frustration. It was not lost on anyone that the underlying cause was that the company's culture was strong, pervasive, and unforgiving of newcomers who did not accommodate to it. The company engaged us to help design and deliver an on-boarding program for incoming new executives.

A senior executive was recruited away from a competitor to the great dismay of that competitor—so much so that a legal non-compete was imposed on the incoming executive for the first year. This hire was a tremendous coup from a business and technical perspective, and the CEO who recruited him on the basis of a prior working relationship felt he had put a proud feather in his cap by pulling this off. The executive was assigned to go through the company's new on-boarding program. In the course of conducting the initial assessment of this newly arrived executive, it became clear that his philosophy of leadership could be summed up as "Create a vision and swing for the fences." In the first ten days of his tenure, what appeared to be a bold and decisive leadership style was experienced by his peers and direct report co-workers as arrogant and shoot-from-the-hip. The consultant coached this new executive around precisely this cultural and personality difference, explaining that the company was more methodical, and valued thoughtful and collaborative decision making more highly than "rock-star" independent home runs. The incoming executive, a bright and capable leader who had been rewarded over many years at his own company for "hitting home runs," took in this coaching, realizing that he would not be successful if he persisted in this culture without some course correction. He began listening more, reframing his leadership direction as modifications to successful strategies, rather than issuing bold new directives that were experienced as uninformed and arrogant. One year later, during a human capital calibration, he was seen as the top successor to the chief technical officer.

In the four years since the initation of that program, twenty-five new executives have been hired; all but one are still with the company. The company is making visible progress toward its ambitious transformational goals, keeping the "baby" of its highly successful culture while throwing out the "bathwater" of those cultural attributes that are misaligned with the new business strategy.

New-hire orientation is another important tool to codify the culture and set expectations for those first entering the organization. All three of these talent selection and integration levers (selection, on-boarding, and new-hire orientation) are tactical methods for ensuring that the Vision Culture is consistently propagated to the greatest extent possible

Leadership Development, Training, Calibration, and Succession Planning. Development of new leaders and managers must, of course, reflect the Vision Culture—both in specific leadership traits and competencies as well as in core values. Development and training of fresh leaders is one of the longer-cycle levers of change, which serves to cascade the Vision Culture down into the organization and propagate the wave toward its realization. Unlike compensation, which can change in a quarter, leadership development takes time, generating more nuanced outcomes that are sometimes only visible over years. As with the other human capital levers, it may be necessary to substantially upgrade a weak or nonexistent leadership-development function or, if the function is in good order, to simply ensure that the content of the target behaviors is brought into alignment with the Vision Culture.

In Condition Red, development and training are less likely to have an immediate effect and may not be forceful enough to produce a result quickly enough for this level of urgency. In Condition Yellow, and when they are actively linked to the Vision Culture, senior-level leadership-development programs can be valuable ways to communicate important expectations about leadership effectiveness in the new culture. Such a program, that might include a one-time "360-degree feedback" and leadership style assessment, becomes a powerful mechanism to convey the Vision Culture in practical, actionable terms for the "willing but unable" (Figure 6.2).

The "360-degree feedback" paradigm of individual assessment and feedback is useful for matching leadership-development efforts with the R-Y-G level of culture change urgency. The primary value of this 360-degree process is to differentiate those in the organization who are aligned with values but need development of new capabilities, versus those who are fundamentally

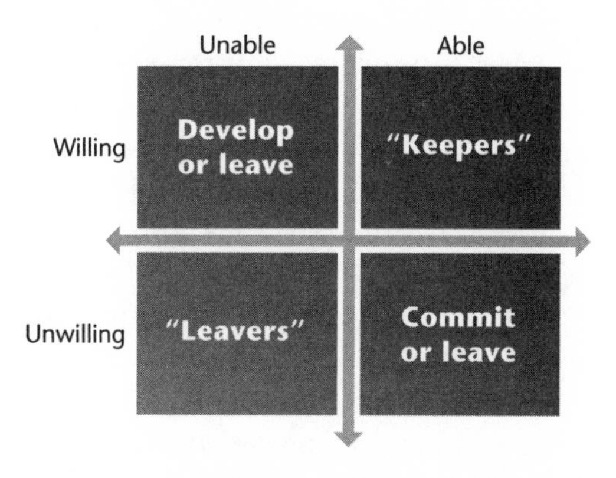

FIGURE 6.2. Two-by-two willing-and-able matrix

resistant to the Vision Culture and the changes that are in motion. It begins as a diagnostic exercise but quickly moves to high-impact action: develop, promote, separate, educate. There are many possible motives for the "unwilling"—whether able or not. Sometimes the resistance is caused by a true difference in values. In other cases, there is a misunderstanding or misperception of what the expected change is. The reason this is such a useful tool is that it helps those leading the change determine the best action for different reactions to the culture change expectation:

- The willing and able are already sponsors or agents actively involved in promoting the culture change.
- The unable and willing need training, development, and candid feedback about whether it is realistic for them to develop in the ways that are necessary for them to be successful in the Vision Culture.
- The able and unwilling need confrontation about their resistance to accelerate their decision to move on as sponsors, or move on out of the organization.
- Finally, the unable and unwilling group presents the clearest target source of action—though of course these individuals deserve an opportunity to understand how they have been evaluated and to respond.

The appropriate action to address culture change resistance depends entirely on the *cause* of that resistance. As Figure 6.3 outlines,

- A true misunderstanding about the Vision Culture requires education as a remedy. Despite best efforts of the culture change sponsors, the word does not always get out to the right people in a timely way. The Vision Culture message that starts out with a serious Condition Yellow rationale may be diluted or distorted in transit to final targets of the message in the farther reaches of the organization.
- Gaps in competence or capability require development or training that ends with demonstrable improvement. How much improvement and how long that takes are two of the thorniest questions leaders will face. There are some wrong answers (taking too long or not showing enough change), but many right answers depending on the individual in question, the R-Y-G condition, and the business circumstance.
- Resistance to the Vision Culture *after an appropriate period of ratification* during which reasonable questions to the initial Vision Culture draft are encouraged, must be confronted. Depending on

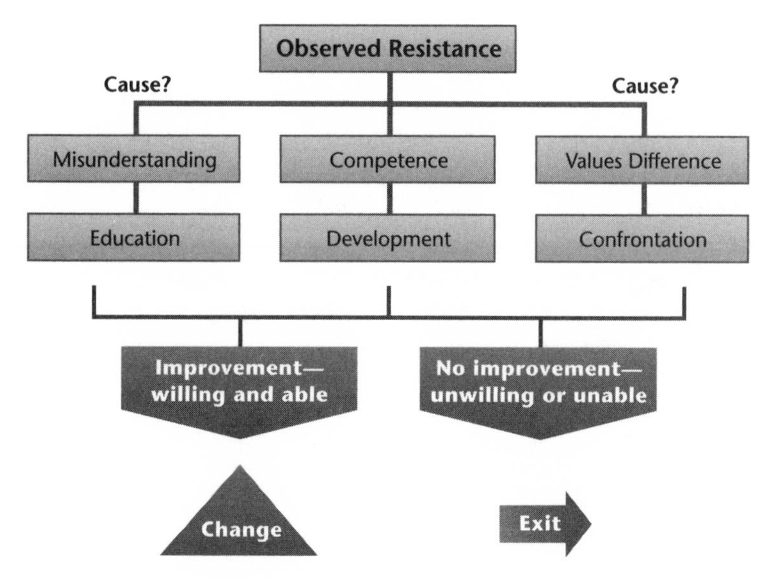

FIGURE 6.3. Diagnosing resistance to change

the specifics of the Vision Culture, tolerance for dissension may vary considerably. Whatever tolerance for dissent is spelled out in the Vision Culture, the senior executive who cannot, or will not, support the Vision Culture must be forced to make a decision. Case 6.6 is a typical example.

Case 6.6. Francois Gets Fired

Francois, a fifty-year-old senior executive at a large West Coast financial institution, had been heard to say that the new Vision Culture was "one more in a long line of fads" that the company's chairman was promoting via his recently appointed CEO. The new CEO arrived a year ago, getting the job that Francois had been a candidate for (as well as once previously) but had been passed for over due to his long-standing criticism of the chairman. Francois was technically brilliant—largely the architect of the bank's credit culture, though considered too aggressive by some—and highly successful over his twenty years with the company. Francois was vocal about what he thought should be included in the Vision Culture during the Get Real Tool exercise in the top team—mostly themes related to aligning the mainstream culture with the more aggressive culture of the credit committee policies that he had put in place over the years.

Seeing the gap between Francois' core beliefs and the Vision Culture, the new CEO asked him whether he could support the Vision Culture during the ratification stage. He said "yes," but had not been entirely honest with himself, continuing to privately hope that others would share his view and not support the new CEO's culture initiative.

Two months after the Vision Culture was rolled out, the CEO continued to hear second-hand reports of how the agreed-upon messaging was not being faithfully communicated down into Francois' organization. Far worse, Francois seemed to be growing more bold and vocal about his own dissent to the Vision Culture. The CEO called Francois in and gave him two alternatives: to resign that afternoon, or be terminated on Monday. Six months later the CEO, speaking to the author about lessons learned, indicated that he regretted waiting so long to confront Francois, observing that the Vision Culture had taken a quantum leap forward after his decision to remove him. Not only had a cynic been removed from destructive nay-saying but, far more important, the CEO's action was a public statement that calibrated what degree of dissent from the Vision Culture would be tolerated at the highest level of the organization. Subsequent to Francois' departure, a number of long-tenured senior staff also decided that they could not support the new Vision Culture, and elected to leave through retirement or other employment. The departure of Francois was considered to be the "tipping point" of the culture change.

The example in Case 6.6, which I, as a CEO advisor, have experienced in one form or another in almost every yellow or red culture change, is another powerful rationale for why the CEO must understand the Willing-and-Able Matrix and take an active role in calibrating it both conceptually and, eventually, in actions like those taken with Francois. This is not a task to be delegated to anyone. Another lesson from the Francois example was that much of what appeared to be values-based resistance down through Francois' organization turned out, after his departure, to be "informational" and "educational." Francois simply did not embrace the new Vision Culture and made only half-hearted attempts to represent the reasons for the change to those under his formal and informal influence.

It is important that the CEO take a visible and active role in calibrating the four willing-and-able" categories to the level of culture change urgency and the Vision Culture content. People decisions such as that concerning Francois are often painful and easily avoided. The CEO and top team must demonstrate "where the bar" is for those reporting to them, and perhaps to others beyond that immediate circle, depending on circumstance.

In the section on modeling executive authenticity, I will expand on the "bar" that the CEO set in the Francois example. Before we move on to that, let us turn to the systemic impact of where the "bar" is set in the process of calibration and succession planning.

Formal Calibration, Succession, and the Willing-and-Able Matrix. The "calibration" and succession or career planning processes run by Human Resources can and should be "repurposed" to serve the culture change. Like the other human capital levers, these may require a range of focus that spans from simple alignment of the Vision Culture with existing systems to a completely new "installation" of basic calibration and succession processes.

"Formal calibration" is typically an annual human resource process—sometimes irreverently referred to as "rack and stack"—in which senior managers rate their direct reports in a top-to-bottom forced ranking. There are numerous variations on the theme, but all share a central goal: to "raise the bar" by imposing an evaluative discipline on managers as they provide feedback to direct reports about performance, career potential, and alignment with the culture. The process is particularly powerful, if not always successful, because it uses peer pressure and assumptions inherent in the normal distribution across departments to create a higher standard. The "normal distribution" assumption is simply that not everyone can be "outstanding." The majority—68 percent or so—will function in the middle, half above and half below the mean. A minority will fall two, three, or more standard deviations from the mean at either end—as "stars" or as "poor performers."

Many organizations wrap several of these objectives (calibration, succession, and incentive rewards) into a single "people review" that focuses action on the top and bottom few. A common practice at the beginning of a culture change is to set a policy that the bottom 5 or 10 percent be put on some form of "requires improvement" formal notification. This is a particularly useful practice in changing "support" cultures that have become complacent or value loyalty and long tenure. However, this practice, made famous at General Electric by Welch, can be equally destructive after several cycles, when there is an expectation that 10 percent or more of the leadership should be "sloughed off" every year to drive continuous upgrade of the workforce.

As in the example case of "Francois," imposing higher or Vision Culture–driven new standards and values is absolutely essential to make the culture change real. The CEO must be involved in setting the top and bottom bars so that the process does not fall entirely into mechanistic human resource hands or become diluted by "legacy culture" forces that do not wish to see their own security jeopardized. Both in visible decisions about key people and in stated policy, it is the CEO's responsibility to set clear expectations about where this cultural standard is set.

Succession planning is a practical necessity to ensure business continuity and organizational stability. It is also, like all the other talent management levers, a powerful tool to signal how recognition and reward via promotion and career success will reflect the new Vision Culture. The combination of the two—calibration and succession planning—provides the practical tools to literally reshape the composition of the executive team and the fundamental cultural DNA of the company.

There are many ways to accomplish this, as I have outlined in the preceding discussions of key human resources levers. Of course, the tactical implementation details of a calibration or succession are never the job of the CEO. The CEO's job for all of these culture change human capital levers is the same:

1. Ensure that the basic capability is in place and insist that it be "installed" if it is not present and working.
2. Ensure that the contents of the performance management, rewards, metrics succession, and calibration are aligned with the Vision Culture.
3. Take an active role in defining where the bar is set for these levers, remembering that the bar may be set at different levels in years one, two, and three.

Process Improvement

I have called out several human resource processes that are key levers in the culture change. These human resource processes (performance and talent management, rewards, organizational design) are really a subset of a much larger category of processes that exist at all levels of the organization. An organizational process is a collection of actions or "steps" that, when assembled as a whole, create value. There are processes within every functional area that help complete its primary task—for example, quality and efficiency processes to ensure product integrity or safety in the manufacturing area. There are processes that cut across the entire organization, for example, annual budgeting and planning processes. The performance management process in human resources is another example of an enterprise-wide process.

There are innumerable organizational processes beyond those behavioral-focused human capital levers that may become the focus of a culture change. These processes outside of the human resource area may sometimes serve as the centerpiece of the Vision Culture. Following are some examples:

- *Innovation*. Leaders of a company that found itself caught in the downward spiral of commoditization realized, after repeated attempts to cost-cut their way to better margins, that they would never get there with their existing strategy. A centerpiece of their

Vision Culture was a shift toward greater innovation. The Culture Change Roadmap included a constellation of initiatives aimed at creating these capabilities:

  - A complete overhaul and rethinking of the product-development process, which had historically been buried in the marketing function with little involvement from other functions
  - A company-wide initiative to remove numerous other cultural barriers to innovation from top to bottom
  - A core set of innovation leadership competencies translated into performance management and rewards
  - A newly established cross-functional innovation team charged with breaking down internal barriers to innovation across departments and looking outside the company for new ideas

- *Agility.* This company realized that becoming more flexible, agile, and responsive to customers was a competitive advantage, and could threaten survival over the next five years if left unaddressed. This "agility and flexibility" centerpiece of its Vision Culture was translated into a number of large and small initiatives on the Culture Change Roadmap:
  - A complete overhaul of authorization protocol and procedures aimed at giving more "local" authority and discretion to staff dealing directly with customers. This included top-to-bottom changes in controls related to signature authority for managers as well as a department-level initiative aimed at review of all "standard procedures" with the goal of elimination or simplification.
  - Metrics for departmental success were changed to focus greater attention on cycle time and internal customer satisfaction related to responsiveness. Rewards for functional department heads would now include a much greater focus on reducing "speed bumps."
  - It also included a set of behavioral competencies focused on creation and reward of leadership behaviors related to flexibility, proactive initiative, and risk-taking. These new "agility" competencies were then translated into human capital levers such as performance management, succession and bonus criteria, and so on.
  - A new organizational design included elimination of several central control departments along with creation of local positions with increased authority for a wide range of what were previously corporate headquarters' decisions.

- *Strategic Management.* Finally, a company realized, in the course of its Launch phase culture assessment and the Get Real process of integrating the Shadow Cultures, that it must change the existing culture of reactivity that lacked sufficient forward vision and planning. The top team realized, with chagrin, that several important external events that had thrown the entire company off balance could have been easily anticipated and avoided, if only there had been more time spent simply asking the question, Where are we headed and what are likely scenarios? In addition to a focus on strategic leadership competencies related to vision, time management, and prioritization capabilities, the Culture Change Roadmap also included the following:
  - A complete overhaul of the annual planning and budgeting process, which had previously been little more than a budget negotiation driven by the CFO to incremental growth targets, and a sales pitch to the board to secure authorization.
  - A commitment was also made to installation of some balanced scorecard software that would streamline communication and ensure better documentation and follow-up to final strategies.

Like the human resource processes that we discussed earlier, alignment to the Vision Culture in the roadmap could include anything from *de novo* installation of a missing process (for example, the strategy management example) to minor tweaking of an existing process so that it can better support the Vision Culture. The CEO needs to understand the important link between high-level attributes of the Vision Culture and practical implementation through any number of key levers. Obviously, the role of the CEO is not to get involved in process improvement, but he or she does need to be a guiding, and perhaps deciding, force in prioritizing how the Vision Culture is translated into organizational attention and resource allocation.

Let us move now move on to the one area where the CEO must be heavily involved in the details: modeling executive authenticity.

Modeling Executive Authenticity

The third and final change lever that must be used by the CEO and find a place somewhere in the Culture Change Roadmap is the shift toward the Vision Culture by the CEO and top team. We will discuss several key CEO responsibilities in this last section of Propagating the Wave.

Keeping It Real: The One Thing You Cannot Leave Out

The human capital levers that are so important in shaping a culture will not be enough without robust, visible modeling of the new culture by the CEO and top team. After Setup and Launch phases, there is no more powerful accelerator or decelerator in Propagating the Wave than how the top leadership team actually behaves—in both micro-daily and macro-quarterly actions. Without question, and by a significant margin, this is probably the single biggest predictive variable in the culture change equation and the reason it is Critical Success Factors 5.

Minimum best practices for the CEO and top team to "keep it real" include

1. CEO involvement and personal modeling
2. Managing top team dynamics

CEO Involvement and Personal Modeling. The leader of the team sponsoring the culture change—whether CEO or school principal—must actively model the behaviors emblematic of the Vision Culture. As simple and obvious as this seems, it is incredible how *infrequently* it is well executed. There are many rational and irrational reasons for this, but probably the most common one is the "emperor's new clothes" syndrome. Subordinates of the CEO are fearful to point out leadership behavior that is clearly misaligned with the Vision Culture. Sometimes this reticence is based in reality; sometimes it is just cowardice; usually it is reflective of the very leadership style and behaviors that are targeted for removal in the Vision Culture.

Whatever the reasons, the CEO should assume that others—especially direct reports and below—will *not* take the lead in telling their superior about perceived development needs. In my twenty-five years of experience with this phenomenon, the CEO would be well advised to assume that "there is always something." In Condition Red and Condition Yellow, the CEO is historically part of the legacy culture, or has been brought in to change it. Either way, it is virtually a certainty that there are CEO leadership competencies and stylistic qualities that are out of alignment with the Vision Culture. How could there not be? How to best solve this problem?

First, the CEO should find a trusted advisor—ideally someone both internal and external to the team—whom he or she can truly depend on to "speak truth to power." As every CEO knows, this is a more difficult task than might first appear. Difficult, in part, because of the inherently political nature of any executive team; even on the well-functioning, high-performance team, CEO subordinates have agendas and budgets. Finding this advisor is also sometimes difficult because defining the issue may require expertise in behavioral observation and description.

Sometimes the misaligned behavior can be quite nuanced—something everyone feels, but is difficult to pin down in descriptive terms that are actionable. Communication and other more interpersonal kinds of behavior can be difficult to describe in sufficiently clear terms for someone without behavioral expertise. In other cases, the problem behavior revolves around a central trait or passion of the CEO that he or she is unwilling or unable to change. Case 6.7 illustrates how powerfully the top leader's actions can be in shaping the behavior of all employees and, ultimately, the culture.

Case 6.7. The CEO Who Liked the Numbers

The founder and long-time CEO of a mid-sized software firm was a "numbers" person with a conservative and sometimes narrow view of the company that she had started and successfully grown. She had hired weaker CFOs, who were really VPs of finance, in large part because she was the de facto CFO. It was clear that her passion was the financial engineering, and she had little true interest in other areas of the company—paying attention to them just enough to make sure they were working—and generally hiring competent, independent executives to fill those positions that demanded little of her time and attention.

When the company hit the twenty-year mark, there was a major crisis that ensued from this dynamic. Having secured tremendous personal wealth, five years previously the CEO had hired a president to come in and take over daily operations and continue growing the company. This president, like many of the day, was irrationally exuberant and went on a major acquisition binge, only to have it all come crashing down with the "dot-bomb" correction. He was fired, and the CEO felt compelled to step back in and focus on a "culture change." Inappropriately delegating much of the culture change leadership to an outstanding human resources executive, the company proceeded to craft a new Vision Culture. One of the many key attributes of the Vision Culture was a new emphasis on growing internal talent. This attribute was recognized as strategically important due to the very technical nature of the company's target market, which required a combination of software and health care expertise. The Culture Change Roadmap included considerable attention to coaching and development of talent from within the company. Leadership development, calibration, and succession were all called out in the roadmap and provided with significant investment of resources to build a true "leadership pipeline."

In the first cycle of these various human capital levers, managers throughout the organization had received training in a variety of coaching and development events, and it was expected that these events would be conducted with diligence and care by the top leadership of the company. The CEO initially did not find time to do this—though all of her direct reports were taking this small piece of the culture change seriously. The HR executive took it upon himself to mention this to the CEO, pointing out that her direct reports had noticed that these feedback, coaching, and development events had been repeatedly cancelled, or done in perfunctory ways.

The CEO—a generally open and reasonable person—went back to her previous focus on the financial strategy of the company, spending a great deal of time with analysts, investment bankers, and the company's financial staff on questions related to stock buyback, price modeling for the software, and other financial engineering issues. The executive team members went about their business in the culture change, achieving a measure of success in this particular area and many other areas related to realignment to the Vision Culture. In both private conversations and an exec team meeting while the CEO was absent on vacation, they discussed the problem of the CEO's failure to embrace even a minimal level of coaching effectiveness, agreeing that it was "undesirable" but okay, since they all felt committed to this aspect of the Vision Culture. As the second year of the culture change gave way to the second cycle of coaching and performance management, executive team members went at these activities with their own direct reports with far less enthusiasm—beginning to model some of the avoidant and perfunctory pattern of the CEO. The HR exec team member noticed this, and with some encouragement from the author, challenged the CEO about this behavior. This led to an acknowledgment by the CEO of the adverse impact of her behavior and, shortly after, a change in the structure to create a COO-president role, allowing her to remove herself from daily operations and managerial coaching. The new president, a member of the existing executive team, recommitted to the coaching process that was a centerpiece of the Vision Culture, and the culture took an immediate, dramatic step forward. The very fact that the president's promotion was evidence of the "leadership pipeline" working, as well as the acknowledgment that the CEO's failure to model coaching translated to her self-removal from an operating role, gave the culture change an enormous boost, as employees saw their leaders "keeping it real."

Sometimes the problematic behavior is palpable and easily pinpointed, but even executive-level subordinates are reluctant to address it with their superior for fear of being labeled "resistive." Consider, for example, the "impatient CEO" who starts to display nonverbal signs of irritation when subordinates bring him or her news of resistance to the culture change, or when aspects of the culture implementation are questioned in good faith (Case 6.8).

Case 6.8. The Evangelical President

The new president of a large consulting organization came in with an almost evangelical mission: transform the culture of this sleepy government contractor into a dynamic fount of creativity and technical innovation. In the first three years of his presidency he made many courageous and bold moves, earning him the loyalty and respect of his direct report team and many others in the organization. After articulating a clear business vision, he removed noncompliant and incompetent members of his team and created a compelling new Vision Culture that included an innovation methodology and language—all bundled into a two-day training. Things proceeded dynamically and constructively toward real culture change for three years. As the fourth year of the culture change rolled around, the bloom started to come off the rose as his direct reports encountered more and more resistance to the direct pressure and "evangelizing" of the president. The joke was that you didn't want to run into the president over lunch and be buttonholed into a conversation in which your loyalty to the innovation principles would be tested with what seemed to many like a "cross examination" or "loyalty test."

The view of the executive team—who admired the president for his energy, vision, and the changes he brought—was that the organization had embraced as much of the Vision Culture principles as it was capable of, but was now at a point at which dialogue and compromise about fundamental realities of the organization were necessary to go forward. This meant really two things. First, the rank-and-file principal investigators (mostly Ph.D.-level professionals) had changed as much as they were going to, and were now saying "this is as far as we'll go—we are not going to attend another two-day seminar in which we are subjected to the same principles we have heard for the last three years." Second, everyone was fatigued with the president's "bully pulpit" style that never seemed open to dialogue, but only to retransmission of the "gospel" according to the president. He had created his "formula for change" and used it to create a more innovative culture. The original formula was just "out of gas," and repeating the same principles was no longer producing change, but resistance. It was time for course correction and new approaches—which required the president to listen, instead of transmit.

Those bold enough to speak candidly with the president about their concerns and the unintended consequences left the encounter with a feeling of being condescended to at best, and chastised at worst. Attempts by several trusted advisors and consultants to acknowledge this impasse and address it were unsuccessful—ending in the president's termination of, or distancing from, the messenger. The culture change was "stuck" in its own frozen ideas, and despite much progress, was essentially stuck at this impasse to the detriment of all.

The two preceding examples illustrate how CEO traits can create significant obstacles to culture change and ultimately value creation. In both cases, the issue was largely unknown to the CEO and avoided by the top team, and became a significant demotivator for the organization to continue embracing the culture change. Dotlich and Cairo,[9] as well as many others, have described the ways in which CEO stylistic traits and personality create blind spots that hinder overall effectiveness. The point is that CEO blind spots become organizational liabilities, and this is especially so when the entire organization is looking to the CEO to determine "how serious we need to be about really doing this."

Managing Top Team Dynamics. The dynamics of the top team model the systemic dynamics for the entire organization in the same way that the CEO's behavior does. How the top team resolves conflict, communicates, makes decisions, and decides on a myriad of other variables is directly reflected down into the culture of the organization—irrespective of what the deliberate words and intentions of the Vision Culture outline. Indeed, the net behavior of the top team literally becomes the culture. It is a powerful lever for the CEO that absolutely cannot be ignored or underutilized. The power of this lever comes from the fact that it is under the direct influence of the CEO—unlike so many other systemic variables that the CEO may set in motion via delegation or assignment but must then monitor from a distance.

What can the CEO do to shape the team so that it can be that power lever? There is much written about this topic in the organizational development and general management literature. Narrowing our focus to the question of how to shape the team to best influence the culture change, there are three key areas for the CEO to pay particular attention to:

- Composition—Who is on the team?
- Internal team norms—What are the rules of engagement within the team?
- "Keeping it real"—Using regular audits to do so.

Composition. The CEO may or may not get to choose who is on the top team depending on the circumstances. Regardless of whether there is an opportunity to select new members of the top team, the CEO has tremendous influence over everything that occurs in this space. Clearly, when there is the opportunity to select new top team members, it is a major opportunity to shape the culture. After practical issues of experience, domain, and technical position requirements are satisfied, the culture question comes down to this: "How far along is the culture change of the top team in the journey between the existing 'as is' (Actual) culture and the "to be" (Vision) culture?"

If the culture change is in the stages of Setup or early Launch, it is usually an important opportunity for the CEO to demonstrate full commitment to the values and attributes of the Vision Culture. The major risk lies in going too far, too soon, and having resistance in the legacy culture derail or drive off the new executive. Aside from the disruption and discontinuity this kind of "host rejection" creates, it may also reinforce resistance to adoption of the new Vision Culture, or reinforce cynicism by those supportive of the new culture about the possibility of real change.

The other side of this risk, of course, is to hire someone who does not embody the Vision Culture, with the practical result that such a person is less likely to effectively play a leadership role in it just by virtue of who he or she is. There is also the undesirable consequence of a general perception that the CEO and top team are not serious enough about moving to the Vision Culture to hire someone who represents it. This is a tough call—and one of the many reasons why translating the Vision Culture to well-articulated leadership competencies is so valuable.

If the opportunity for a new hire comes later in the culture change process once the Vision Culture has taken hold, the question is simpler in that the competencies and leadership style of the new hire should reinforce the Vision Culture. There is less risk of "host rejection" because the legacy culture has been replaced with Vision Culture.

In both of these situations, and everywhere in between the two extremes, it is well worth the time and expense to conduct an expert professional prehire assessment, and to offer some form of on-boarding so that any misalignments between the new hire and the culture can be quickly identified and coached. These are difficult and largely "lonely at the top" CEO decisions—but of great impact, especially at the early "tipping point" stage before there is momentum to the culture change.

Internal Team Norms—Rules of Engagement. Every team faces a universal set of questions about how members will operate with each other.

- Some of these questions are in the realm of interpersonal chemistry and values—for example, issues of trust and commitment, personal integrity, and mutual support and collaboration.
- Other questions relate to team dynamics that arise in conducting the business of the organization—for example, how are decisions made, how is conflict resolved, how inter-dependent do we need to be? Are we a "track team" in which members operate independently with scores rolling up to a portfolio metric? Or are we a "basketball team" that wins by making interdependent plays? How do we hold each other, and our direct reports, accountable?
- Questions of communication must be answered by every team—for example, what is confidential? How open and direct are we with each other? With the rest of the organization?

How the top team members behave in word and action with each other and downward to their own teams will set the standard for the entire organization. The preceding are a sampling of the most common "universal" questions. There are many other team norms, sometimes identified in context of the particular team, nature of the business, and circumstance.

The critical CEO responsibility relative to a successful culture change is to first ensure that these team norms are discussed, consensual, and explicit. It is to be hoped that, in the context of creating the Vision Culture, many of these issues will have been vetted and resolved. The second, more challenging responsibility is to be the "conscience" and possibly "enforcer" of these norms when there is variance. The logic is simple and compelling:

- Individual and collective behavior of the top team must directly reflect the Vision Culture—or the Vision Culture is an "empty suit."
- The perception and daily experience of the top team by the rest of the organization is the single most visible and impactful influence in modeling the new Vision Culture.
- Only the CEO is formally in a position to be conscience and enforcer of these team norms, and this will only occur after the team has spent dedicated time building consensus about what those norms are and made serious public commitment to living them.

How the CEO builds and optimizes the top team is the subject of a large and vibrant literature that is well treated by Lencioni[10] and Katzenbach,[11] among others, and beyond our scope here. Just as there are many "right" organizational cultures, there are many right ways to create an effective top team. The CEO, as leader of the top team, is in a unique position to directly define and shape these team norms—thus indirectly, though powerfully, shaping the culture of the entire organization. If that responsibility is abdicated, or poorly executed, the culture change will be suboptimized at best or will fail outright, as employees become cynical and disbelieving of the new culture.

Keeping It Real: Making Objective Feedback the Norm. The 360-degree feedback and coaching process is a widely used and extremely valuable way to ensure that predictable blind spots and human frailties are identified, constructively communicated, and addressed. There are many variations on the theme of effective multi-rater feedback—the particular tool and approach are less important than that it be done in a way that feels confidential, safe, and objective.

The importance of performing 360-degree assessments with the top team cannot be overstated. It should, of course, include the CEO and be conducted at the outset of a culture change and on some subsequent cycle—usually every eighteen to twenty-four months. Whatever the specific details, tools, and methods, the CEO must visibly embrace the principle and model the attitudes and behaviors that will normalize the feedback process. This principle, in my view, holds for all top teams, regardless of whether they are engaged in a culture change or not. In the circumstance of a culture change, it is mandatory and should *always* be an item on the roadmap that has the full commitment of the CEO and top team.

Because the 360-degree process for the top team needs to be confidential and objective, it should be done by an outside expert, of which there are many to choose from. At the outset of a culture change, it is important that items on the 360-degree tool include all the key leadership competencies from the Vision Culture. This exercise, when conducted professionally and in good faith, is an ideal way for top team members to get a valid read on how well aligned they are with the values and competencies of the Vision Culture. Subsequent cycles may have a harder "edge" in that there is an expectation that initial improvement areas have been addressed and show progress.

In some cases, the initial feedback is so discrepant that the question comes up: "Can the individual be successful?" At the top team level there is no one but the CEO who can sponsor and follow through on these issues, though clearly the detailed execution of the process from data collection to feedback and possible coaching needs to conducted by an objective expert.

It is a good practice to have the senior leadership beneath the top team also participate in some form of 360-degree assessment specifically aimed at alignment to the Vision Culture. In many cases, there is simply a mandate in the Culture Change Roadmap that all leaders of a certain rank or title will have a 360-degree review. The reason I raise this issue is because these 360-degree processes are often mandated for "senior leadership" without the top team participating—implying naively that the top team members, because they created the Vision Culture, do not need to audit their own actual behavior. The worst possible approach—though regrettably common—is to single out a few "marginal performers" to participate in the 360-degree process, or to exclude the CEO.

Chapter 6 Summary

In Chapter 6 we have explored mandatory and variably optional levers of change that populate the Culture Change Roadmap. The three big levers—change management, human capital levers, and modeling executive authenticity—should always have a place in the Culture Change Roadmap. If you took ten different Culture Change Roadmaps, there would be "boilerplate" categories that would always be the same:

- A clearly defined "to be" Vision Culture
- Change management and communication initiatives
- Human capital levers: performance and talent management, rewards and compensation, and behavioral competencies
- Actions to ensure executive authenticity

In addition to these "basics" there might also be any number of other company-specific items depending on circumstance, but these "big three" culture change levers are the "big three" precisely because they are so uniquely impactful in changing the culture.

We have come a long way on the journey that began with Setup, then Launch, and finally to Propagating the Wave. We turn now to the fourth and final phase of the Culture Change Process: Celebrating Progress.

Setup Launch Wave **Progress**

7 Celebrating Progress

In Chapter 7, I outline the fourth stage in the Culture Change Process after Setup, Launch, and Propagating the Wave. *Celebrating Progress* is the end of a natural cycle, marked by the shared view that the Vision Culture has been largely achieved. Before I outline key actions and issues in the fourth step, it is important to set some timeframe benchmarks for culture change.

Timeframes and the End-to-End Process

Every organization that undertakes the culture change journey is different in too many ways to easily list. One of my goals has been to establish some universal principles to help the CEO and top team develop realistic and best-practice individual yardsticks. I have tried to do this with the red-yellow-green condition continuum and with minimum best practices for each of the four phases: Setup, Launch, Propagating the Wave, and Celebrating Progress. I have not spent much time on the subject of time itself. Before we enter our discussion on Celebrating Progress, it seems appropriate that I outline some general timeframes, in order to set realistic expectations.

Let us assume that the first starting point is during the "four CEO questions" in Setup. This is that important first juncture in which the CEO answers question 3: "Do I have the right organizational culture to execute the strategy?" That question is most likely to come up for a newly appointed CEO, who has a compelling and natural reason to answer the first two preceding questions: "What is expected of me to create value and keep my job?" and "Is the current company strategy a reasonable way to make that happen?" These initial questions may also come up for the long-tenured CEO facing a disruptive external change in the market. In either case, asking these questions is a reasonable "zero point" to set the clock ticking for our culture change timeframe discussion.

From that zero point of first realization that the culture is out of alignment with the strategy, it would be hard to imagine the CEO taking more than a month or two to act on the first steps of Setup. Those first steps include a level of threat assessment ending in the R-Y-G determination and the related strategic communications to get others on board. In my experience this rarely happens in less than a month. If it takes more than three months before the next milestone at the beginning of Launch, something is probably wrong and it may never happen. The other likely outcome is a change of CEO, often directly as a result of this failure, and then the entire cycle resets with a new zero point for the new CEO.

To make the example easy, let us assume that zero point is January 1, 2009. All other things being equal, it is likely that Launch would begin about March 1. Unlike Setup, Launch requires engagement by a larger group and sometimes external experts to help with the assessment of the Actual Culture. Completion of the Get Real Tool for Shadow Culture integration to produce the Vision Culture, and then ratification of that Vision Culture, are the other concrete deliverables that must come out of Launch. A visual, as in Figure 7.1, is always helpful when trying to envision overlapping time horizons.

All in all, three months is probably minimum and six months probably maximum for Launch. From a January 1 starting point, it would be unusual to be at the final Launch milestone—a completed Culture Change Roadmap—before six months, or June 1, 2009. It is important to note the CEO's role in setting the pace and driving the timeline to both this "best practice" metric and the R-Y-G condition level of urgency. The CEO who has arrived in September 2008 and determined a Condition Red culture change priority on January 1, 2009, could easily decide that a completed Culture Change Roadmap was one of the top three priorities and drive the process accordingly to hit a June 1 or earlier beginning of Propagating the Wave.

How long Propagating the Wave takes is to some extent dependent on where the organization sets completion milestones in the Culture Change Roadmap. Assuming the "typical" scenario, this third phase of Propagating the Wave is likely to be about one year. The pace for this third phase is set by the natural cycle of the culture change levers, mostly the human capital levers that typically run on an annual cycle. For example, annual performance and salary reviews, calibration, succession planning, promotions and titling changes, or financial and budget forecasting. So, continuing the

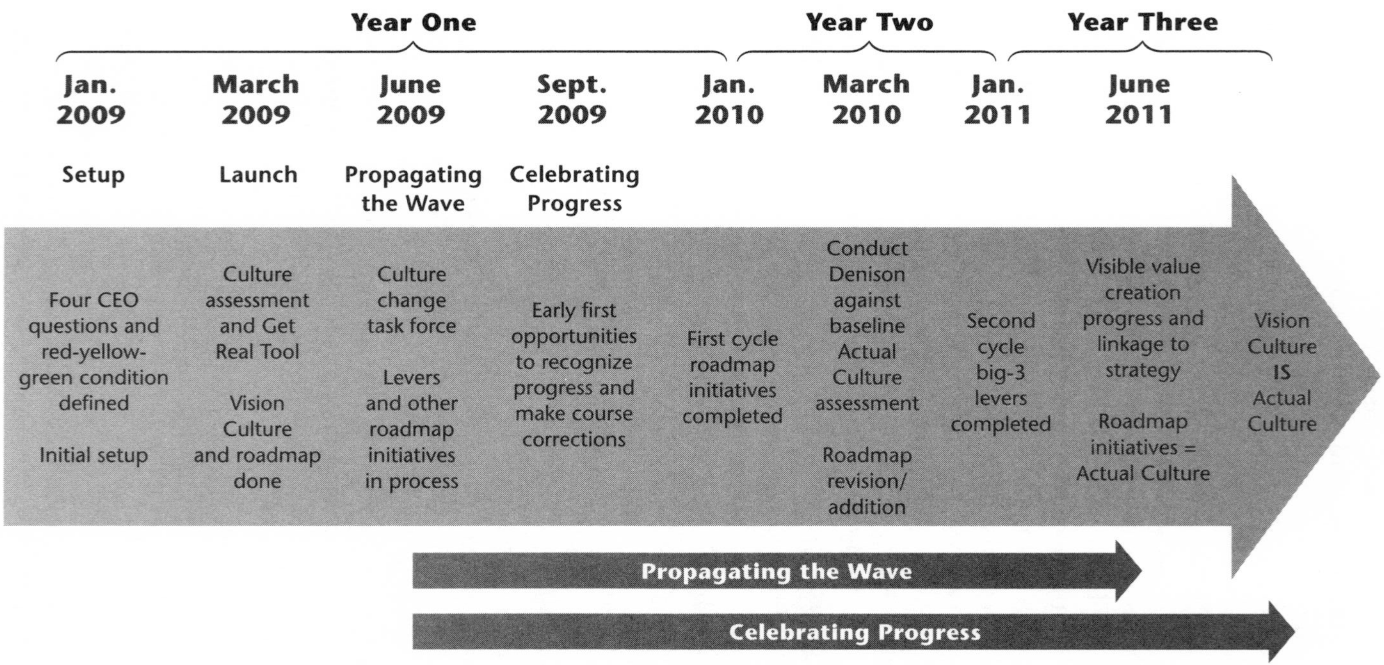

FIGURE 7.1. Culture change long-horizon timeline

January 1, 2009, illustration, by the end of the "typical" culture change, we would be at about eighteen months advanced, or at June 1, 2010. It would not be unusual, in my experience, having been a part of many culture changes over twenty-five years, to have a culture change span two full years before anyone can credibly say "there's been a change."

Celebrating Progress is an important set of activities but is not a time-consuming or labor-intensive activity in the way Launch and Propagating the Wave are, and should be happening to one degree or another from the early days of the culture change. I will have more to say about this as we move on shortly to discuss various approaches to recognizing progress. With regard to timeframe expectations, it is my view that a well-designed and executed culture change can show clear results at eighteen months, and there will be important success milestones along the way. However, it could easily be two full cycles of annual performance appraisals, rewards, departures, and new hires before people are saying, "This is a different place with a different culture." In other words, the proverbial "bottom line" is that culture change is a two- to three-year process.

This decision about how quickly the Culture Change Process unfolds can and should be driven by the CEO's assessment of its priority. Most of the obstacles and gates that would make the Setup and Launch phases twelve or eighteen months are in direct control of the CEO; following are some examples:

- A make or buy decision about the expertise and bandwidth for executing the culture change is a time when the CEO and top team must make important trade-offs that directly affect speed and timeline of the culture change. External consultants will cost more, but expedite the process with experience and proven methods. Internal consultants will cost less (though not "nothing" since their "old jobs" need to be backfilled) but have the advantage of creating an enduring capability and presumably some historical knowledge of the culture. The ideal is probably the consultant who can flexibly move from initial definition of the culture change architecture to training some internal talent and then to stepping back into a shadow consulting role to help the CEO and culture change task force stay on course.
- Offsites for the Get Real exercise require top team calendar prioritization that is clearly in the purview of the CEO to expedite via fiat.
- Town hall ratification events and the appointment of culture change task force members with related delivery dates are also well within the discretionary authority of the CEO to calendar.

Propagating the Wave pace is more susceptible to motivation and potential resistance to what has been set in place by the CEO and top team during Setup and Launch. It is the reason why the change and communication levers are so important to moving the process forward. Certainly, there are actions that the CEO and top team can take to accelerate the implementation activities outlined in the Culture Change Roadmap, but these are less directly influenced.

Let us now move on to concepts, tools, and methods in Celebrating Progress.

Celebrating Progress

There are many ways to "celebrate progress." I have chosen to title this fourth and final phase of the Culture Change Process with an emphasis on "celebrating" rather than "measuring" progress. Euphemistic, perhaps, but of course celebration cannot happen without measurement—how else would we know what to celebrate? This emphasis is more than just a reflection of optimism; it also reflects the inconvenient truth that there is rarely a "definitive end" to culture change. If the change process has been well designed, attention has been paid to critical success factors, and the CEO and top team have been active sponsors of the Culture Change Roadmap, then there will be progress and this progress will be measurable in objective ways. It is unlikely that there will be an "end" because the successfully conceived and executed culture change moves the organization to Condition Green, in which enterprise-wide change effort is not required. Remember that in Condition Green there are still culture-shaping activities occurring, but most of the activities that constitute Setup, Launch, and Propagating the Wave are unnecessary because they have just recently occurred over the past two to three years—though, of course, not necessarily in the ways I describe here. (There are certainly companies with a Condition Green culture that have not necessarily gone through this suggested process but are nevertheless at Condition Green due to good leadership or a similar process.)

The final "metric in the sky" is question 3 of the four CEO questions in Setup: "Is the culture well-aligned with the strategy?" This can, and must be, a "yes" or "no" question for the CEO, but as I have taken pains to point out, the continuum of Condition Green to Condition Yellow to Condition Red will make a tremendous difference in how success is defined, and therefore measured. After a Culture Change Process has achieved the milestones laid out in the Culture Change Roadmap, we know by definition that some important and measurable changes have occurred, and the CEO must determine whether these have added sufficient value to now answer "yes" to question #3. There are unquestionably indicators, large and small, which I will discuss shortly, but the big question #3 is something only the CEO can answer—as only he or she can answer questions 1 and 2: "What do stakeholders expect of me in terms of value creation?" and "Do I have the business strategy in place to create that value?"

I have separated the numerous possible success metrics into three "levels," remembering that this fourth phase of the Culture Change Process is not only about "declaring victory" but also about "creating victory" all along the way in the form of intangible rewards and recognition (Figure 7.2). As will be evident, these three categories vary in their degree of objectivity. Level 1 includes informal encouragement, recognition of early milestones, and "hero stories." Level 2 is formal Culture Change Roadmap metrics. Level 3 involves value creation linkages to the strategy.

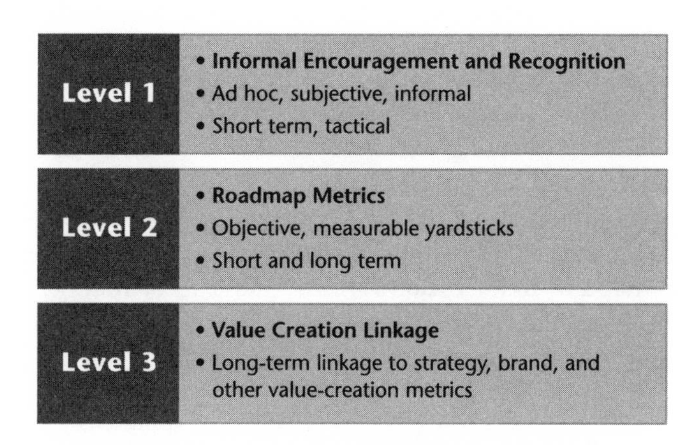

FIGURE 7.2. Three levels of celebrating progress

An apt metaphor for these three ways to Celebrate Progress is to think about a continuum along dimensions of objectivity, timeframe, and immediate versus strategic impact.

1. Level 1: Informal encouragement and recognition are highly subjective, by definition ad hoc and reactive, and a result of immediate impact. The impact may nevertheless be quite material, as our example about the VP of R&D further on will illustrate. This first category is at the "ground" and tactical level of the culture change.

2. Level 2: Roadmap metrics are objective and measurable, but vary in immediacy of impact. They are clearly not reactive or ad hoc in the way informal encouragement or recognition are. Roadmap metrics are the "yardstick" and "punchlist" that tell us where we are in completing the "project" of culture change. They are quite important for this reason because they bring objectivity to subjective phenomena.
3. Level 3: Finally, value creation linkage to the business strategy is the most powerful and has the highest impact, but it is difficult to be fully objective about and usually a "post-hoc," lagging indicator.

Let us look at examples and best practices in each of these categories of Celebrating Progress.

Informal Encouragement and Recognition

This first category of culture change success may appear "soft" relative to the other two—and in the usual sense of the word it is. This category, by definition, does not include objective measures but only subjective ones. Despite this qualification, make no mistake about how important this activity is for the CEO, top team, and anyone in a position to recognize and reward progress in the culture change.

Case 7.1 is an example of this category that illustrates several important dimensions: continued motivation of risk-taking individuals who begin to act in accordance with the Vision Culture, public recognition of a desired Vision Culture attitude or behavior, and the power of urban myths to generate momentum for the culture change.

Case 7.1. The Recognition Watershed Event

A global industrial company headquartered in the midwest had determined that the bar had been significantly lowered over the years, with the result that there were many "C" and even some "D" players that had simply not been held accountable but were "passed along" review after review. The Vision Culture specifically called out the goal of raising the bar to once again be a world-class company—a general theme of fighting complacency and confronting substandard technical talent was specifically mentioned. This Vision Culture "kernel" was translated in the roadmap to numerous human capital initiatives, one of which specifically set the metric of a 10 percent "needs improvement" bottom ranking across the major functions and business units. This expectation was finalized and became public in the middle of the annual calibration cycle, and so the roadmap detail was actually worded in such a way that this 10 percent calibration was not expected for sixteen months, after a full year of performance could be taken into account. The top team agreed that in the shortly upcoming first calibration cycle they would "move in that direction" but would not hold themselves accountable until the following year. The vice president of R&D had already started "raising the bar" before the culture change was formalized into a set of roadmap metrics. When the top team met several months later to perform this calibration exercise, he came with that 10 percent "needs improvement" identified, and had already begun having conversations with his own team about setting that standard. The top team was shocked, and in the end somewhat jealous, that he had taken this somewhat unpleasant and unpopular initiative so proactively. Later that week the CEO called the VP of R&D in for a private compliment, and then in their executive team regular meeting made a public statement of congratulations to him. All through the next couple of weeks, the CEO portrayed this VP of R&D as someone emblematic of the Vision Culture. At the end-of-year compensation committee with the board, the CEO requested a special bonus for the VP of R&D. Other top team members, putting aside their envy and realizing that this was well intended, went back to their staffs with messages along the lines of, "I guess we're really serious about this" and "Let's think about how we can raise the bar right now, without waiting for the next calibration cycle—we all know who is in that bottom 10 percent."

This is a perfect example of how the CEO can put tremendous wind to the sails of a culture change in the very early phase. No metric was formally achieved, nor was the "culture changed," yet it should be clear to anyone hearing this example that a tremendously important milestone was achieved because the CEO took the initiative to lionize a member of his staff. The message was instantaneously clear to everyone on the top team, who reported it to their staffs, after which it quickly became an urban legend.

Formal Culture Change Roadmap Metrics

This one is straightforward and largely self-explanatory. As long as the Culture Change Roadmap has been thoughtfully constructed and key milestones entered as timelined and measurable, the obvious action is simply to review and celebrate achievements as these are accomplished. Of course, good judgment should be used about which roadmap achievements are called out in which venues. Some metrics deserve to be called out in company-wide meetings, others departmentally, others with external stakeholders such as customers or other strategic partners.

Three other "project management" best practices are recommended:

1. Establish a regular review of the Culture Change Roadmap. Depending on the size and complexity of the organization and the

roadmap, this is sometimes done more regularly by the Culture Change Task Force, with occasional report of "variance" to the top team. In Condition Yellow or Condition Red, this should be done more frequently by the top team. The CEO can and should make this determination and drive it forward as a function of the R-Y-G condition and progress over time.

2. Readminister the Denison Organizational Culture Survey—or whatever key assessment tools were established as baseline in the Launch phase. One of the many good reasons to use such a tool is how easy it becomes to mark progress against that original baseline. It is not worth doing in anything less than a year from original administration; I advise something closer to fifteen months, though more than two years is probably a missed opportunity. In anything less than twelve months, there may simply not be enough progress to make it worth the investment of attention and energy. Without "stacking the deck," it is wise not to measure culture change progress before there is an opportunity for real progress to be made. It can only be discouraging, and may even be destructive if sufficient time for some of the human capital levers to play out through a cycle or two has not occurred. Fifteen months is ideal for most culture change initiatives, in my experience. Naturally the CEO and top team sponsors of the culture change have a vested interest in showing progress, particularly when this has been in the high-visibility top-five priorities. It is important for the top team not to "hover" over progress assessment like anxious parents waiting to see scores in their child's gymnastic event.

   Another practical consideration, though secondary, is that in organizations of any size there may be some "survey fatigue"; less intrusion is always better. Readministering a survey or other assessment procedure is worth thinking carefully about. Results are hard to take back, and the impact on the broader culture change effort can create defining moments. The Denison or another survey tool provides a uniquely objective perspective into culture change progress; it should be elevated to the status of sole or final arbiter to the question, "Has the culture changed?" It is an important metric to commit to in the Culture Change Roadmap, but should not eclipse all other metrics on the roadmap.

3. Missed deadlines must be carefully considered—in the same way they would be for any high-impact project being tracked. Most roadmap metrics will be easy to determine as achieved or not achieved—and the best approach is to note these and celebrate as

appropriate. It is important for the CEO to balance two opposing objectives: measuring of real progress objectively, and celebrating success. These are generally not in conflict but rather a "step one and step two" aimed toward the same goal. There are a small number of cases in which there could be a conflict between competing interests: one motivated by objective assessment of progress, the other by the need to be encouraging and positive about a difficult task.

In principle, this decision about how to respond to a missed deadline is really no different than many others the CEO must make related to the "carrot or stick." Other variables, such as key attributes of the Vision Culture related to timely achievement, or an accumulation of successes or failures, might also influence this decision. When a high-impact or time-sensitive culture change milestone has not been achieved, this is never a good thing. Once again, if the Culture Change Roadmap and task force have been set up as recommended here, there should be a flow of information to the CEO so that significant milestone failures are not sudden or big surprises. Case 7.2 provides a good example of how the effective CEO should appropriately step in to shape a high-impact culture decision around timing of performance reviews. This is likely a decision the CEO would never be involved with were it not for the material influence on the culture change initiative.

Case 7.2. Myerson CEO Makes a Key Timing Decision

Myerson & Company's Vision Culture and roadmap were highly focused on creating more professional discipline and accountability—all in context of the desire to create value within a new competitive environment in which larger, more highly automated and disciplined financial institutions were beginning to enter the company's previously uncompetitive space. Its roadmap included a number of newly created behavioral competencies that served as the content basis for a number of human capital levers. Chief among these was the planned implementation of a new performance management system. The roadmap was finished in early March, and the natural performance review discussion was usually held in June. In May, for a variety of reasons—forced resignation of the HR director being the most important—it became clearer to the CEO that the performance management implementation milestone was going to slip, with high-impact consequences. Missing the June implementation window meant that this very significant lever of culture change would be delayed a year as well as would delay the mechanism to provide feedback to weak performers. The CEO emphasized how unacceptable he thought these delays were and raised the question to the top team (also the culture change task force in this organization, due to its size) about potential solutions. After some "out of the box" thinking, the team decided that there was no compelling reason to have the performance review process in June, and that moving it to July would not make a material difference, but would allow the basic manager training and completion of other documentation and IT issues that needed to precede any credible attempt at implementing this new system. Though not widely communicated, it was clear to all that this first cycle would be a learning experience, allowing the next cycle in twelve months to benefit from that learning.

Value Creation Linkages to the Strategy

Culture is an engine of value creation *when it is aligned with a good strategy*. Section I of the book was devoted to explaining that linkage, and Section II has focused on describing the tools, methods, and leadership actions required to change the culture. Monitoring roadmap metrics and celebrating progress are absolutely critical steps, but the "end of the day" measure of culture change is value creation, not check-off of items on the roadmap or urban legends.

The project management analogy is useful to illuminate this point (Case 7.3).

Case 7.3. Quantum ERP Roadmap

Quantum, a top-five disk drive manufacturer in the mid-1990s, determined that it needed to increase the speed and efficiency with which the salesforce was able to let customers know about available inventory—both as a way to offer superior customer service and to improve the salesforce's ability to counter competitive offers related to available quantities and time of delivery. This was a capability deemed by all to be one of several competitive differentiators in the increasingly commoditized fixed-disk-drives market. The centerpiece initiative of this capability was a "big bang" enterprise resource planning (ERP) implementation of thirteen Oracle modules (typical at the time was implementation of two to three modules successively over a multiyear period). A massive initiative with a final price tag in the neighborhood of $75 million was launched over an eighteen-month period. The project plan was close to two thousand lines at one point. At the successful final launch of this ERP system there were numerous high-, medium-, and low-level success milestones that were achieved. The system "worked" (eventually, not right away). One set of success metrics was the roadmap milestones that were gradually accomplished over the eighteen-month period. The real "end of the day" success metric for this was linkage to the value creation strategy around order and shipment transparency for customers into Quantum's multiple manufacturing locations. The ERP project was a success when measured by the standard of roadmap completion, but the "real" success metric was the way in which this multifunction ERP capability increased the company's ability to differentiate itself from competitors—therefore ultimately adding value to shareholders. In other words, successful roadmap completion is a necessary, but not sufficient condition to ensure value creation.

This is precisely the reason why linkage of the Vision Culture to value creation strategies is so important a variable to include in the Get Real Tool process. Remember, one of the two Shadow Cultures—the Required Culture—comprises those attributes that are necessary to execute the strategy—in turn linked to value creation. The final determinant of whether the culture has changed is whether value has been created in those specific ways outlined in the Vision Culture.

Relative to evaluating culture change through determining the success of impact and linkage to strategic variables, five practical points for the CEO are important to keep in mind:

1. Begin with the end in mind. The CEO and top team's ability to link successful Culture Change Roadmap outcomes with strategic capabilities and value creation is entirely dependent on initial framing of those linkages in the creation of the Vision Culture and the roadmap aimed at achieving it. The CEO has a unique opportunity during the Setup phase to define the linkage between competitive capabilities and culture to create enduring strategic value.
2. Maintain focus in creation of the roadmap on "critical path" items. When the top team goes through the Get Real exercise during Launch it is important to fully vet the Actual, Ideal, and Required cultures while maintaining a laser focus on the short list of cultural attributes that link to strategy in the Required Culture. To a large extent, *the Vision Culture is the Required Culture, modified by the aspiration of the Ideal Culture and the practical realities of the Actual Culture.* In other words, the degree to which the top team navigates that compromise will determine the strength of the linkage between strategic necessity and the Vision Culture.
3. Linkage is not causality. Even the successfully completed Culture Change Roadmap cannot guarantee that the desired value will be created. But this is no more or less the case with the successfully completed budget. If the budget is well designed to focus on profitability, and then well executed, there is no guarantee of value creation. As with the well-designed and executed Culture Change Roadmap, there is a greatly increased probability, and the "reasonable person" can weigh the variables and conclude that "yes," value has been created or "no," it has not. Over an extended period, and

evaluated by multiple parties (essentially what the market does to determine share price), the link between strategy, culture, and value can be seen more clearly, but it is difficult to say with finality that a certain capability, culture, or strategy has created value. The point is that knowledgeable inside and outside observers of the company can reasonably claim that value has been created due to certain leadership actions over a period of years, but as long as diligent practices have been followed in equal amounts, there is no reason to think this is more true for a set of financial practices than for a set of cultural practices.

This is one of several tenets of the book: *the future value of the well-aligned culture cannot fairly be compared to other organizational success predictors when there are sloppy or entirely subjective methods used to build the culture.*

4. Shape perceptions. As in the first category of Celebrating Progress, informal encouragement and recognition, the CEO has considerable ability to define reality by shaping perceptions related to commonsense linkages between specific culture outcomes and broader value creation metrics such as market share, market capitalization, share price, organizational effectiveness, and so on. Case 7.4 will help illustrate this.

Case 7.4. Customer Intimacy Success Milestone

At the two-year mark of a culture change, all of the roadmap milestones had been successfully achieved and were moving to that stage of being invisibly integrated into normal activity instead of being "initiatives." The focus of the Vision Culture had been on "customer intimacy," and the roadmap showed investments in developing different attitudes toward customer responsiveness, listening, and trusted advisor kinds of strategic relationships in which customer decisions were made with top executives at the table. Other initiatives included investments in new customer relationship management software, but the centerpiece was really a shift in values and attitudes toward true attentiveness to "delighted customers." The culture change was clearly a "success" in the "level 2" sense of achieved Culture Change Roadmap metrics. Market share, sales volume, and customer perceptions of the brand had all jumped up dramatically since the culture change began two years previously. In his communications to the board and stockholders in the annual report, and less formally to employees in internal communications, the CEO called out the successful culture change as the key to their success, using these other metrics as evidence that the culture had changed and needed to continue in the same direction.

In this example, did the change in culture absolutely, positively cause the uptick in overall company value as measured by share price, market capitalization, and various customer metrics? There is no way really to prove or disprove that. Did everyone inside and outside the company believe it—absolutely!

To put a point on this, in year two of a culture change, if key value-creation metrics called out in the roadmap are "down," the culture change should not be counted a success yet. This assessment and how to communicate it requires careful thought by the CEO and top team since those value-creation metrics may simply require a third, instead of only a second, year of progress. The unintended consequences of being too harsh too soon are potentially very damaging. Like the economy, a portion of culture change relies on confidence and optimism about the future. If this optimism is prematurely or mistakenly erased, the self-fulfilling prophesy effect is a likely consequence—and obviously an undesirable one.

5. Initiatives become standard practice. A fifth and final way to measure the success of a culture change is to note the disappearance of any distinction between "aspired" and "actual" behaviors, processes, and other systemic organizational patterns. The Vision Culture and implementation roadmap describe "to be" objectives that do not currently exist. When the proportion of "to be" attributes goes to zero, the company is in Condition Green and the culture change is over. In the messy real world, this never happens finally or completely, and is one of the reasons why culture change takes at least two to three years—and longer, depending on what standard of completion one chooses to impose.

As the second cycle of the annual human capital levers is passed, there are useful objective and subjective criteria to help evaluate the degree of overall culture change success. For example, if one of the roadmap initiatives is installation of a new coaching and career development process, an easy objective metric to evaluate success can be found in simple "number of coaching sessions per manager completed." If the goal is once per quarter, this is a measurable occurrence. In year one, if there is 75 percent occurrence, one could say "we are three-quarters of the way there on this metric." In year two, if there is 93 percent occurrence, we could say we're probably as far as we can expect to be. At this year two of 93 percent level of occurrence, it would also be fair to say that this is no longer an "initiative" but is now an integral part of the organization's collective behavior.

An excellent way to determine the success of a culture change is to assess the number of aspired-to practices that are no longer "new," but the "way we are." In other words, the Vision Culture is now the Actual Culture.

Chapter 7 Summary

In Chapter 7, Celebrating Progress, I have noted the close relationship between measuring and celebrating progress. We explored three levels of conducting this fourth phase of the Culture Change Process: informal encouragement and recognition, formal roadmap metrics, and linkage to value creation. We also discussed benchmarks for the overall timeframe of a culture change, and what the CEO can do to accelerate the change process.

Chapter 7 marks the end of Section II, which has focused on the four stages of the Culture Change Process: Setup, Launch, Propagating the Wave, and Celebrating Progress. We move now to Section III, where the topic is common culture change scenarios, and I end the book with a discussion of leadership capabilities for the leaders of culture change.

Section III

Practical Applications

In the third and final section of the book we move first, in Chapter 8, to three illustrations of common business situations in which culture change is clearly needed and outline general suggestions on how to proceed in each of them. Finally, in Chapter 9 we conclude the book with a discussion of leadership best practices for culture change, identifying a handful of behavioral competencies for the culture change leader.

8 Three Common Culture Change Scenarios

In what follows I describe some common scenarios to illustrate how culture change plays out in the real world. By "real world," I mean that in these examples not everything turns out picture perfect. Organizational culture change is often a messy and complicated affair that does not proceed in the orderly way I've outlined, from Setup to Launch to Propagating the Wave, and ending with Celebrating Progress. And though the map is not the territory, it is still invaluable in this messy world to have a map. The maps for culture change I've provided in the book are the benchmark and best-practices maps but, more important, the customized Vision Culture, Culture Change Roadmap, and Five Critical Success Factors for Culture Change.

The scenarios that I will describe each follow the same format: first, an outline of a very common business circumstance brought about by either a trend in the broader economy or internal developmental stage. Second, a real case illustration from a company I am familiar with. And third, lessons learned for dealing with the commonly occurring business circumstance. The three topics from which I draw our examples are innovation, scaling culture to match growth, and the merger and acquisition scenario, or, stated differently:

1. Creating the innovation culture
2. Creating the discipline or performance culture in the rapidly growing, early stage, complacent or family-owned company
3. Creating the high-engagement culture, integrating different cultures in a merger

Creating the Innovation Culture

Many products go through a predictable cycle of commoditization: demand for the product causes increased volumes, the cost-per-unit goes down, and eventually so does the price, putting pressure on all those offering the product to differentiate a product that is no longer unique. The "bargaining power" of customers is increased, and companies offering the product must find ways to compete on price or value. This is a predictable cycle, though particulars of the cycle vary with the product, the company's management of the cycle, and macroeconomic forces related to demand.

This cycle has happened repeatedly in the technology industry, notably with cell phones, printers, and computers. Despite a complex set of factors including economic climate and unique product or company situations, we can simplify by saying that as this commoditization cycle has become more common, the generally accepted remedy is "continuous innovation." There are other remedies that may arise out of distribution, branding, and marketing strategies, but these are largely "delaying" strategies that will not stop the inexorable economic changes of reduced margins, increased volume, and decreased differentiation of producers of the product in question. The innovation concept has spread like wildfire in the popular business press. The basic idea as far as business strategy can be summed up with a few simple propositions:

1. The cycle of commoditization is accelerating exponentially. What used to be a ten-year adoption and commoditization cycle for "product X" is now a five-year cycle, and will become a two-year cycle in the future.
2. This accelerates the "creative destruction" cycle in which the birth and death of companies will also accelerate at a much higher rate than previously.
3. The only real solution to this new external reality is "continuous innovation" as a strategy, organizational capability, and culture. The companies that can most effectively read what customers want and rapidly develop new offerings to meet those needs will "win." They will win competitively and therefore create value over time, avoiding the increasingly likely fate of becoming casualties of Darwinian selection.

At the end of the day, most products will gradually reduce in cost if the product appeals to a high-volume market that can shop around for features and prices. Creating new products or other material innovations to the fundamental value of the product is one of only two ways out of this "cycle downward into commodity hell," in which margins are low and customers have significant bargaining power. As a result of this new accelerated birth-death cycle for products and entire companies, there has been an increasing focus on how companies can become "more innovative." The literature on innovation is large and growing; we would refer the reader who wishes to know more to Davila, Epstein, and Shelton's practical handbook in this area[1] or Fagerberg, Mowery, and Nelson's more academic review of the field.[2] Typical of such books, issues of culture are not thoroughly addressed—but there is little question that this has become a mainstream concern for many companies.

Many organizations are now working hard to become "innovative" companies, for innovation is a strategic solution to the economic law that new products eventually become commoditized, reducing overall value for the company and in some cases causing the company to disappear as competitors find better ways to survive this commodity cycle. Applying the paradigm that we have developed earlier in the book, let us assume that a company has understood the need to become more innovative, and also has the wisdom to realize that this will only happen if the organizational culture makes the transition as well.

We can safely assume that the company that has operated on the strategic assumption that it is providing a certain value with relatively fixed margins will have a culture that is not highly innovative—precisely the reason that they wish to *become* innovative. We can also safely assume that as this new strategic reality is first realized, there will be Condition Yellow or Condition Red discrepancy between the new strategy and the Actual Culture.

Case 8.1 is a real-world illustration of how things can go wrong when a key strategic initiative goes forward against the tide of a misaligned culture.

Case 8.1. A Case of Innovation False Start at The Food Company

One of the largest producers of fruits and vegetables in the world arrived at the sudden realization that margins were eroding more quickly than expected and a trend was clearly in motion. Strange as it may sound, this company had enjoyed, for many years, a "premium brand" differentiator based on quality and branding. A sticker on the banana or pineapple allowed the company to charge premium prices, and margins were maintained for a surprising number of years, delaying the inevitable descent into "commodity hell" for a short time. Eventually the trend in margin erosion was so great that it was hard to ignore. The first response of the company was to cut costs—which it did, burning through a president or two in the process. The company had a long tradition of highly centralized financial control from its headquarters in North America. This private company was controlled by a chairman with a majority interest who, understandably, expected a return on his investment. The lack of this return was actively driving pressure on senior management to improve margins—which translated into several budget cycles of tightening.

The third president in six years arrived and quickly realized that further cost-cutting was not going to fix the problem. He focused on renegotiation of contracts with customers to raise pricing and some tough restrictions on capital expenses. For the first time, the idea of an innovation initiative surfaced—from the chairman, not the president. As is often the case, the chairman read an article about product innovation in a business periodical and was suddenly "converted." He issued a company-wide challenge for more innovation. An innovation program was initiated that included

- A request for new ideas across the five-thousand-employee international workforce
- Revision of the new product development
- Creation of a cross-functional innovation team
- Innovation training
- A reward structure to recognize ideas that truly came to fruition as new product ideas were established.

After six months, the program was a widely acknowledged failure. Why? The reasons were plain for all with eyes to see—though not always easy to talk about openly in this culture:

- The newly created "innovation database of ideas" surprised everyone by totaling out at fifteen thousand new ideas, unfortunately, about a third of them in languages other than English. On a sampling basis, it was estimated that five thousand of these were duplicates; 50 percent of them were "trivial," such as, "The restroom at our plant in Ecuador should be repainted—lime green this time"; and 15 percent of them were "personal attacks," such as, "Fire my boss and his boss, and you'll have plenty of innovation." It would take a small team several weeks to categorize these issues into some meaningful database, but then what? The innovation team was stuck: *Who* would use these ideas, and *how* would they be used?
- The new product-development process, though well thought out, focused largely on new packaging of existing products, such as fruit cups and small packages of snack vegetables. A significant universe of opportunities related to innovative changes in other areas were left unaddressed. For example, innovation within the business model (such as marketing more directly to the end-customer rather than allowing wholesalers to set those terms); innovation in process improvement up and down the supply chain; research and develop-

ment innovation related to new varieties and pest control. In other words the product or brand focus was far too narrow. Many of these innovative ideas outside of the product area did not require new investment but allowed savings and future potential revenue opportunity as innovations blossomed. These were not considered "innovations" by the chairman, who wanted "blockbuster" new products that would quickly generate revenue. Significant opportunities for innovation—and revenue—were lost.

- The top team was politely enthusiastic, saying all the right things in front of the chairman but privately rolling their eyes. Without exception, the common view was that without some investment of capital, innovation was little more than a pipe dream—not necessarily enormous amounts of capital, but something in the reverse direction from "cut another 9 percent" for next year's budget. Even small expenses—addition of a new scientist focused on new products versus quality control—were not being looked favorably on by the chairman in the environment of eroding margins.
- Related to this concern was the unwillingness of the chairman to allow the necessary "ramp up" time for any new product to achieve profitability—usually a year or two. Even the company's historical "blockbuster" new products operated at a loss initially as they were adopted. New product ideas were often never presented due to the anticipated failure of meeting this hurdle rate.
- Finally, there was the tremendous fear of the chairman himself. A bright, entrepreneurial man who had built a diversified portfolio over the years (to which he added The Food Company), he had an often toxic, abusive leadership style that the top team found humiliating, but tolerated, and the next levels found terrifying. In the first six months of the innovation program, the innovation team generated six new product ideas for presentation to the chairman. With great pride and excitement they worked these ideas up into a high-quality presentation. The chairman was demeaning and dismissive of all the new ideas, ranting that they were just "the same old stuff repackaged" or that he should just fire everyone on the team for the time of his they wasted. The team left shell-shocked, and then became discouraged.

The author was engaged to help revive the moribund innovation program shortly after this disastrous "shutdown" experience of the team. In the course of a relatively brief engagement, the following assessments were made:

1. The root cause of the failure was primarily cultural and had little to do with some of the innovation procedures. A disdain for expert outsiders with proven tools and methods was really a symptom of two things: an insular cultural isolation that hated paying for what internal staff should already know (according to the chairman) and the real harm that a slash-and-burn cost-reduction

program led by a brand-name East Coast consulting firm had caused during the recent era of "cost-cut our way to profitability." This cultural insularity had led the innovation team to open the spigot of the fifteen thousand ideas and focus narrowly on marketing innovation, leading to further cynicism by the operating presidents, and the innovation program had come to a standstill.

2. A culture of fear, caution, and passivity was a direct result of the chairman's toxic leadership style. Those who challenged him were terminated, or banished to remote regions of the company where they had no voice.

   Those that remained were pressured into making unrealistic promises for margin reduction and profitability, without real possibility of anything other than re-creating a "culture of scarcity" and fear.

3. A historical culture of complacency had arisen, in part from the fear-inducing style of the chairman but also because the company had not really had to deal with a worldwide commoditization of its best-selling products, previously living in the "value" zone in which profit margins were high and stable for many years.

This crisis led to a "cry for help" for outside expertise that resulted in the culture change recommendation and commitment to create a Vision Culture with innovation as the centerpiece and a Culture Change Roadmap that was populated with these key initiatives:

1. Integrate the "orphan" innovation program with the formal leadership hierarchy so that the president and top team were sponsors of the innovation initiative, rather than being observers of the innovation task force. The top leadership team—corporate president and operating unit presidents—went on a two-day Silicon Valley innovation tour to several Northern California companies known for their innovation capabilities.
2. Hire a Ph.D.-level VP of innovation with the technical background and organizational leadership skills to design an enterprise-wide innovation program.
3. Train the current innovation task force so that members would be more knowledgeable as they created an enterprise-innovation program informed by current best practices and not hampered by the "home-grown" insularity that the previous attempt had been victim to.
4. Empower local geography directors of innovation that would report to the soon-to-be-hired VP of innovation.
5. Define new innovation-focused leadership competencies that could be translated into the existing human capital levers.
6. Encourage sharing of ideas across geographies and divisions, and outside the company.

Unfortunately, a week after the innovation task force had delineated these plans and had them ratified by the operating top team, the corporate president resigned—expressing the view that what the chairman desired by way of financial results was unachievable in this environment with the existing constraints.

In a day all of the progress that had been made on a true innovation Vision Culture was put on hold and essentially "canceled." A new president, the fourth in seven years, was appointed, and he stated at the outset that "innovation was important" but that it would have to wait six months or so due to other "survival"-level financial pressures. The innovation initiative languished—and essentially went quietly into the night.

Lessons and Recommendations

We can learn many things from this case example about creating a culture of innovation; here are a few:

1. A well-designed culture program will *never* succeed without the active sponsorship of the CEO and top team—a bold statement, I realize, but true nonetheless. This company's innovation initiative was started as a task force special project, outside of the formal chain of command, for several complex political reasons, the most important of which was that the chairman did not think the operating group presidents were "innovative" and they needed a challenge or jumpstart from bright young managers with new ideas. This was a mistake. The people who are going to lead the innovation initiative must be the top team, otherwise it is just a bunch of employees, bright ones perhaps, holding a "book club."
2. The top team must model the behaviors and attitudes that it wants to propagate down into the organization. A culture change from cautious complacency to innovation always includes a cluster of leadership competencies along these lines: risk-taking with new ideas and methods, challenging superiors or established ways of thinking and doing things, tolerance for failure from the top team—just to name the most common values and competencies that must serve as the foundation for an innovative culture. The Food Company sometimes modeled these behaviors at the second and third levels of management—but the CEO and chairman actually modeled the exact opposite of these values, creating a chilling effect on new ideas and magnifying the fear of failure and punishment.
3. Yes, best-practice innovation tools and methods are important—as the fifteen-thousand-ideas mistake illustrated at The Food Company.

But these innovation technologies are empty tricks without a culture that fosters innovation.

4. The innovation-focused Culture Change Roadmap at The Food Company was a well-conceived roadmap informed by best practices and introduced to the company by experts. Yet it was not enough, and never is, without a sincere focus on aligning the culture in which the innovation strategy will operate. The list of actions and initiatives on the Food Company roadmap is an excellent example of the kinds of commitments that are required to move toward an innovation culture.
5. If the company labels its culture change initiative the "Innovation Process," this is purely a "headlining" decision for what is still a genuine culture change process. The question is not the name, so much as what is "underneath the hood": Is it a real culture change process informed by the Five Critical Success Factors, or an internal publicity campaign? It is quite common for a business process initiative to be launched and run into culture-related troubles, motivating the top team to address the underlying culture issues that will make the initiative successful and create lasting value. The brand-new CEO has more latitude to shape the initiative in a way that can follow the culture change sequence from Setup through Celebrating Progress. We are well advised to remember that many culture change initiatives start in the midst of something else, triggered by realization that the culture is misaligned at a red or yellow condition and must be addressed for other elements of the strategy to go forward.
6. Another lesson worth noting in the Food Company example has to do with the unique culture challenges of the "mature" or "plateaued" company in context of the developmental cycle that all companies go through. Briefly, this evolutionary cycle outlines predictable, universal challenges that every company will face as it grows. In a company's early phases, "Startup," "Infancy," and "Go-Go," challenges are related to survival and customer adoption of the new company's offering. In the next main phase the challenge is building and scaling—90 percent of all new companies never go beyond this phase of roughly $20 million annual revenues, either disappearing or remaining small. We will take up this challenge in the next scenario. For those companies that successfully scale to continued growth the challenge becomes maintaining stable growth. The period of time that a company stays in this "maturity" phase can vary from a few years to decades, but it is never "forever."

The Food Company is an example of a company that has been in business for a hundred years, growing over seventy-five years to become a stable, profitable company creating new value for shareholders every year. As the company lost some of its ability to innovate it went into decline instead of reinventing itself. As it became more focused on maintaining margins and profitability by reducing costs instead of reinventing itself, it went into further decline until it was indeed in "commodity hell": costs are as low as they can be to maintain short-term profitability, no investments have been made in creating new products, and suddenly the external market becomes more competitive.

By contrast, a company such as IBM in the 1990s when Lou Gerstner took over was able to reinvent itself and escape the commoditization unfolding in the PC industry that took the lives of Digital Equipment, Wang, and many others that did not survive. General Motors provides another poignant example of what happens when a previously successful company does not change its culture in the "maturity" phase. The reason the evolution cycle of these companies is so predictable is largely due to the predictable human reactions to the various phases in the cycle:

- In the early phases the challenge seeks its own level: you "go-go" or you die.
- In the middle phases, the challenge is to grow and stabilize—the culture changes to one that can systematize, stabilize, and scale or it does not, remaining the same size, perhaps for a long time.
- In the mature phase the company has "arrived"; the biggest challenge is complacency or "not having a challenge." It is simply a fact of human nature that a steady state seeks to perpetuate the steady state. The failure to successfully recognize and meet the culture challenge of maturity and decline is what we see in The Food Company and GM, though not in Hewlett-Packard or IBM. HP and IBM certainly reached maturity and looked into the abyss of decline—both were successful in reinventing themselves, HP through its Compaq merger that allowed it to compete in the PC space, and IBM in its acquisition of PricewaterhouseCoopers, allowing it to bundle consulting with sales of technology and hardware.
- The last phase leads down into decline and death—where The Food Company was headed—or up into reinvention, in which another cycle of "go-go" challenge can begin.

Creating the Discipline or Performance Culture

Many companies find themselves surprised or ambushed by a sudden change in the competitive landscape that is clearly the result of prior complacency. PowerBar was a company that fell prey to this problem. It had essentially invented the nutrition bar category and for many years had 80 percent-plus market share, looking upon the few emerging competitors as no threat to its continued dominance. In a remarkably rapid timeframe the company's leaders were shocked to learn that their market share had slipped to 60 percent and that several of these "upstarts"—Clif Bar for example—had managed to grab hold of a big chunk of their share.

At the same time that this competitive reality grabbed their attention, they began the necessary steps to go public, creating liquidity for the founders. These two strategic realities converged in the awareness that they needed a more professional, disciplined, and therefore scalable culture to create the necessary medium for their three key strategies: grow the business to create value for the founders and the next generation of owners and managers, professionalize the culture to make the initial public offering (IPO) possible, and understand the events that had led to such a dramatic loss in market share so it could be proactively managed and reversed (Case 8.2).

Case 8.2. PowerBar Makes the Transition to a More Disciplined Culture

The Actual Culture of this company was a textbook example of the small family business. Relationships were long-standing and highly valued in the PowerBar culture. The founder, a champion marathon runner, was altruistic and competitive, but had created a family-like business in which many friends and family were in senior positions. As with all such firms that grow successfully, there comes a time when some of those individuals will not have the technical or domain expertise to provide the leadership needed by the company to do what needs to be done. The bar needs to be raised around basic managerial competence. The culture-as-personality climate was tolerant and relationship-oriented—some staff worked very hard, others did not. Creation and preservation of relationships was a reality of the Actual Culture that the founder and his team were not always ready to acknowledge—in part because the founder himself was uncomfortable confronting poor performance, coaching, and managing difficult people issues. The culture-as-capability had all the predictable gaps that one would expect to find in a small company that had grown rapidly: there was little in the way of disciplined management processes in areas such as strategic planning, performance management, and information systems infrastructure. Several functional areas critical to the new strategy—marketing and operations—were suboptimized at every level, from the people to the systems.

A Vision Culture was created by the CEO and top team that identified the culture—values, personality, and capabilities—that would be necessary to scale the company, take back market share, and create the procedural infrastructure required for an IPO. A well-designed, honest Culture Change Roadmap was created and well managed by the CEO and top team. Early in the course of the culture change, several senior executives departed and were replaced with higher-caliber talent. The new leadership team was suddenly a notch above where it had been and was raising the bar for its direct report teams—in line with actions specified in the Culture Change Roadmap. The team had some typical garden-variety "new team" issues, but for the most part worked well together.

PowerBar was able to accomplish virtually all of its strategic objectives as a direct result of leadership's swift and decisive commitment to a change in culture that would support those strategies. For sound financial strategy reasons, they elected to sell the company to Nestlé rather than pursue the IPO, which worked out quite well for the shareholders (though tragically, the founder died suddenly of a heart attack, only a few years after the Nestlé sale). This is a success story in which the founder and leaders of the company were able to transform their culture to match the reality of their revenue growth and related competitive threats that accompanied that success. PowerBar "reinvented" itself through the merger with Nestlé, essentially growing itself one-hundred-fold in a single event. PowerBar is no longer a trendy Berkeley company, but a business unit in a gigantic multinational.

The Bank of Hawaii, though many years older and larger than PowerBar, faced a similar culture challenge, as did Myerson & Company. The common thread through all three is the painful transition from a comfortable, "familial" environment in which supportive relationships are held in the culture at a higher priority than results, which can come only when there is a focused discipline on accountability and performance.

Lessons and Recommendations

What can we learn from these three cases that illustrate transition from a complacent comfort zone?

1. In most cases, this is a painful transition—rather than an "exciting" transition like innovation. The people who cannot make the journey usually have to leave the organization—sometimes after having spent their entire careers there.
2. This reality of painful transition, combined with the fact that the founder is the creator and likely the biggest influence on the Actual

Culture, tends to move these culture changes to outcomes like those of PowerBar and Myerson & Company. The existing top team, even after it moves toward the Vision Culture, may not be able to take the company to the next level, and value is created by merger, acquisition, or outright sale to new owners who come with a fresh perspective.

In the Bank of Hawaii case, there was a wholehearted and painful attempt to change the culture, but in the end it was not enough of a change to create the financial performance required of the board. Three years after the culture had already successfully gone through a painful move away from a supportive, relationship-oriented culture to an achievement-oriented culture, the CEO and all but one of the top team who accomplished that significant achievement had left the organization. The lesson here is this: it is very difficult to change the culture that you are a product of. It can be done, but more easily in a smaller company.

3. I decided to fold the culture transition required of fast-growing companies into the scenario of movement out of the relationship-oriented culture because they almost always go together, and the culture change issues are similar. The small, rapidly growing company, whether literally family-owned or not, cannot help but take on some of the cultural characteristics caused by size. No matter what the climate, you can probably get to know everyone in a company with fewer than one hundred to three hundred employees. They can probably all fit in the cafeteria at one time. When prompted by rapid growth to address the need for more efficient infrastructure, discipline, accountability, and domain expertise, it is hard to imagine that there would not be this sense of loss of a comfortable social environment. Even when the Actual Culture is not highly support- and relationship-oriented, but more achievement- and performance-oriented, many of those in a smaller organization are attracted to that environment because of the informality and lack of procedures. For different reasons than in the relationship culture, there is loss and a sense of resistance to more procedures, bureaucracy, and a general depersonalization of the culture.

   A. One of the "selling" points that is worth making to mitigate this resistance to greater process discipline is that *thoughtful* and efficient processes can actually make the work environment *more* flexible and responsive internally. One of the issues that is common in this "scaling" transition from small to medium-sized company is the parochial silos or "tribes" that focus on their own priorities, with less concern for horizontal dependencies that are needed to coordinate important activities across departments.

B. Small companies suddenly faced with sales volume that breaks down existing processes and systems are usually welcoming of less reactivity and crisis mode operations. These are personally stressful, and always inferior to a thoughtfully designed path toward scaling these systems, processes, and structure to anticipate future growth.

C. The thoughtfully designed organization structure combined with regular communication can mitigate this concern about "depersonalization" and inflexibility. Unfortunately, there are no similar elegant solutions for issues of technical and managerial competence.

4. As a brief passing comment—that deserves much greater attention—it is interesting to note the generational influence on culture. In this "transition to the performance culture" that is more characteristic of companies run by "baby boomer" leaders, we should acknowledge the "Jerry McGuire" phenomenon—"X" and "Y" generation leaders and employees who are happy to exchange financial performance and cut-throat competitive politics for less money and less stress.

Creating the High-Engagement Culture

This is an important topic, about which surprisingly little has been written, considering the number of acquisitions and mergers and their very high failure rate—most commonly due to culture-fit issues. Stahl and Mendenhall have offered a comprehensive look at this topic.[3] It is a complex problem-set with many aspects and angles of approach. As in any culture change challenge, the first question is always, "What does the strategy require of the merger?" or "What presumed value creation will occur as a result of the merger?" There is a famous quip about mergers: "Whatever they're calling it, it's always really an acquisition." There is truth to this in that actual strategic partnerships of co-equals is rare. Usually one company is reaching out to initiate a relationship with the presumption that it will bring value. There is usually a dominant party; even when the small firm initiates acquisition talks with a larger potential partner, the larger partner will most likely be in the driver's seat.

A good place to start our discussion of value creation through culture alignment in the M&A (merger and acquisition) situations is with the question, "Why do so many of them fail?" There are various statistics published on what that percentage of failure really is—most likely because different authors use different criteria to define success and failure. Estimates range from 60 percent success to 90 percent failure. Of course, some companies—for example Cisco—have created a powerful and enduring culture and capability around acquiring other companies. The most reliable recent figures I have seen show that 83 percent of all deals fail to deliver shareholder value at the level originally expected. Fifty-three percent actually destroyed value versus creating it![4] Even a very small acquisition in dollar terms can eat up a disproportionate amount of executive time and create considerable disruption. It is a tricky business at every level. As is the case in the single-company culture that we have mostly been focused on, the Vision Culture that will create value is directly linked to the strategy.

There are many reasons for a company to consider an acquisition, but from the big-picture level there are really only two: a strategic reason or a financial reason. Apologies to the experts in the field for this gross oversimplification: the strategic acquisition is aimed at adding new value through acquisition of a capability, market, or technology that will further the acquiring company's existing strategy—rather than "organically" growing it over time. There are numerous reasons and ways to do this which we will not dive into. The financial acquisition aims to capture value by purchasing a company that is considered to be undervalued and likely to rise in value. The strategic motive may or may not also be there, but by definition it is not primary.

The strategic acquisition is the more frequent, since financial acquisitions are mostly done by larger companies with the capital to do so as a way to balance their overall portfolio. This strategic versus financial distinction is important for culture change because in the strategic acquisition it is much more important to stabilize and capture the strategically valuable component of the business. In the financial acquisition, other than to eliminate duplicative costs, the acquired entity likely will continue to operate as is, and issues of cultural integration create less risk for the acquiring company.

Putting aside the financial acquisition, the second key question is how much integration between the two cultures there will be. In Case 8.3, let's look at one M&A situation I helped with.

Case 8.3. The Battery Company Acquires The Charger Company

The acquiring company—The Battery Company—was a market leader that produced "mission critical" batteries—for defibrillators, military equipment, and assorted other markets in which the battery "has to work, every time, or someone"s life is at risk." The company's leaders saw the opportunity to acquire a charging company that was known to them over many years in their common ecosystem. Acquisition of The Charger Company would give the acquirer a "total solution" for customers who sometimes went to the acquired company for better solutions—charging complex batteries turns out to be a fairly complex task that requires sophisticated and innovative engineering capability. The strategic rationale was sound, and if the company was all it appeared to be, would produce a leap forward in both revenue and competitive advantage.

After all the financial and legal due diligence was completed, the deal was consummated. The acquiring company was in Portland, Oregon, the acquired company in Redmond, Washington, close to Microsoft. It was determined early in the due diligence, through a fair and objective assessment of the two companies, that over time most functions in the much smaller acquired company would be absorbed in the acquiring company—things such as manufacturing and most of the administrative services, which were less well developed in the smaller company and duplicative.

The crown jewel of the acquired company was its engineering function—a small department of about ten extremely talented engineers in this specialized space. Though this was never spoken aloud, in order to avoid offending others, this engineering talent was actually the primary reason for the acquisition, in addition to the company's customer list and ongoing revenue stream.

Everything was proceeding according to plan in the first month after the deal was completed. As the dust around the acquisition began to settle, it became more and more obvious that there was quite a significant cultural difference between the two companies—much of it centered on the two engineering cultures. A slide was created to try to capture those differences in a way that would lead to constructive dialogue:

Portland	**Redmond**
Financially focused	Technical innovation focused
Evolutionary	Revolutionary
Managers = Deliverers	Managers = Builders and planners
Structured, formal	Unstructured, informal
Strong production	Strong engineering
Near-term execution to conservative targets	Longer-term innovation and vision
Internal focus on scaling and process	External focus on customers

The issue that surfaced as critical to value creation through the acquisition was that the VP of engineering at The Battery Company—a very competent senior engineering manager—had been hired several years previously to help The Battery Company scale from $20 million to $100 million. In pursuit of that goal, he and the entire top team had focused on shaping the culture to become more disciplined, systematic, and process-driven than the prior culture, which had caused the company to languish at $20 million for several years, unable to grow. The VP of engineering had done precisely what he was charged with doing, creating an engineering culture that was scalable, disciplined, and capable of consistently supporting the growth needs of the sales and marketing function that were outselling more and more business.

The Redmond charger company ascribed its considerable success to the fact that it was a highly innovative environment that encouraged creativity. Gradually a crisis emerged in the form of the Redmond engineers threatening to quit if they were going to be "crushed" by the Portland company engineering-process-driven culture that they felt was slowly extinguishing their creativity.

The solution that emerged after many individual discussions was an offsite specifically aimed at a constructive merge of the two cultures. Expectations built into the design of the working session included the following:

- There was an assumption that both cultures had strengths and weaknesses.
- The Battery Company was not presumed to be "more right" in its cultural assumptions than The Charger Company—though all business decisions that affected investor requirements, such as removing unnecessary duplicative administrative costs and merging of systems, were presumed to be The Battery Company's final decision.
- The objective of the session was to outline the Vision Culture of the merged entity and then create the Culture Change Roadmap to make that happen.

To make a long story short, the working session was the beginning of a real change in which the two cultures identified their Actual, Ideal, and Required cultures individually and then drew from those lists to outline a shared Required Culture and finally a single Vision Culture and roadmap for the now "merged" entity. The Battery and Charger Company, though in different locations, is now one company, growing successfully and exceeding investor requirements. Value was created through the acquisition because attention was paid to integrating culture.

Lessons and Recommendations

What lessons can we learn from The Battery Company acquisition case?

Ideally, a process such as the one just described should be done as early as possible to avoid the kind of culture clash crisis that is often the beginning of years of unproductive distancing and failure to collaborate. This usually cannot occur in a collaborative working session until the legal and financial proceedings are complete—for obvious reasons: it is simply not worth the time and energy to invest in creating a shared Vision Culture before the deal is final—they do fall apart, as Dow Chemical learned in early 2009.

Recognizing this practical contingency and acknowledging that culture *is* the engine of value creation, it is a travesty that acquiring—and acquired—companies do not conduct more rigorous culture-fit due diligence in advance of the enormous risk that culture misalignment poses. Before the deal is complete, it is probably not realistic to conduct a full culture assessment like the one described in Launch, but there are few barriers to conducting informal, unobtrusive culture assessments through private discussions with current and departed senior members of the acquired company.

The more significant barrier is the same one facing the single-company culture change: appreciating the high-impact risk of culture misalignment and translating this to the same level of risk that the financial, legal, and marketing risks pose. Once an acquiring company has decided to "go out hunting," many possibilities are rejected or accepted as possibilities—usually for financial or market-driven value creation reasons, rarely for reasons of culture-driven risk factors. This is foolish, value-destruction leadership, and almost certainly a prime suspect in the high M&A failure rate. No competent CEO would continue with an acquisition after discovering that the target was more burdened with debt than previously realized, creating a balance sheet risk for the acquiring company. Nor would a CEO proceed realizing that the two companies would actually lose market share if they combined. Why would a competent CEO and top team proceed with an acquisition in which the culture of the target company was realized clearly to be so different that reconciliation would be impossible without terminating most of the leadership of the company, and consequently flushing those leaders who would create the value in the acquisition? Nevertheless, it happens every day, and serves as testament to the damage of general ignorance concerning culture in modern organizations.

In the more frequent situation, the deal has been done and both companies realize that value will be created through finding ways to better understand the two cultures. This must start with the value creation strategy of the acquiring company: "What is the strategic rationale of the acquisition and how can that best be translated to a culture integration and alignment roadmap?" The next driving question is usually related to organizational design and structure. When the new acquisition is structured as an additional business unit or division, the challenges are quite different from a more complete restructuring of both companies. The answer to this question of how merged the culture must be to create value, of course, varies widely with the circumstance, but generally speaking there is a continuum that ranges from "full integration" to "no integration" and everything in between. We will explore examples of "low integration" and "full integration" on the culture change task.

Low Integration Between Microsoft and Yahoo

The two cultures of Microsoft and Yahoo are so different that integration is undesirable and presumed to be value destroying, rather than creating. When Microsoft courted Yahoo in the summer of 2008, its strategic rationale was to capture the media and search capabilities that Yahoo had and Microsoft was missing. Realizing the great differences between the two cultures and the historical animosity, Microsoft's leaders went into the deal with the thought that perhaps there would not be an aggressive culture-integration process, but that the company would be slowly integrated over time through "culture exchange" programs that allowed voluntary cross-fertilization of the two cultures. As a practical matter, these were the words, but Microsoft had done many previous acquisitions that had earned it the title of "the Borg" (from *Star Trek,* a machine-like species that absorbed the individuality and creativity of all in its path).

Microsoft	**Yahoo**
Highly competitive, less collaborative	Collaborative consensus-building, less comfortable with conflict
Office culture: team members work independently on their own piece of a project	Cubicle culture: people team on projects and work in open office setting
Technology company: inventor, innovators, engineers, programmers are dominant	Creative "media" company: advertising content, media development, planning and placement

The deal fell apart because the Yahoo CEO and founder, Jerry Yang, was loathe to be overrun by the Microsoft barbarians, who he probably rightly assumed would extract the key media and search capabilities, throwing out the rest of Yahoo as husk. This cost him his job but illustrates the interesting situation in which there is a compelling market-value motive for the acquisition in sharp juxtaposition to the culture differences. In the case of the Microsoft-Yahoo deal, it is fair to say that Yahoo's culture was so different—encompassed in the behavior of Jerry Yang—that the deal fell apart for truly cultural reasons before it could happen. Yang continued to have the full support of his board throughout the negotiation with Microsoft's Steve Ballmer—until major shareholder Carl Icahn pressured the board to oust him, which they did.

Full Integration—Fast and Slow

The strategic premise is that value can only be created through full integration of the two companies. Let us assume that there are "garden variety" culture differences—such as those in the Battery Company acquisition—that require a well-designed and fully sponsored integration process. This is largely a variation on the Culture Change Process described in Section II of this book. If the cultures are dramatically different, or opposing, this might be a reason to maintain more separate structures and avoid active attempts to merge the cultures, and, perhaps, a reason not to do the deal. That may not be an option when the deal is already done. With sufficient value creation upside and CEO conviction, any culture can be merged. The question is simply how much value will be destroyed in that process, thus raising the question of whether there is value to be created. The far end of this continuum is the famous "Neutron Jack" fable of how Jack Welch of GE acquired companies with a management style that "nuked" all the people, leaving the buildings, equipment, and other assets untouched, like a neutron bomb. It is hard to imagine a situation in which the people, even if only in a targeted portion of the acquired company, would not be necessary to maintain the hoped-for value. This is why the "financial" acquisition is a different animal than the "strategic" acquisition. In the "financial" acquisition, the acquirer assumes that the culture will remain largely untouched, so that it can add its current financial success to the acquiring company—often an Investment firm, or portfolio manager of some kind.

Exceptions to the Basic Culture Change Model

A few best practices and procedural guidelines that differ slightly from the Culture Change Process described earlier in Section II are worth noting.

Culture Change Structures That Reinforce Shared Decision Making. Design the process in such a way that the first step is creation of a joint culture change task force that is fairly composed of respected leaders from both organizations. A key component in The Battery Company's successful negotiation of the engineering culture crisis was that all stakeholders were invited to the table to resolve the conflict combined with the value premise that the acquiring culture is not "right" by default in the case of differences. In large measure, these two design elements determined a successful outcome because they neutralized control and respect issues that are always present as an undercurrent in an acquisition. This is an inescapable dynamic in acquisitions. Some value has been paid for or "bought" by the acquirer, and the acquired company is now the "property" of the acquirer that paid for it. Successful acquirers find ways to quickly take this issue off the table so that a meaningful dialogue about the merged culture can focus on integration—ultimately what creates value. What destroys value in any M&A event is any real or perceived experiences of devaluation, competition, or disrespect. In some cases, the culture of the acquiring company is by nature aggressive, arrogant, and ill-suited for collaborative partnerships. This has likely been a source of value-creation in the win-lose competitive environment, but is value destroying when the task is to "bring new members into the family."

The Culture Change Process in Postmerger Integration. The Culture Change Process in postmerger integration should follow more or less the same principles and steps outlined in Chapters 4 and 5:

- Ideally a culture assessment should be performed on both companies so there are factual data for the culture integration team to work with.
- The Shadow Cultures should be delineated using the Get Real Tool—first separately, so there is a shared awareness of differences. In the interest of time, since this is solely a means to the end of a shared Vision Culture, this might be less exhaustive and in-depth than for the culture change. Because the goal is integration, not change (though clearly change may be involved), my experience has been that the majority of time is best invested in crafting the shared Vision Culture from brief "bullet style" summaries. This will vary as a function of the R-Y-G condition in both companies, and on other time-related factors.
- The urgency level for integration of the two cultures will vary as a function of the strategic rationale, degree of conflict between the cultures, and perhaps other factors unique to the situation. All other things being equal, a culture integration is almost always a Condition Yellow or greater urgency level. The sooner the cultures are integrated, the lower the chance of unconstructive mutual exchanges and negative perceptions.
- The framing question for the final task of creating a shared Vision Culture and roadmap is this: "What attributes from these Shadow

Cultures will create the most value?" Presumably, the Required Culture of the acquired company will have changed as a result of the merger, since its strategy is now subsumed in the acquirer's strategy. It is important to get an accurate and objective read on the two Actual and Ideal cultures as distinct from each other. It is only in doing this that the team can appreciate where the alignment and misalignment are in regards to the Required Culture. For the most part, with the exception that there are two sets of Actual and Ideal culture attributes instead of one, the principles and methods of the Get Real Tool should be applied as described previously. Given the additional complexity of two data sets, and the undercurrent of company chauvinism, expert and directive facilitation is essential. The CEOs of both companies must set the tone, and should be present for the final discussion of the Vision Culture, so that it does not have to be taken to another level for ratification. Time may prevent the CEOs from being present during all of the "working through," but they must be present and active when all the data are collected and consensus areas are separated from dissension.

- Once the Vision Culture is crafted, a shared roadmap should be created. In most respects this is no different than the Culture Change Roadmap paradigm I have described earlier in the book, except that there will be action items that vary according to each company. The "to be" Vision Culture target will produce different gaps for each company relative to the Actual Culture for each. It is important—symbolically and practically—that there be only one Culture Change Roadmap with shared and company-specific action items in one place for both companies. For example, the acquiring company might see value in adoption of some best practice from the acquired company—a new product-development process or manufacturing practice.
- It is important that the culture change task force hold true to the principle of taking best practices and values from *both* companies against the metric of what will best serve the Required Culture. This cannot be emphasized enough, but requires considerable maturity and objectivity on the part of both companies—not always in great supply, unfortunately. When viewed correctly, the acquisition process may provide a unique opportunity for the acquiring company to question and change aspects of its Actual Culture that are poorly aligned with the Required Culture.

Practical Exceptions. To be practical, there are situations in which a robust culture integration effort are not required:

- When the relative size of the acquired company is much smaller, it may be silly to talk of "mutual" change. The smaller company should be respected, and strengths capitalized on by the acquiring company—but the tail should not wag the dog.
- The shared Culture Change Roadmap may stretch out over a much longer time period than usual, simply due to practical constraints of time, money, and bandwidth. Integration of sales territories and customers may be sensitive. Integration of larger systems may be complex and expensive.

Chapter 8 Summary

In Chapter 8 I used three common culture scenarios—the innovation challenge, the early- and late-stage developmental challenge, and the merger-acquisition challenge to illustrate how the Culture Change Process can create value. We move now to Chapter 9 for a discussion of the competencies necessary for leaders to develop in order to more effectively use culture as an engine of value creation.

9 Culture Change Leadership Competencies

What kind of leader does it take to lead a successful culture change? This final topic is especially important because culture change can only occur when the CEO leads the effort. Like many of the topics we have touched on previously, this one is vast, and I make no pretense of a comprehensive review in the larger space of CEO competencies. As I have tried to emphasize throughout the book, there are many implementation aspects of culture change that will be handled by the senior human resources executive and other leaders. However, there are a handful of critical decisions and actions that only the CEO can perform. In what follows I will first review that list of CEO-imperative responsibilities and then move on to the "critical few" list of leadership competencies necessary to effect a successful culture change. I will also briefly outline what capabilities the CEO needs from the senior HR executive in a culture change.

What Is the CEO's Role in the Culture Change?

I have organized the answer to this first question sequentially around the four culture change stages: Setup, Launch, Propagating the Wave, and Celebrating Progress.

Setup

1. Answer the four CEO questions
   A. What is expected of me to create value and keep my job? (Hopefully the same thing!)

B. Is the current company strategy a reasonable way to create that value?
C. Do I have the right organizational culture to execute that strategy?
D. Do I have the right team to mostly do all of the preceding?

Deciding to begin a culture change is truly a task that cannot be delegated, though of course never a decision to be made without data gathering and consultation with trusted advisors, the board, and perhaps other stakeholders. It is certainly the proverbial "lonely at the top" decision that must be made by the top leader of the organization. It is important to remember that even a cautious "non-decision" due to avoidance, uncertainty, or timidity is still a decision of major impact.

2. Determine the red-yellow-green level of culture change urgency. I will not repeat the relative risks of false positive and false negative mistakes that were reviewed in Chapter 4. Clearly a mistake by the CEO here has high-impact consequences. No one but the CEO can, or should, make this final decision about where the culture change effort will be prioritized.

3. Frame and define the Culture Change Process as a reflection of the R-Y-G condition.

A. Is it in the top three, top five, or top ten priorities for the company?
B. Do we have the internal expertise and bandwidth to realistically address that urgency assessment?

4. Communicate the persuasive rationale behind both the R-Y-G urgency level and the rationale behind the resourcing question. In a Condition Yellow or Condition Red situation, energize and motivate the top team and the entire organization to focus the right amount of time and energy on the culture change.

Launch

5. Sponsor and lead the Culture Change Process and calendar, ensuring that key deliverables are produced quickly but thoughtfully. These include

A. *Culture assessment*. This is a task requiring technical expertise—certainly nothing the CEO should be directly involved in conducting. The CEO's role for this deliverable is to ensure that the minimum best practices are met and that it is conducted expeditiously. This is likely something to be sponsored by the senior HR executive, who may be managing outside experts to get this done.

B. *Get Real Tool.* Manage the Get Real Tool process ending with creation of a Vision Culture.

   i. The CEO should develop an opinion on the Shadow Cultures and the Vision Culture—though typically should not "mandate" or insist on this view unless there are special circumstances in the top team or important stakeholders are in denial or resisting.

   ii. The CEO should be present and actively leading the final steps leading up to the Vision Culture. This does not necessarily mean imposing specific viewpoints, but it does mean resolving conflict, driving to closure, and ensuring that the top team does not fall off into a ditch or drill holes in the sky.

C. *Culture Change Roadmap.* Sponsor and guide as required the creation of the Culture Change Roadmap. This is a detailed project plan that the CEO should not be down in the details of. Like the company's budget, the CEO must know what is in this document, then formally approve and sponsor it. This and the assessment are activities that likely require minimal direct involvement by the CEO—perhaps as little as framing the task and monitoring the outcome.

D. *Ratification.* This is a complex series of communication events that the CEO should not personally be planning and choreographing. The CEO must be visible, persuasive, and confident in communicating the Vision Culture and roadmap to all key groups of stakeholders.

Propagating the Wave

6. Formally charter and sponsor the culture change task force—the primary agent in moving the culture change forward. Key resourcing conflicts that arise in selecting the membership of this team and adjusting other priorities accordingly may come up to the CEO for escalation. At the outcome level, the CEO's responsibility is to ensure that this is a strong, cross-functional team with competent leadership and membership. Remember that not all culture change initiatives require a culture change task force—in smaller organizations the top team may serve in that function, obviating the need for a separate culture change task force. This decision is, of course, also one for the CEO, to be based on an assessment of requirements of the culture change relative to available resources.

7. Be sufficiently knowledgeable about change acceleration and the human capital levers to have an intelligent opinion on the strategic decisions that may escalate to your level. Most of this area is technical in nature; things such as behavioral competencies, organizational design, metrics and rewards, talent management, and process improvement are not areas that the CEO is likely to have technical expertise in. It is essential that CEOs understand minimum best practices in all of these areas, but the design and execution of these key roadmap initiatives is not a good use of their time. These are potentially significant resource questions that have been resolved with the collective wisdom of the top team and culture change task force.

A. In extreme Condition Yellow or Condition Red, the CEO will likely be involved in establishing where the bar should be set for the willing-and-able calibration and metrics and rewards decisions. It is critical that this decision faithfully reflect the Vision Culture—and it can be a subject in which there is frequent backpedaling and avoidance of tough action. The CEO must visibly model the administration of these human capital levers with his or her own team. The design and administration of almost all the human capital levers is the job of Human Resources.

8. Model executive authenticity. The CEO is the *only* person in the organization who can set the standard through modeling his or her own behavior and create decisive action to ensure the same standard with direct reports. Only the CEO can initiate a challenge to misaligned executive behavior, and only the CEO can terminate a top executive.

A. Composing the membership and building a top team that is well functioning and models the Vision Culture is something the CEO may engage expert help with. Clearly, only the CEO is going to make the material value decisions about what kind of team should exist and how it will operate.

Celebrating Progress

9. Define progress. There will be many opinions about whether the culture has changed at all, or enough at various milestone points. If the roadmap has been well-constructed with objective milestones, there will be plenty of data as years one, two, and three roll around. It is important for the CEO to be proactive in striking the right balance between proclaiming "victory" and things "still to do"—and to proactively define progress with reference to these data. As we discussed in Chapter 7, on Celebrating Progress, a culture change is never absolutely "done." However, there is a

point at which the Vision Culture *is* the Actual Culture, and this must be celebrated by the CEO.

A. As success milestones are achieved, the CEO should initiate, or respond to top team requests for, the dismantling of various culture change activities and structures. Some of these may be obvious, others may be less so and will require CEO adjudication.

10. Set and drive the organization's "master calendar." Although with recommendations from the top team and culture change task force, the CEO is the only one who perform this task. The CEO must determine when to assess culture change progress and what the right message is. Some of these decisions are self-evident default-related decisions flagged in the Culture Change Roadmap

11. Celebrate and model celebration. As the culture change unfolds and various milestones are achieved or revised, the tone and quality of how these events are celebrated, revised, or criticized will come from the CEO's modeling at these points. None of these are unilateral or "lonely at the top" decisions, and they should include top team and culture change task force input.

The Five Critical Success Factors

Every culture change process is unique, but it is the CEO's responsibility to ensure that the Five Critical Success Factors for Culture Change are in the forefront, and that the company's culture change initiative meets with these minimum basic success factors.

Success Factor 1: Define the level of urgency and the reason for culture change

Success Factor 2: Define the "new" and "legacy" cultures

Success Factor 3: Build a culture change roadmap

Success Factor 4: Translate the vision culture into observable behaviors and measurable events

Success Factor 5: Model executive authenticity

A Different Kind of Leader

Now that we've reviewed the list of CEO responsibilities necessary to make a successful culture change, we turn to this question: "What are the leadership competencies that the effective CEO leading a culture change would need?" Many of the required competencies are no different from those required of all CEOs to create value, and they comprise far too long a list to fully enumerate here: vision, courage, confident conviction, cognitive flexibility, and perseverance, to name a few. (This field of "important CEO competencies" has been well mined for many years—the interested reader is referred to Kotter's classic work on change leadership.[1])

There are four competencies that I have found to be highly correlated with successful culture change—these are the "critical few":

1. Dual-horizon vision
2. Self-awareness
3. Team leadership
4. Source of inspiration

In what follows, I will outline a more rigorous behavioral competency description for each of these.

Dual-Horizon Vision

Linking traditional "lagging indicator" metrics with "leading indicator" value-creation metrics

Dual-horizon vision means that the CEO has the ability to see the farther horizon of continuing value creation, balanced with immediate metrics of organizational performance for shareholders. Making the Vision Culture and the actions necessary to achieve it is an example of dual-horizon vision.

The one-dimensional CEO as financial leader is a dinosaur. For many reasons, not the least of them the selfish demands of Wall Street (aka *we the investors*) for quarterly profits, there are still many of these dinosaurs running big and small companies. As Jim Collins has so convincingly set forth in his books *Built to Last*[2] and *Good to Great,*[3] true value is only created over a period of years. I would add an important corollary to Collins's assertion, that an aligned culture is a powerful tool, if not the most powerful tool, to create enduring value. True value creation does not happen in quarters, or even single years, but in multiple years and decades.

- There is a cognitive component to this competency in balancing strategic and tactical actions and timeframes.
- There is also an emotional component to this competency around courage, conviction, perseverance, and confidence when the farther horizon value is important enough to justify lowering of shareholder returns in the short term. At the personal values level, this

requires some measure of short-term sacrifice in professional and career goals. It requires the confidence to withstand pressure from stakeholders who want short-term value.

- It requires a conceptual appreciation of the relationship between leading and lagging indicators, in general, and specifically in any particular company. Financial indicators are critically important. To the extent that they become central to the exclusion of culture, the company is going forward by looking through the rear-view mirror: a relatively "safe" but "unsound" way to lead a company.
    - To change culture you need to believe that culture is important. To create enduring value, you need to believe and intend for that to happen, or of course, it will not. Dual-horizon vision simply means that the CEO has taken the time to educate him- or herself about what constitutes enduring value creation and not fallen prey to any of the five distorted views of what organizational culture is (irrelevant, fatalistic, overly complex, mechanistic, and personally influenced). The leader clinging to one of these views is unlikely to be a successful sponsor of culture change. Dual-horizon vision demands a level of awareness about the ways in which culture is an accelerator, gate, and prime mover of value creation.
    - For any CEO with "eyes to see it," dismissing the importance of culture with any of these five "limiting views" of culture is a liability.

Self-Awareness

Understanding one's own strengths and weaknesses and doing something about it

Critical Success Factor 5—modeling executive authenticity—hinges almost entirely on the CEO's ability for self-knowledge, openness to feedback, and a willingness to make adjustments in the interest of aligning with the Vision Culture. This does not require perfection, only a willingness to strive for it in matters related to personal behaviors. I have provided several examples of effectively designed and launched culture change initiatives which founder for the sole reason of the CEO's misaligned behavior (for example, The Food Company case).

- This competency requires not only the "good intentions" to be self-aware and open but also the commitment to the regular, objective auditing that can "keep it real." There is no malice or attempt to evade presumed here. The inescapable fact for any of us who come into a culture from the outside is that there are always suggestions—and sometimes "unspeakables"—that all see but that have not been communicated to the CEO. A commitment to self-awareness must begin with a commitment to the premise of the Johari Window, which assumes that there will *always* be aspects of our impact on others that we are blind to. That awareness demands regular objective input from those who have no conflict of interest in speaking truth to power.

- Extending the implications of this Johari Window premise, commitment to self-awareness also demands that the CEO attempt to create an atmosphere in which "keeping it real" is expected, requested, and rewarded. My experience is that the "reward" for speaking truth to power need not always be a dramatic change in behavior, though this is always desirable. It does require that when truth is spoken to power, it is not punished or ignored but acknowledged and followed by visible effort.
- At the bottom level of this competency is a mature confidence that can take in constructive, well-intended feedback without worry about loss of stature or authority. Many CEOs are fearful that if they start acknowledging weaknesses, the sharks will smell blood and their position will be undermined or threatened. This could not be farther from the truth—others see strength in the ability to accept real input about misalignment.
    - It is certainly true that a defensive, guilty, or panicked response to on-target feedback will create unintended and undesirable consequences. This is one of the many reasons why such feedback must be conducted formally by an outside expert—to minimize politicization and maximize a safe environment for feedback.

Team Leadership

Shaping the top team to be primary DNA for the culture

As I emphasized in Chapter 7, "Propagating the Wave," the dynamics of the top team visibly model how the organization should work cross-functionally. The top team also models the tone and quality of how the "tribes" of the organization should interact with each other. This makes it one of the most powerful levers that the CEO has direct influence over. The Vision Culture that calls out attributes around teamwork and collaboration is contradicted by the CEO who manages in a "spokes of the wheel" fashion that minimizes the fact of peer-to-peer interdependency and collaboration.

- This competency requires, at the outset, that the CEO have a modern understanding of what a high-performance team is and how to create it. Many CEOs have had neither education nor coaching in how to be an effective team leader. They may appreciate the one-to-one principles of goal-setting, performance management, and problem solving with direct reports because the goal of meeting strategic objectives demands it. This means an appreciation of the team as a system capable of delivering value that is greater than the sum of the parts. A thorough review of this knowledge base is not possible here, but there are certainly innumerable resources to gain it. The reader is referred to Katzenbach[4] or Lencioni,[5] who approach the topic with the CEO in mind as audience.
- Underlying the basic knowledge about "what" a high-performance team is, and "how" to create it, are several cognitive and emotional competencies:
    - Cognitively, effective team leadership requires the ability to see the "forest" of the team dynamic, distinct from the "trees" of individual behavior. Every team has a clear "signature" that is the net effect of the individual personalities and history. The team composed of very independent entrepreneurs may gravitate toward operating independently without the bother of acknowledging interdependence that is necessary for optimum value creation. The team composed of polite, mild-mannered executives may meet frequently but leave many elephants in the room. The universe of possible systemic dynamics is endless and is further complicated by changing team membership—a team is only as old as its latest arrival.
    - In the emotional dimension, the "emotional intelligence" construct made world famous by Daniel Goleman is a useful paradigm to capture this dimension of the team leadership competency.[6] This is the ability to "feel"—that is, sense or intuit without explicit factual data—the unspoken emotional undercurrent of the team, and use this information as a guide to take actions that address obstacles or enhance performance of the team-as-team.

Source of Inspiration

Motivating others to believe in the Vision Culture and act on it

The last and fourth of the critical few culture change leadership competencies is the ability to "sell the plan" to others in a way that is ethical, compelling, and, when possible, inspiring. Culture change, as I have seen it unfold successfully in numerous ways, is always dependent on the CEO playing an active role as "chief sponsor." There are many ways to motivate and inspire—not all of them are "evangelical," elegant, or eloquent. In fact, depending on the industry sector, "inspirational and compelling" communication may require convincing charts and graphs presented in a factual, low-key manner.

- The central competency beneath the ultimate outcome measure—"Are they motivated to act accordingly?"—is more about understanding the "currency" of what will motivate various target audiences and then translating that to a language that speaks to that need.
  - There are communications and organizational effectiveness experts to help with both; CEOs do not need to generate this work product from a blank page. They *do* need to appreciate the importance of the task and their symbolic role in conveying it through multiple channels inside and outside the organization, and they must act as final "copyeditor" on the messaging.
- It is also important to emphasize those myriad nonverbal actions that communicate more loudly than words in motivating and inspiring others to act in accordance with the Vision Culture. After the CEO delivers a well-crafted message, there is only one real question in the minds of every audience, irrespective of who they are: "Will she or he maintain focus?" In other words, "Will she or he make it happen through leadership actions that set priorities, model tough choices, model the right kind of sacrifices in her or his sphere of influence?" "Will the walk fit the talk?" When people see that the CEO is following through by doing what she or he says, there is no greater inspiration possible. The CEO that treats these public and private communications as "stakeholder management" or "press releases" is conveying a value-destroying message: "This isn't for real—I'm telling you what you need to hear, instead of the truth."

The New Human Resources Executive

This book is directed to CEOs in the broadest sense of the term, with the intent to include any top leader who has the authority and responsibility to establish the priorities and resources for a culture change. Though I hope that human resource professionals, organizational development experts, and others in positions to advise the CEO will find something useful, appealing to this non-CEO audience was not the primary objective. Given the important role that the senior human resources executive will likely play in any culture change, I thought it important to include a brief note to the CEO about what the competencies and sensibilities of a senior human resources executive capable of adding value to a culture looks like.

Human resources is a function in transition—failing in some cases and being redefined in others, depending on the person, the company, and your point of view. The senior human resources specialist will continue to play an important role, as do controllers in the finance function. Often missing is the HR executive who can be a thought partner to the CEO in the way a strong CFO is. Someone who is an expert in human resource matters yet also has the strategic understanding of culture that allows him or her to initiate and lead and has a "seat at the big table" to influence both the CEO and top team on human resources *and culture*—as a peer.

One of the reasons I believe strongly that the CEO needs to know as much about culture change as I have suggested throughout the book is because many HR executives do not appreciate, or appreciate and cannot step up to, their potential leadership role and the value they add as chief architects and advocates for this "engine of value creation." There are many reasons for this—not the least of which are the same for CEOs regarding dual-horizon vision: the obsession with short-term financial metrics by demanding investors has relegated the "people function" to "optional" second-class status—and attracted talent to the field accordingly.

There are many extremely talented HR executives who can and do play a trusted advisor role, and I have had the pleasure to work with many of them over the course of my career helping organizations shape and change culture. Too many HR executives allow themselves to be defined as implementers of the human capital levers but not as the "chief culture officers" or "chief capability officers" that are peers of the chief financial officer, chief marketing officer or chief information officer. Titles are not the issue here—but in my experience too many HR executives do not have a seat at the "grown-ups' table." They report to the CFO or other executive reporting to the CEO. The reasons for this are historically shaped—a result of the "five fallacies" about culture that I outlined in Chapter 2. My point here is not to fix human resources but simply to acknowledge the fact of the function's inability to serve as chief culture and capability officer. In theory, were the human resources function operating at this higher level, the CEO could delegate more of what I have defined as CEO responsibilities. Indeed, in a handful of organizations with true "chief culture officers," this is the reality. Sadly, this is the very small minority. Even in these exceptions, it is my strong view that the CEO must step up to be the visible and proactive sponsor of culture alignment to the strategy.

This issue is noteworthy here in context of the harm that this "second class" function does to the value creation potential of culture. Insofar as the CEO assumes that culture as engine of value creation is the realm of the HR executive (because it is less important or because he or she is under mistaken assumptions about the capability of that HR executive and the function), the overall value creation of culture alignment is diminished to some small or great degree.

The result is that an important pathway to value creation is diminished or lost altogether.

Key competencies for the new HR executive or chief culture officer include the following:

1. A sophisticated and thorough understanding of the strategy and workings of the business equal to that of other top team members.
2. The ability to make the conceptual and practical case for culture as an engine of value creation in the currency and language of the business, not the specialized language of human resources or organizational development.
3. Management and leadership skills capable of building or maintaining a human resources transactional team that reliably turns the crank on important human resource administrative procedures.

   In my view of the chief culture officer, this team might include not only the traditional HR functions (staffing, benefits, compensation, talent development, and generalists) but other key functions such as process improvement, quality assurance, and organizational development.
4. Expertise in culture change tools and methodology as well as the strategic dimension of all the human capital levers. The chief culture officer should have an understanding of everything in this book (actually quite a bit more that) that surpasses the CEO and all other top team members. He or she should be the top team's strategic and tactical expert in exactly the same way the CFO or CIO would be.

A useful metric is that similar expectation for CFOs: they are subject matter specialists in treasury, accounting, and so on, and may have spent early portions of their careers in one or several of these. Nobody sees them anymore as specialists—they have sufficient knowledge about all the functions that report to them to make strategic alignment decisions.

5. Strategic thinking capability that can add can value to the brainpower of the top team as it considers all the complexities of the Shadow Cultures, the Vision Culture, and alignment of these to the business strategy.

A tall order, I admit, but HR executives of this caliber are out there—and until there are more of them, culture change will remain the responsibility of the CEO. There is, of course, a growing voice in the human resources community supporting this theme of becoming more "strategic" and less "transactional": what I have outlined here is hardly a new thought in modern HR thinking. My view is that this evolution in the HR discipline is necessary but not sufficient. At the end of the day, change will occur only if there is a shift in CEO thinking that demands a higher standard, in turn translated to selection criteria and commensurate organizational authority suitable to be an effective sponsor for culture change. The HR community needs to continue building to meet that future need—which will come, but only when CEOs escape from the "five fallacies" of culture distortion to fully appreciate culture as engine of value creation. For the moment, it remains the primary responsibility of the CEO to select HR executives who are equal to the task of aligning culture with strategy—just as would be done for a CFO for financial strategy.

Chapter 9 Summary

In Chapter 9, I described four leadership competencies that are particularly important for the success of any culture change: dual-horizon vision, self-awareness, team leadership, and the ability to inspire others to act. I also discussed the importance of clearly delineating the role of the strategic human resources executive in a culture change initiative, and how this may expand or contract the role of the CEO.

In Chapter 10, I describe a current example of how culture has an impact on shareholder value.

Epilogue

10 Culture, the Economy, and Survival of the Fittest

In July 2009, the world found itself in an economic crisis that no one under the age of seventy had ever experienced. Rick Waggoner, who arrived as the savior of General Motors in 2000, was asked by the U.S. president to step down from his post as CEO. The world's largest automaker, and the crown jewel of American industry for seventy-five years, was bankrupt and would emerge as a completely different company after restructuring. GM's fate remains uncertain. In that same month, Tesla Motors, in Silicon Valley, announced that its electric-powered car would be in production by late 2010. Before that, in the fall of 2008, the largest brand names in financial services—Bear Stearns and Lehman Brothers—literally blinked out of existence. Compare this dramatic story to that of Goldman-Sachs. It was knocked back by the external environment but emerged six months later to unprecedented profitability and a $16 billion bonus pool. What conclusion should we draw? Value cannot be created when you're extinct! Strong cultures not only survive but emerge stronger than they were before the herd is thinned.

We witnessed in 2008 and 2009 an incredible and unprecedented eclipse of what were formerly the strongest, most profitable companies in the world, as though Shiva the Destroyer had cut a swath right down the middle of Wall Street. Yet some of those institutions—Wells Fargo, Apple, Google, and Toyota, for example—are not just surviving but thriving through the collapse. These "terrible winters" or adverse periods in history provide a treasure trove of learning. For example, there are some forms of brain damage that no one will ever see except as the result of war. The advances made in neurology during World Wars I and II, due to our new understanding of brain injury and how to treat it, would never have come during peacetime. This recent period in the economy was the "terrible winter" that is thinning out the herd—fortunately, even the worst winter does finally end, and there is more food and shelter for a smaller herd.

The global economic downturn of late 2008 to 2010 similarly supplies us with tremendous learning about the myriad ways in which culture acts as a prime mover, accelerator, or gate to create or destroy shareholder value. The "terrible winter" that descended on the American and world economies is a test of who has invested in an enduring culture aligned with a sound strategy. To use the "terrible winter" analogy, there are some very strong members of the herd that, through simple bad luck, are going to slip off a cliff into a ravine to their deaths while looking for food in dangerous places. But across the entire herd there will emerge some who have the capabilities—perhaps in several different ways—to survive the storm. These are not cultures, strategies, or capabilities that were quickly created as the intensity of the storm became apparent, but enduring strengths developed over years and in periods when there was no external pressure to do so.

The financial services sector is a dramatic, largely public microcosm of how culture has created or destroyed value in a cohort of companies that all appeared to be more or less peers on the same level playing field just a short year ago. Two years ago Citigroup was considered to be a blue-chip stock—solid as a rock. Its stock was trading at a high in January 2007 of 57. On October 1, 2009, it was trading at 4.46 with pressure for the current CEO to be dismissed. I think we can all agree that a great deal of value was destroyed. In the same period, Wells Fargo Bank also lost some value, going from a high of 39 to a later 26 and rising. Bank of America went from 55 to 6.36 during that same period. AIG went from 73 to 1 in the same period. Now we shouldn't make too much of just the stock price because there are other indicators of value creation and destruction, but as a rough measure of how well individual members of the "herd" are faring, stock price is a reasonable proxy for "how well is the company doing" and "how much value has been created or destroyed" in this same three-year period.

Let us look now quickly at the performance, strategy, and cultures of two of these companies, Citigroup and Wells Fargo, to illustrate how culture creates and destroys value.

- Citigroup was founded in 1812 in New York, operating initially as a regional bank but quickly moving to become a "super-regional" and financial center. In 1998 it combined with Travelers Group to form the world's largest financial services company and at last accounting had $1.9 trillion in assets in 107 countries, 12,000 offices, and more than 300,000 employees. CEO John Reed in the 1980s, Sandy Weill in the 1990s, and Charlie Prince more recently all had reputations for ruthless, results-driven, ethically questionable and opportunistic leadership styles. They pursued a strategy of rapid growth through acquisition in highly diverse industries that included brokerage, hedge funds, and other extremely lucrative but risky businesses. In the fall of 2008, the company was caught in the subprime mortgage and credit default swap excesses. On the verge of collapse and bankruptcy it was saved by the federal government with $25 billion in emergency aid because it was "too big to fail." Further government bailout money has followed, and Citigroup's value, though underestimated in the view of most, is considered questionable by all—as suggested by its stock price.

- Wells Fargo was founded in 1852, operating for many years as a regional bank and then a super-regional on the West Coast. Its managers pursued a conservative growth strategy, always maintaining a strong balance sheet and making occasional strategic acquisitions—Crocker Bank in 1986 and Norwest in 1998. They showed a steady commitment to technology that facilitated customer interface. They were early adopters and investors in the automated teller machine, and later online banking. Total assets are $1.42 trillion, and the bank has roughly 279,000 employees. Managers never invested heavily in tangential financial service products such as insurance or the exotic derivative instruments that entranced so many other bankers, nor did they in international geographic expansion. In 2007 Wells Fargo was nominated "Safest Bank in the World" by peers. In the fall of 2008, the bank was forced to accept $25 billion from Secretary Hank Paulson, which its managers indicated they did not need. As of this writing they expressed their wish to return the $25 billion (though have not yet done so), unlike Citigroup, which has accepted another $25 billion because it needed the money to survive.

Citibank for the past fifteen years has been famous for its ruthless, voracious, and diverse acquisitions; its risk taking; and its extravagant—but always "so darn successful and profitable"—strategy and culture. During that same period Wells Fargo has been known for its conservative yet strategically thoughtful key acquisitions and investment in technology to leverage a smaller physical footprint. In 1990 Wells and Citi were considered "equals" and competitive rivals in a small club of super-regionals.

Without much controversy, we can safely conclude the following:

- In the past three years, Citigroup has destroyed most or all of the value it created for shareholders over the previous ten years, the result of an aggressive, acquisitive, and highly risk-tolerant culture that acted entrepreneurially to pursue a strategy of unprecedented expansion. Its existence is in question—and whatever the outcome, it will almost certainly cease to exist in its present form and be sold off in pieces.
- Wells Fargo, though certainly suffering the effects of the "most terrible winter on record" has lost far less of its value. The result of the past ten years of its conservative, cautious, but value-creation-focused culture expanded so slowly that it was often called "boring" and openly ridiculed in the business press for its failure to capitalize on the explosive growth of the Internet and housing booms. Its continued existence and confidence that it will create value, even now before the "terrible winter" is not over yet, is a certainty. It is not dependent on the government and has a strong balance sheet, and, barring an "Ice Age" in which everything living dies, Wells Fargo will survive and create value again.

The Citi culture is one in which means justify the ends, high rewards justify high risk, and ethical boundaries are relativist and easily bent to serve individual agendas. Most important, it is one that promotes a high degree of win or lose internal competition, reinforcing a sense of individual power, results, and personal achievement. This is a culture of "carnivores" who conquer and control, and therefore require a continuing diet of new growth opportunities—acquisitions. In the end, Citi, like AIG, probably grew so large as to be ungovernable. The opportunists in the credit default swaps and hedge fund units at Citi, AIG, and many other similar institutions were spawned by this kind of "predatory" culture and then essentially unsupervised by both the company and the government. This kind of personal risk-taking that jeopardizes the entire entity would be unthinkable in a culture that exercised even modest supervisory control in context of a culture of conservatism. Cultures that create mercenary individualism are less likely to create lasting value that can survive terrible winters.

In contrast, Wells Fargo has a tradition of slow, conservative growth with a longer view. There are certainly politics and internal competition, but not the lionization of CEO rock stars like Weill and Prince. Kovacevich and Stumpf, Wells's chairman and CEO, respectively, are not Wall Street celebrities who have inspired a cult of personality. Their strategy included steady growth and some acquisitions, yet these are certainly not "gentle" bankers who are not competitive street fighters. Wells Fargo has a culture of achievement and results—and while there are competitive politics, results in this environment require cooperation. Value creation in the long run requires some measure of self-serving altruism. This is not a culture of "self-serving carnivores" that allowed billions of dollars of value to be destroyed through personal greed, ego, and relaxation of the most basic of banking core values: don't risk your capital. To be fair, there are many fair and ethical people at Citigroup and AIG—they just weren't the ones running the show.

In closing, I would underscore this most central point of the book: culture is the medium within, and the engine through which, value will be created or destroyed. It is the environment out of which an aggressive and unethical or a conservative and thoughtful business strategy will arise. And finally, culture is the accelerator or the barrier to the execution of that strategy—depending on how well aligned it is. As the many examples of this book have illustrated, and as this newest financial crisis dramatically illustrates, culture is inextricably linked to value creation in numerous ways. The CEO who has not answered the question, "How do I shape my culture to accelerate strategy and value creation?" and taken steps accordingly, is simply not doing his or her job.

Appendix: Dawson Culture Change Lexicon

This "Culture Change Lexicon" has been useful for some executive teams as a "prompt" to get discussion flowing about the Shadow Cultures. It is neither an exhaustive nor scientifically rigorous tool—just a list to prevent wasted time by the top team in looking at a "blank page."

Rewards

- Promotions—Who gets them and how?
- Salary—What behaviors are reinforced with compensation?
- Incentives—What is focused on?
- Educational opportunities
- Physical space—office location
- Punishments—Who is not rewarded? And why?
- What is rewarded (or punished) and why?
- What are rewards based on? Merit? Tenure? Personal relationships? Performance?
    - Is this fair or unfair?
    - Is it measured and databased?

Social Norms

Conflict

- How are disagreements handled?
    - Directly or indirectly?
    - Are they avoided, denied, smoothed, explosive?

- Regarding public versus private confrontation norms, what's the level of "decorum"
  - What is the level of "face saving" versus open and direct challenge?

Respect for Differences—Empathy

- Are respect and empathy for each other important values—or not?
- In terms of diversity, are individual differences tolerated, celebrated, or ignored?

Competition

- How "political" is competition over scarce resources?
- Is there a hardball or softball tolerance of political influence?

Authority

- Regarding the "obedience" quotient, how acceptable are challenge and dissent?
- How is "order" maintained? How are rules enforced?
  - Through logic, guilt, public disgrace, or intimidation?
- What happens to people who disobey the "rules"?
  - The emperor has clothes.
  - The emperor does not have clothes.

Team

- Do teams have primacy over the individual ethic?
- Are teams valued and rewarded on a par with individual performance?
  - Teams are an important mechanism for getting things done.
  - Teams are a necessary evil to create cross-functional buy-off.

Trust and Closeness

- How "social" are members of the organization?
- Are they friends outside of work?
- Are there close, long-standing personal relationships or more distant work relationships?

Dress, Speech, and Appearance

- Are these formal or informal?
- Are relations polite and polished or rough and colloquial?

Work-Life Balance

- How would the number of hours and level of commitment to work be measured?
  - High—medium—low
- Is consideration given to family and personal circumstances?
- Is work a "fun" place to be—are people energized when they're there?

Organizational Patterns and Dynamics

Communication

- How are the quality and quantity of communication from top to bottom?
  - Open and free flowing or constricted and controlled?
- Regarding horizontal communication—how does information flow across departments?
  - Through the formal organizational structure, or more informally?
- What are the primary communication vehicles?
  - E-mail, paper, voicemail, direct contact?
  - People listen to each other in an attempt to understand and develop true dialogue.
  - People "transmit" without any genuine interest in dialogue.

Decision Making

- How do important decisions get made? What is the style and quality of those decisions?
- Are decisions participative and inclusive—consensus-oriented versus directive and authoritarian?
- Are they paternalistic or autocratic?
- Are they efficient, decisive, crisp?
- Are they slow, indecisive, ponderous, ambiguous?
- Are they rapid, decisive, reactive with unintended consequences?
- Are they accurate—that is, are "smart" and correct decisions made?
- Are decisions made with data, or intuitively, without data?

Problem Solving

- Is there disciplined planning versus reactive responses?
- Is problem solving creative and innovative versus standardized?

- Is it long term versus short term?
- Is it empirical versus intuitive?
- Is it flexible and spontaneous versus rigid and structured?

Quality, Innovation, and Continuous Improvement

- Are innovation and new thinking encouraged and reinforced?
    - Are mistakes considered "evidence of risk taking"?
    - Are mistakes considered "evidence of individual incompetence"?
    - Are mistakes considered "evidence of organizational misalignment"?
- Are new ideas rewarded?
- Are new ideas suppressed and do they rarely emerge?
    - Messengers are usually shot.
    - Messengers are rarely shot.

Customers

Resource Priority and Allocation

- Do customers get priority treatment in the larger resource allocation scheme?
- Are customers "stakeholder #1"?
- Do customers get whatever they need, when they need it?

Informal Attitudes

- Are the following true?
    - We really like our customers—some of them are our friends.
    - Some of our best employees come from customers.
    - We share values with many of our customers.
    - We have loyal customers who really value us as trusted advisors.
    - Other than friendly teasing, customers are spoken of respectfully and positively out of their presence.

Leadership-Employee Relationship

- Does the leadership "do what it says it will"?
- Is leadership fair, respectful, and concerned about employees?

- Is leadership committed to creating a positive environment for employees?
- Are employees loyal and committed to the mission of the firm?

Management Practices

Performance Management

- Do disciplined, standardized performance reviews and supervisory feedback occur regularly?
- Is accountability king?
- Are objectives fair, reasonable, and resourced?
- Are objectives mutually negotiated?

Coaching and Mentoring

- Are coaching and mentoring important activities that managers make time for?
- Are the art and science of management recognized and valued as important competencies beyond technical and industry expertise?

Culture Polarity Adjectives and Typology

In the following figure, either end of the dimension can be effective, given the strategy.

Speed and agility	Slow moving
Customization	Standardization
Disciplined processes	Informal processes
High achievement	Modest achievement
Empowering	Controlling
Conventional	Innovative
Conservative	Risk-taking
High quality	Modest quality
Execution commitment	Execution lack of commitment
High cross-functional coordination	Silos and low coordination
High involvement	Low involvement
Customer always first	Customer important, but second
Profits	Employees
Open communication, systems, processes	Closed

FIGURE A.1. Culture dimensions expressed as polar opposites

Power Culture	**Achievement Culture**
Strong and charismatic leader Leaders take care of their own—reward loyalty Demanding, but fair Compliance with authority prevents innovation or dissent People afraid to deliver bad news Favoritism for "loyal followers" Charismatic leadership valued	Sense of shared urgency about attaining "big goals" Self-motivation and teamwork High morale drawn from sense of being elite and special Rules and regulations easily dispensed with End may justify the means Intolerant work-family balance—exploitation Dissent and criticism stifled—group has difficulty self-correcting and acknowledging failure
Support Culture	**Role Culture**
Harmony and cooperation are highly valued Consensus decision making dominates, slow Respect, caring, and support of one another Familial, sense of belonging and connection Tough people decisions avoided—mediocrity looms People of unequal contribution may receive same rewards, discouraging the ambitious and talented	Individual performance judged against written policies Reward for playing by the rules, dependable service Clear objectives, systems, procedures reduce ambiguity Ask permission, not forgiveness Little room for innovation and creativity Slow, steady, risk-averse, reliable decision making Individual leadership less important

FIGURE A.2. Harrison and Stokes's four culture types
SOURCE: Adapted from Roger Harrison and Herb Stokes.

Notes

Chapter 2

1. Edgar Schein, *Organizational Culture and Leadership* (San Francisco: Jossey-Bass, 1992).

2. Terence E. Deal and Allan A. Kennedy, *Corporate Cultures: The Rites and Rituals of Corporate Life* (Addison-Wesley, 1982).

3. Charles Handy, *Understanding Organizations,* 3rd Edition (New York: Oxford University Press, 1993).

4. Anne Schaef and Diane Fassel, *The Addictive Organization: Why We Overwork, Cover Up, Pick Up the Pieces, Please the Boss, and Perpetuate Sick Organizations* (New York: HarperCollins, 1988).

5. Dave Ulrich and Dale Lake, *Organizational Capability: Competing from the Inside Out* (New York: John Wiley and Sons, 1990).

6. Jim Collins, *Good to Great* (New York: HarperCollins, 2001).

7. David A. Nadler, Marc S. Gerstein, Robert B. Shaw *Organizational Architecture* (San Francisco: Jossey-Bass, 1992)

8. John Kotter and James Heskett, *Corporate Culture and Performance* (New York: The Free Press, 1992).

9. Thomas Peters and Robert Waterman Jr., *In Search of Excellence: Lessons from America's Best-Run Companies* (New York: Warner Books, 1982).

10. Ulrich and Lake, *Organizational Capability.*

11. Edward Lawler III, Susan Mohrman, and Gerald Ledford Jr., *Creating High Performance Organizations* (San Francisco: Jossey-Bass, 1995).

12. Daniel Denison, *Denison Marketing Materials: ROE of Successful and Unsuccessful Cultures,* personal communication, used with permission.

Chapter 4

1. "Global Change Study," *IBM Corporation,* 2008.

Chapter 5

1. Joseph Luft, *Of Human Interaction* (Palo Alto, CA: National Press, 1969).

2. Denison Consulting, www.denisonconsulting.com.

3. Geert Hofstede and Gert Jan Hofstede, *Cultures and Organizations: Software for the Mind* (New York: McGraw-Hill, 2005).

4. Kim Cameron and Robert Quinn, *Diagnosing and Changing Organizational Culture* (San Francisco: Jossey-Bass, 2006).

5. Roger Harrison and Herb Stokes, *Diagnosing Organizational Culture* (San Francisco: Jossey-Bass/Pfeiffer, 1992).

Chapter 6

1. William Bridges, *Managing Transitions: Making the Most of Change* (New York: Perseus Books, 1991).

2. John Kotter, "Leading Change: Why Transformation Efforts Fail." *Harvard Business Review,* March-April 1995, pp. 59–67.

3. Elisabeth Kübler-Ross, *On Death and Dying* (New York: Touchstone, 1969).

4. Daryl Conner, *Managing at the Speed of Change* (New York: Villard Books, 1992).

5. Timothy Galpin, *The Human Side of Change* (San Francisco: Jossey-Bass, 1996).

6. Amy Kates and Jay Galbraith, *Designing Your Organization: Using the STAR Model to Solve 5 Critical Design Challenges* (San Francisco: Jossey-Bass, 2007).

7. Samuel Culbert, "Get Rid of the Performance Review!" *Wall Street Journal,* October 20, 2008.

8. Robert Kaplan and David Norton, *The Balanced Scorecard: Translating Strategy into Action* (Boston: Harvard University Press, 1996).

9. David Dotlich and Peter Cairo, *Why CEOs Fail: The 11 Behaviors That Can Derail Your Climb to the Top and How to Manage Them* (San Francisco, Jossey-Bass, 2002).

10. Patrick Lencioni, *The Five Dysfunctions of a Team: A Leadership Fable* (San Francisco: Jossey-Bass, 2002).

11. Jon Katzenbach, *Teams at the Top* (San Francisco: McKinsey & Company, 1998).

Chapter 8

1. Tony Davila, Marc Epstein, and Robert Shelton, *Making Innovation Work: How to Manage It, Measure It, and Profit from It* (New Jersey: Pearson Education, 2006).

2. Jan Fagerberg, David C. Mowery, and Richard R. Nelson, *The Oxford Handbook of Innovation* (Oxford: Oxford University Press, 2005).

3. Gunter Stahl and Mark Mendenhall, *Mergers and Acquisitions; Managing Culture and Human Resources* (Palo Alto, CA: Stanford University Press, 2005).

4. Susan Cartwright, "Mergers and Acquisitions: An Update and Appraisal," in *International Review of Industrial and Organizational Psychology 2005, Volume 20*, ed. Gerard P. Hodgkinson and Kevin J. Ford (New York: John Wiley & Sons, 2005).

Chapter 9

1. John Kotter, *Leading Change* (Boston: Harvard University Press, 1996).
2. Jim Collins and Jerry Porras, *Built to Last: Successful Habits of Visionary Companies* (New York: HarperCollins, 1997).
3. Jim Collins, *Good to Great: Why Some Companies Make the Leap . . . and Others Don't* (New York: HarperCollins, 2001).
4. Jon Katzenbach, *Teams at the Top* (San Francisco: McKinsey & Company, 1998).
5. Patrick Lencioni, *The Five Dysfunctions of a Team: A Leadership Fable* (San Francisco: Jossey-Bass, 2002).
6. Daniel Goleman, *Emotional Intelligence: Why It Can Matter More Than IQ* (New York: Bantam Books, 1997).

Index